Nature
in
Trust

Nature in Trust

The History of Nature Conservation in Britain

JOHN SHEAIL

Blackie
Glasgow & London

Published by
Blackie and Son Limited
Bishopbriggs, Glasgow G64 2NZ
450/452 Edgware Road, London W2 1EG

© John Sheail 1976
First published 1976

ISBN   0 216 90122 7

Printed in Great Britain by
Thomson Litho Limited, East Kilbride, Scotland

For Gillian and Andrew

Acknowledgements

A very great number of people have helped me in the preparation of this book—I only wish that I had room to thank them all.

My greatest debt is to Gillian, my wife, without whose constant encouragement and advice the book would never have been written or completed.

I am grateful for the support given me by Professor K. Mellanby, Dr E. Duffey, Dr F. H. Perring and the many other members of the Monks Wood Experimental Station (Institute of Terrestrial Ecology). Miss Patricia Fox and Mr B. Buck drew the maps. It is a pleasure to record all the help given me by Mr A. E. Smith, and Mr W. H. Dawson and Mr R. C. Hallett of the SPNR, and Mr P. J. Conder and Miss D. Rook of the RSPB. Mr C. S. Elton, Dr S. R. Eyre, Dr R. S. R. Fitter, Mr E. M. Nicholson and Dr A. S. Watt very kindly commented on drafts of the manuscript. Naturally, I am alone responsible for any errors that remain.

The British Ecological Society, Nature Conservancy Council, Royal Society for the Protection of Birds, and Society for the Promotion of Nature Reserves very kindly gave permission for me to refer to material preserved in their archives.

Hilton, 1975   *John Sheail*

Contents

List of Figures

List of Tables

Preface

This book is concerned with man's attitude toward wildlife in the past and, more especially, the development of the nature conservation movement. The term wildlife includes all plants and animals, even those which have been introduced from other parts of the world, but it excludes domesticated animals and those plants which exist only as food crops for the human population.

The conservation of wildlife has become an important issue. Many people believe plants and animals have a right to exist and be preserved from persecution and extinction. Probably many more think we have an obligation to protect and enhance our heritage of wildlife for the sake of our children and later generations to enjoy. The presence of a variety of wild plants and animals makes our lives more interesting: most people are excited to see beautiful and distinctive flowers, or discover the tracks of a badger. Wildlife is a popular subject for books and programmes on the radio and television, and ecology is an increasingly popular subject for study and research.

Wildlife has an important place in the total environment, and there have been attempts to attach a monetary value to it as a resource. This has proved extremely difficult, and many people prefer to regard wild plants and animals as a priceless part of their national heritage, comparable in value with historic buildings, the English language and such concepts as British justice.

There has been a tremendous growth of interest in wildlife conservation during recent years. By 1975, 180,000 people had joined the Royal Society for the Protection of Birds (RSPB), and the County Naturalists' Trusts had a membership of over 100,000.

Such events as European Conservation Year have helped to focus attention on our attitude toward wildlife. The destruction of wildlife by farmers and foresters, industrial and mining ventures, has been graphically illustrated on film and in print. Steps have been taken to control harmful practices and the use of toxic substances.

Very often, these activities and discussions have prompted various questions. What was the attitude of people to wildlife in the past? How did the conservation movement evolve in Britain? What was the influence of individual persons, voluntary bodies, and the government? It is the purpose of this book to answer some of these questions.

During the nineteenth century, naturalists believed cruelty and over-collecting were the greatest threats to wildlife, and such bodies as the Royal Society for the Prevention of Cruelty to Animals (RSPCA) and the Royal Society for the Protection of Birds (RSPB) were founded to fight such evils. It was widely believed that legislation would be the most effective way of controlling human behaviour, and consequently a great deal of attention was given to securing wild bird protection acts and county by-laws for preserving wild plants. It was hoped that lessons at school, posters, pamphlets and other forms of propaganda would facilitate law enforcement and win greater public sympathy for wildlife.

During the present century, the many changes in land use and management have brought an even greater threat to wildlife through the destruction of their habitats. Naturalists realised that the most effective way of preserving wildlife was to establish nature reserves, where the land would be primarily used and managed for wildlife conservation. The Society for the Promotion of Nature Reserves (SPNR) was formed specifically to help the National Trust and local bodies in obtaining such sites. Naturalists, nevertheless, were so weak in countering the ever-increasing dangers to key areas that it was logical for them to participate in the wider concern for the countryside, and especially the preservation of amenity. Consequently, they took part in the many discussions and committees of enquiry on the objectives, location and administration of national parks.

Little was achieved until the 1940s when the government became more closely involved in land-use planning and accepted the concept of national parks. Since wildlife was regarded as an essential ingredient of these parks, the government also accepted some responsibility for nature conservation. Lists of proposed National Nature Reserves were compiled, and the book ends by reviewing early experience in acquiring and managing reserves. It describes the creation of the Nature Conservancy and the first County Naturalists' Trusts. These bodies were designed to acquire and manage reserves, and to assist in protecting wildlife throughout Britain.

This book is largely based on primary data, namely original reports, minute books and correspondence. The personal papers of various naturalists, biologists, geologists and planners have been consulted.

Considerable use is made of the archives of such voluntary bodies as the Society for the Promotion of Nature Reserves and Royal Society for the Protection of Birds, and of such learned societies as the British Ecological Society. The relevant official records have been studied in the Public Record Office, including those of the Cabinet, Ministry of Town and County Planning, and the Forestry Commission. Of course, not all the relevant manuscripts have survived or are available for study. The Hon. N. C. Rothschild and W. H. Hudson, both of whom played a major role in the nature conservation movement, left instructions with their executors to destroy all manuscript notebooks, letters and scraps of written paper. All government papers deposited in the Public Record Office remain closed to public inspection for a minimum of thirty years, and this means that it is much harder to gain a detailed view of all sectors of the nature conservation movement from the late 1940s onwards. For this reason, less attention is given to the decades of the 1950s and 1960s in this book. This period should be made the subject of another book whenever the source material becomes available.

It is hoped that one of the by-products of this book will be to encourage individuals, societies and official departments to take greater care in preserving their papers, whether related to policy decisions or the contemporary status of individual species and sites. These records will play a vital part in studying the nature conservation movement of the 1970s. We do not know what questions the historian of the environment will be asking in ten, thirty, or fifty years' time, but his dependence on documentary evidence will be no less than it is today. As responsible members of the nature conservation movement, we have perhaps a moral duty to help him in his task.

Chapter One

The Preservation of Nature

Man has always been interested in those plants and animals which helped him in his daily life. Various wild plants were a clue to the fertility of the soil: maiden-hair grass, wild carrot, horse mint, wild thyme and birds-foot trefoil were thought to indicate poor soils, whereas yarrow and the black thistle were associated with more fertile soils. Plants were collected for the preparation of medicines, colouring materials and cosmetics. Indeed, they were the most important form of medicine, and most botanists were medical men until the seventeenth century. William Turner is regarded as the Father of British Botany, but he was essentially interested in plants for their medical properties.[1]

Likewise, a keen interest was taken in those wild animals which were hunted for food or sport. Their meat helped to vary the staple diet, especially in winter: on the coast, seabirds were often taken in order to eke out the normal diet of fish and vegetables. Each year, raids were mounted on the puffin colonies of Ailsa Craig. Robert Gray described how nets were spread over the rocks at night, enclosing the puffins which sat on their eggs or beside their young. He wrote, 'in the morning, about an hour after sunrise, the men returned for their spoil; and, after twisting the necks of the fluttering captives, threw the bodies into the sea, where they were picked up by one of the fowlers . . . in a boat.'[2]

The exploitation of these natural resources was so important that sometimes even Parliament intervened to preserve individual species of wildlife. An Act of 1533 sought to protect the eggs of wildfowl between 1 March and 30 June each year and to prohibit the slaughter of wildfowl between 31 May and 31 August. The Act noted how various persons were taking large numbers of birds

> . . . in the somer season at such tyme as the seid olde fowle be mowted and not replenysshed with fethers to flye nor the yonge fowle fully fetherede perfectlye to flye.

There were already signs of a serious decline in the number of 'dukkes mallardes wygeons teales wyldgeese and dyverse other kyndes of wyld-fowle', which threatened supplies of eggs and meat to the tables of the nobility and the markets of every town in the kingdom.[3]

It is clear that concern for plants and animals was conditional on their being of direct value to man. Very little sympathy or interest was shown for wildlife itself. Botany did not emerge as an independent science until the seventeenth century, when in 1629 Thomas Johnson published his book *Iter . . . in agrum Cantianum* which treated plants as plants, rather than as herbs for medical use. His book described over 250 plants which were found during a tour of parts of Kent.

The foundation of the Royal Society in 1663 is regarded by many as representing the beginnings of modern science, and for many years it was the only organised national society for the study of natural history as a whole. Fitter has distinguished two trends from the early eighteenth century, the first being the establishment of frequently ephemeral learned societies or clubs. The Aurelian Club may have been the earliest entomological society in the world, founded in 1745, but it soon came to an untimely end following a fire which destroyed its library and collections in 1748. A Society for Promoting Natural History was created in 1782, but achieved so little that a group of dissatisfied members founded the Linnean Society of London in 1788, which soon became the foremost natural history society in Britain.

Meanwhile, a second trend was developing; that of establishing philosophical clubs where interested persons could meet and discuss natural phenomena of all kinds. By the mid-nineteenth century, many had evolved into natural history societies and clubs: for example, the Cotteswold Naturalists' Field Club and the county societies for Somerset and Worcestershire were established in the 1840s, and by the 1890s almost every part of the British Isles was served by a local society. The preservation of wildlife was included among the objectives of some of these new societies: a speaker at the foundation dinner of the Wilt-shire Archaeological and Natural History Society in 1854 expressed the hope that the Society would help in reducing the losses of wildlife in the county. In his view, birds and animals were persecuted out of ignorance, superstition and the sheer love of cruelty, and he expected the Society to play its part in educating and disciplining people in their conduct toward wildlife.[4]

But naturalists and their associations were exceptional in their out-look on wild plants and animals, and most people, including Parlia-ment, continued to be interested in wildlife only when it impinged on their livelihood and well-being. It was not until the mid-nineteenth century that any significant progress in wildlife protection was made, and that was when public interest was stimulated by reports of cruelty toward birds and instances of over-collecting of specimens, leading to the increasing rarity and local extinction of plant and bird species.

The perception of these two threats to wildlife led to the formation of national and local societies, and chapter two will examine how they initiated and exploited the various Acts of Parliament, county orders and by-laws. Legislation was regarded as the most effective way of regulating cruelty and over-collecting, but in the longer term, improvements in education were equally important. Both adults and children had to be taught to understand and respect all forms of wildlife. This chapter will conclude by demonstrating the essential role played by research in providing the guidelines as to how these objectives could be secured.

The Sportsman and Cruelty to Animals

Although the establishment of Royal Forests and Chases indicates an early interest in hunting, both for food and pleasure, relatively few wild animals were killed until the eighteenth century when the widespread use of the breech-loading, double-barrelled gun and central-fire percussion cartridges made it possible to kill very large numbers, even in a single drive. The game bags of pheasants and partridges became so heavy that sportsmen had to buy fresh breeding stock in readiness for the following year. But there were no attempts to replace the other birds killed in the game coverts during the shoots.

There are many accounts of this slaughter, but one of the most graphic appears in Osgood Mackenzie's memoirs, *A hundred years in the Highlands*, published in 1921. Mackenzie boasted that he had, for example, shot 1,900 head of birds and animals on his estate in Wester Ross in 1868. This included 1,314 grouse, 33 black game, 49 partridges, 110 golden plover, 35 wild duck, 53 snipe, 91 blue rock pigeons, and 184 hares. He had no compunction in shooting 'anything that moved'. Mackenzie recorded how he was shooting snipe one day on the Isle of Ewe when he started 'a thrush which had a broad white ring round its throat, just like that of a ring ousel. I promptly shot it', and he described how 'on another day on the same island we kept putting up nearly as many short-eared owls as grouse and snipe . . . I shot five'.[5]

This kind of slaughter was not exceptional, and it may have been no coincidence that Mackenzie himself reported a dramatic decline in the number of most birds in the late nineteenth century. He described how 350 snipe used to be shot on a neighbouring estate and how 'they bred in considerable numbers on my grounds and gave me a lot of sport. Now there is hardly a snipe to be seen anywhere. The rock pigeons which used to provide such good practice for our guns, have also pretty well disappeard. The great northern diver is becoming quite scarce, whereas it used to be common.'

The journalist, Richard Jefferies, provided an equally grim view of the future of wildlife in lowland England, along the river Thames, where, 'the moorhens are shot, the kingfishers have been nearly exterminated or driven away from some parts. . . . The result is that the osier-beds on the eyots and by the backwaters—the copses of the river—are almost devoid of life. A few moorhens creep under the aquatic grasses and conceal themselves beneath the bushes, water-voles hide among the flags, but the once extensive host of water-fowl and river life has been reduced to the smallest limits.'[6]

But the impoverishment of the wildlife of the countryside by so-called sportsmen aroused comparatively little concern: it was only when they caused obvious cruelty and suffering to individual birds that the public conscience was aroused. Nature preservation in its early days was almost entirely an emotional issue, fired by outrage at the barbarity of fellow-man. It is significant that one of the first successful campaigns on behalf of preservation was directed toward stopping parties of 'sportsmen', mostly from towns, from slaughtering seabirds during the breeding season, when it was easier to kill very large numbers of birds.

The first battues at Flamborough Head occurred in 1830 when a steamer took parties of twelve to thirty 'gentlemen' daily to shoot the birds as they rose in fright from the cliffs. Charles Waterton described the consequent cruelty and waste in his *Essays on Natural History*, published in 1838. He wrote, 'no profit attends the carnage; the poor unfortunate birds serve merely as marks to aim at, and they are generally left where they fall. Did these heartless gunmen reflect, but for one moment, how many innocent birds their shot destroys; how many fall disabled on the waves, there to linger for hours, perhaps for days in torture and in anguish; did they but consider how many helpless young ones will never see again their parents coming to the rock with food; they would, methinks, adopt some other plan to try their skill, or cheat the lingering hour.'[7]

These excursions became more frequent following the building of the railways, and various tradesmen soon began to exploit this cheap source of plumage by offering payments for the wings and other choice parts of the young kittiwakes and other birds. In order to secure even greater profits, the fashion of decorating ladies' hats with bird plumage was encouraged, and John Cordeaux described in the *Zoologist* in 1867 how London and provincial dealers offered a shilling each for 'white gulls' and one man had boasted of having killed 4,000 gulls in one season. Another had obtained a contract for the supply of 10,000 birds to a London dealer. A Member of Parliament, Howard Saunders, recalled in the 1860s how he had watched the plumage hunters at work, 'often cutting their wings off and flinging the victims into the sea, to struggle with feet and head until death slowly came to their relief'. He recalled, 'I have seen the cliffs absolutely spotted with the fledglings which had died of starvation.'[8]

The cruelty and dramatic fall in the number of seabirds at Flamborough Head and elsewhere aroused little concern until 1868 when Professor Alfred Newton referred to the battues in his address to the British Association conference at Norwich. He remarked, 'fair and innocent as the snowy plumes may appear on a lady's hat, I must tell the wearer the truth—she bears the murderer's brand on her forehead'. Newton attacked the hypocrisy of a nation which censured the Spaniards for their love of bull-fighting and yet connived at the agony inflicted on thousands of birds and their young each year.[9]

The inhabitants of the countryside were equally guilty of cruel practices. W. H. Hudson provided several examples of callousness toward birds in Cornwall in his work *The Land's End*, published in 1908. Thousands of redwing, thrushes, larks, fieldfares and other species flew westward toward Land's End whenever waves of cold air, with snow, struck southern England, and on such occasions many birds dropped exhausted among the sand dunes or towans where men and boys had prepared hideous devices called teagles. These consisted of sets of twenty or thirty baited hooks, fastened with short threads to a string, two or three feet long. They were placed on a strip of ground from where the snow had been cleared. The hungry birds seized the bait on the hooks, oblivious of the struggles of victims already caught by the teagles. Many succeeded in freeing themselves by breaking the thread, but the birds eventually died since the barbed, bent wire remained in their beaks or was swallowed.[10]

Only the larger birds were taken as food: the remainder were simply thrown to one side, mortally injured. Hudson was appalled both at the callousness of these trappers and the attitude of their fellow countrymen who tolerated this behaviour. Hudson censured in particular the attitude of 'landlords, who are absent or else shut up and inaccessible in their houses where they see nothing and hear nothing; the local editors; the ministers of religion; and above all the authorities, and county and borough councillors and magistrates. They are all very careful of their "position" and their "reputation" and cannot afford to and dare not denounce or interfere with these old pastimes or customs of the people.'

Wildlife and the Collector

During the nineteenth century, there was growing concern over another form of disturbance. As the number of visitors to the country-side rose (see page 68), so there were complaints of more and more damage to wild plants and animals. There were warnings that rare plants would disappear, and the common species would become rare, as visitors and holiday-makers picked, dug up and trampled on the plants.

Primroses vanished from hedgerows and woodlands in the vicinity of towns, bluebells were damaged by trampling, and many distinctive flowering species became locally extinct. According to a correspondent to *The Times*, 'the danger is becoming far greater nowadays than it was for there are few parts of the country which are not accessible by motor-car. It is quite easy to drive almost anywhere, load a car with roots and flowers, and get away without being observed.' The pasque flower *Pulsatilla vulgaris* was relatively common on Therfield or Royston Heath in Hertfordshire but, according to S. F. Harmer: 'as soon as it begins to flower, it is ruthlessly attacked by the natives of Royston and by motorists from a distance. . . . During the present year (1929) I found thirty people, mostly young women, engaged in picking every flower they could find, one fine Sunday afternoon.'

Not content with picking the plants, some visitors dug them up and took them away. A. J. Wilmott visited one part of the South Downs every year to see two patches of ten and twelve specimens of the lizard orchid *Himantoglossum hircinum*, but then, in one year, he found all the plants had been dug up, simply leaving ten and twelve holes in the ground.[11]

Most plants were picked or dug up by families and individuals, visiting the countryside on a casual basis, but some organised excursions were arranged. 'Charabancs were driven down to desirable localities' filled with women all intending to come home laden with primroses and bluebells. The Great Western Railway organised 'a daffodil express' on Easter Sunday, 1934, which travelled from Paddington to Gloucester, where the passengers transferred to a bus which took them to Newent Woods in order 'to spend an hour or so gathering as many daffodils as they could tear up in the time'.

Perhaps the most serious trend was the practice of collecting plants for sale in shops and nurseries. A correspondent to *The Times* in 1929 reported seeing hundreds of bunches of snakes-head fritillary *Fritillaria meleagris* for sale in a shop window in Bath, which had been picked in the meadows of Cricklade, 30 miles away in Wiltshire. Not only the foliage, but the roots, were taken of rare ferns during the fern-collecting crazes of the nineteenth century. In his *Flora of Cornwall*, published in 1909, F. Hamilton Davey referred to the 'shameful plundering' of the royal fern *Osmunda regalis* by local and itinerant fern-vendors. He recalled how one professional collector boasted of having sent an entire truck-load of roots, weighing over five tons, from a railway station in Cornwall. At times, the demand for ferns was so high that even the more common species became rare in accessible places.[12]

There was equal concern over the parallel traffic in caged wild birds. Large numbers of small, colourful birds, and song-birds, were caught. In 1913, an inspector of the RSPB reported seeing hundreds of gold-finches for sale for a shilling each in the street markets of east London. Box after box of newly-caught birds were sent from the suburbs and further afield in Bedfordshire and Cambridgeshire to the shops and Sunday stalls of Shoreditch and Bethnal Green. There is some evidence of an increase in this trade in the late nineteenth century, reflecting perhaps the increasing affluence of people who were able to afford for the first time such 'luxuries' as a caged bird. Bird-catching was usually a spare-time activity which became more important as the working week grew shorter. The trade may have become more profitable as transport became faster and cheaper.[13]

The nineteenth century was also a time of growing interest in natural history, and Nicholson has drawn attention to the tremendous strides made in ornithology following the publication of works by George Montague and Gilbert White. Gilmour has described how 'top-hatted Victorians' travelled by train to the Lizard or Teesdale, armed with the latest flora. But this interest did not always benefit the species under study. T. H. Mason described how dealers visited Saltee Island, off the coast of County Wexford, and carried away boat-loads of guillemot eggs for sale to oologists in England. The eggs exhibited such a variety of markings that collectors paid high prices for each, and so systematic was the robbery of nests that the number of guillemots had declined dramatically on the island by the First World War.[14]

Whereas most zoologists and botanists contented themselves with sufficient specimens for their immediate use, some allowed their collecting to become an obsession. For them, science was the 'cloak for miserly accumulation'. Far from contributing to knowledge, these kleptomaniacs often impeded the research of others, for so many specimens were removed that it became almost impossible to study the natural distribution and behaviour of rare species. Although there were already thousands of eggs in public and private collections, oologists still went to great lengths to secure further specimens. There were reports from Epping Forest, for example, of collectors who drilled holes in the trunks of trees with a brace and bit, then used a key-hole saw to enlarge the holes, in order to take the eggs of the woodpecker. This was repeated not once but many times until the collector had worked systematically through the area.[15]

Apologists for collecting claimed that only a small number of specimens was taken compared with those destroyed by natural causes.

They described how the hard winter of 1916–17 had almost exterminated the long-tailed tit and Dartford warbler. They pointed out how gamekeepers inflicted far greater losses in the course of a year than even the most zealous collector of birds and eggs. E. M. Nicholson accepted this view in his book *Birds in England*, published in 1926, and agreed that the blackbird, for example, 'could afford to supply a thousand times as many specimens' before it came within danger of extinction. But he also pointed to the irony of the situation whereby these collectors took only one pair of blackbirds, whereas they sought as many golden orioles and other rare species as possible. Unlike Nature and the game-preserver, they concentrated their destructive power on the rare, and as the number fell so the value of each specimen rose and the stimulus for collecting it increased. In the eyes of many, this made the collector the greatest villain in the preservation of rare species.[16]

The apologists for collecting fell back on the argument that the removal of a single egg from a clutch, or the first clutch of a season, would have virtually no impact on the population, but T. A. Coward refuted these arguments by pointing out how impossible it was for the collector to know whether he was taking the first egg or clutch.[17]

The impact of the collector on individual species may be illustrated with reference to the Dartford warbler *Sylvia undata*, Cornish chough *Pyrrhocorax pyrrhocorax*, and kite *Milvus* spp. The former was often called the furze wren on account of its association with large areas of furze on the heaths and downs of lowland England. It is probable that numbers fell from the seventeenth century onwards as farmers reclaimed areas for cultivation, but the main reason for the dramatic fall in numbers in the nineteenth century was over-collecting. It was relatively easy to find the birds in the distinctive and locally distributed habitat. The Cornish chough was another threatened species, and even E. T. Booth, one of the most active collectors, had to admit, 'the cause of their scarcity on the Cornish coast is not hard to find. There is a great demand for young birds: all that are taken command a ready sale. Consequently, as the nests are not, as a rule, in situations very difficult to be reached by those accustomed to the use of ropes, at the end of the breeding-season there are few besides old birds left. If such wholesale robbery is continued, the result is not difficult to anticipate, and its accomplishment can hardly be long delayed.'[18]

As a class, birds of prey were particularly vulnerable to collectors since they were already sparsely distributed. The kite was traditionally an important scavenger in the streets of London and other urban centres, and the general improvement in sanitation during the post-medieval period may have been the first cause of its decline in numbers. From the eighteenth century onwards, the population of rural birds began to decline as guns became more efficient, and farmers and game-preservers used them to slaughter the alleged predators of poultry runs and game preserves. Collectors may have been 'the straw which broke the camel's back', for they systematically and persistently hunted down the birds. The last eggs in England were taken at Wragby, Lincolnshire, in the 1870s, and in Scotland about ten years later. By the 1920s, only five pairs of kite survived in the more solitary, upland parts of Wales. In spite of efforts to safeguard the nests, collectors still succeeded in robbing the nests or causing the birds to desert in thirteen of the years between 1900 and 1945. In 1937, Miss Dorothy Raikes launched a Kite Preservation Fund to reward farmers who helped in trying to fend off the collectors.[19]

Although the collectors of birds and eggs won the greatest notoriety, the collectors of local and distinctive insect fauna posed an equally serious threat. The decline and extinction of various insect species were variously attributed to weather conditions, microscopical fungoid diseases, parasites, the predations of birds, the advances of cultivation, and the poisoning of food plants and the atmosphere by chemicals, but W. G. Sheldon, writing in the *Entomologist* in 1925, placed the blame squarely with the collector of insects. Although the other factors might reduce the number of insects, they rarely caused the extinction of a species. But the chances of recovery were greatly diminished if the number of specimens had previously been reduced by collecting: there was a stronger possibility of the remaining specimens being eradicated by a natural cataclysm.[20]

In his paper, Sheldon illustrated the decline of a number of species of Rhapalocera, including the famous large copper butterfly *Lycaena dispar* Haw. in the late 1840s. This followed the discovery that the butterfly always laid its eggs on the food plant, the great water dock, which was very conspicuous and could be seen towering above the tallest growth from far afield. The number of plants diminished following the drainage and cultivation of large parts of the Huntingdonshire fen in the mid-nineteenth century, and it was comparatively easy for dealers and local people to collect all the larvae from the few surviving food plants.

The RSPCA

The growing interest in wild plants and animals in the nineteenth century drew attention to the increasing incidence of cruelty and over-collecting. Such activities not only harmed wildlife but human society itself, for the perpetrators were guilty of bestial, thoughtless or selfish acts. The protectionists believed that in saving wildlife, they were also helping to preserve the very fabric of society.

In making a plea for protecting all forms of wildlife on the River Thames, Richard Jefferies emphasised how most of the 'mischief done on the river is really the work of a small number, a mere fraction of the thousands of all classes who frequent it'. He attacked the thoughtlessness and selfishness of this minority of 'sportsmen': society had to discipline them. Likewise, the RSPB drew attention to the corrupt and evil influence of collectors in human society. Many were 'men of wealth and position, officers in the Army, clergymen, "ornithologists" popularly known for their utmost interest in bird life and even for their pronouncements in print on bird-protection'. In truth, 'these collectors not only snap their fingers at the law and take pride in evading and transgressing its provisions, but employ trade agents and dealers to work for them and give heavy bribes to poorer men—men in the responsible positions of keepers and coastguards, and also fishermen, shepherds and others whose ignorance and poverty render them ready catspaws'. In the Society's view, such men not only threatened bird life, but they were an insidious and evil influence on human society itself.[21]

Against this background, protectionist societies were founded, which modelled themselves on existing pressure groups, such as the Anti-Slavery Society. The first to be founded was the Royal Society for the Prevention of Cruelty to Animals (RSPCA), which was primarily concerned with reducing cruelty to domesticated animals.[22] This society in turn became the model for later ventures, including the Selborne Society and the Society for the Protection of Birds, founded in the 1880s.

The Society for the Prevention of Cruelty to Animals was founded in 1824, and obtained its royal charter in 1840. It initially concentrated on suppressing cruelty to horses and cattle in large urban markets. Having met with some success, especially in London, the Society agitated for the suppression of all forms of baiting and fighting, and an Act of 1835 (page 22) gave the Society's inspectors the power to prosecute those organising such activities as bear-baiting and cockfighting.[23]

By the middle of the nineteenth century, the RSPCA had become involved in protecting wild birds and their nests and eggs. It used the data provided by leading ornithologists and local societies to promote legislation, and played a leading role in securing the Sea Birds Protection Act of 1869. During the 1870s, it began campaigning against cruelty arising from vivisection, and became embroiled in trying to defend all kinds of wild animals from deliberately cruel acts of sport. In 1871, the Society inspected pigeon-shooting matches at Hurlingham, and it tried to curb the worst forms of stag-hunting and rabbit-coursing. Although only modest advances were made, a close time for hares was enacted in 1892, and a general measure for the protection of all wild animals was secured in 1900.[24]

By concerning itself with a wide range of issues, the RSPCA secured the support of a larger number of people. Like all voluntary bodies, it had to retain the support of zealots and yet stop such people from alienating more moderate opinion. This was achieved by creating distinct groups within the Society for such causes as protecting birds and opposing hunting and vivisection. In this way, the Society could benefit from the zealots' energy, imagination and resourcefulness, and yet avoid full responsibility for their tactical errors and political naivety.

Although the Society cultivated wide support, it appealed to the government or powerful public figures whenever faced with a problem. It preferred to use private pressure rather than a public outcry to achieve its ends. Far from viewing the government with deep suspicion, the Society welcomed its support and sought to extend government powers. Two of the government's school inspectors were elected to the executive committee in 1857: the Society tried' to strengthen liaison between its own inspectors and the police and mines inspectors: it agitated for the replacement of private slaughterhouses by public slaughterhouses where the treatment of animals could be better regulated.

This strategy of moderation and prudence was reinforced by the professionalism of the Society in raising funds, conducting legal cases, and in promoting legislation. Although the Society did not flinch from appealing to emotion and sentiment when attacking cruelty, it also became a leading authority on animal questions, and was conseqeuntly used as an advisory service by government, various organisations and individual people.

Whilst the RSPCA was primarily concerned with cruelty to domesticated animals, it took a leading role in promoting the first legislation to protect wild birds. But its indirect contribution to the nature preservation movement was even more important. It demonstrated the great potential of pressure groups in changing public attitudes and behaviour. It survived the ridicule of those who accused the Society of putting dogs before men. It gained a reputation for patience, skill, tact and perseverance. New societies could draw on this experience, and some of its members played a key role in founding new wildlife preservation societies. The first meetings of the Society for the Protection of Birds were held in the offices of the RSPCA.

The RSPB

The first national organisation specifically concerned with protecting wildlife was the Selborne Society for the Protection of Birds, Plants and Pleasant Places, founded in 1885. It was a logical extension of the RSPCA in trying to extend humanity to all forms of wildlife. The association with the memory of Gilbert White, the great naturalist of Selborne, was particularly appropriate since White was the first person to study wildlife with warmth and sympathy, showing how animals and plants were an essential part of the larger world.

The Society had the following four objectives:

a) to preserve from unnecessary destruction such wild birds, animals, and plants, as are harmless, beautiful, or rare;

b) to discourage the wearing and use for ornament of birds and their plumage, except when the birds are killed for food or reared for their plumage;

c) to protect places and objects of interest or natural beauty from ill-treatment or destruction;

d) to promote the study of natural history.

Anyone could become a member of the Society by paying a subscription: those who gave over half-a-crown per annum were eligible to hold office. It was hoped each person would form a branch, and by 1886 eleven branches had been established, mostly in Hampshire and Surrey.[25]

The Sea Birds Protection Act of 1869 (page 23) helped to check the destruction of kittiwakes and produced a temporary lull in the fashion for 'white wigs' on the heads of ladies, but new supplies of plumage were discovered in the tropics. Between December 1884 and April 1885, for example, the plumage of 6,828 birds of paradise, 4,974 Impeyan pheasants, 770 Argus pheasants, 404,464 West Indian and Brazilian birds, and 356,389 East Indian birds was sold on the London market. This trend aroused widespread concern, and a Plumage League was founded in 1885 which demanded from its members a pledge never to wear feathers. A year later, the League merged with the Selborne Society and even more people became aware of the scandals of the plumage trade. But the Selborne Society had a wider range of objectives and could not devote its resources specifically to bird protection. Its members were not required to give a pledge against wearing plumage.[26]

In this vacuum, Mrs Robert W. Williamson of Didsbury, Manchester, formed a Society for the Protection of Birds in 1889, specifically to stop thousands of egrets, herons, and birds of paradise being slaughtered each year for their plumes. Meanwhile, Mrs Edward Phillips held occasional 'Fur, Fin and Feather' afternoons at her house in Croydon, near London, attended by such distinguished persons as W. H. Hudson. The members of these two groups tried to persuade their friends not to wear bird plumage, and wrote letters to newspapers at every opportunity. Mrs M. Lemon recalled in later life how she attended the 'Fur, Fin and Feather' afternoons, and on Sundays she noted which women wore plumed hats in church. These women received letters from Mrs Lemon on the following Monday morning, pointing out 'the cruelty of a practice which meant starvation and death for numberless orphaned fledglings' whose parents had been killed by the plumage-hunters.[27]

By 1891, the size of the Society for the Protection of Birds had outstripped the resources of the founder members in Manchester, and its affairs were transferred to Miss Hannah Poland in London. At this point, the Society obtained the support of those attending the 'Fur, Fin and Feather' afternoons. A meeting was held and a formal constitution was drawn up by F. E. Lemon and accepted. For the first year or so, all the officers were women, but W. H. Hudson succeeded Mrs Phillips as chairman in 1892. He was a great inspiration to the infant Society but a bad administrator, and he was succeeded in 1895 by Montagu Sharpe, who remained chairman of the Society until 1942. Miss Poland was succeeded as secretary in 1892 by Mrs Lemon, who superintended the bulk of the Society's work until the late 1930s.

The rules of the infant Society demanded:

i) that members shall discourage the wanton destruction of Birds, and interest themselves in their protection;

ii) that Lady-members shall refrain from wearing the feathers of any bird not killed for the purposes of food, the ostrich excepted.

The Society believed the best way of destroying the plumage trade was to secure as many members as possible, who would sign the pledge never to wear plumage. It was hoped these members would set an example to others who would in turn become members and stop wearing feather-bedecked hats. This was thought to be far more effective than legislation, posters and public appeals. Accordingly, the Society created as many branches as possible, with local secretaries who subscribed one shilling per annum each. Ordinary members paid only two pence as a registration fee, and by 1898 there were 152 branches and 20,000 ordinary members. Branches were set up overseas, and the branch in India secured the first measure against the plumage trade, namely an order from the Indian government in 1902 which banned the export of bird skins and feathers.[28]

A large part of the Society's resources was directed toward promoting Plumage Bills to destroy the imperial and international traffic in plumage. Speakers and writers used the 'storehouse of statistics and first-hand information' belonging to the Society to publicise the cruelty and selfishness of the trade. In 1911, the Hon. Mrs Arthur Henniker organised a demonstration on behalf of the Society, which consisted of sandwich-men parading in the West End of London during August and just before Christmas. They carried pictures telling the story of the egrets, with a placard showing a hat trimmed with osprey. The men distributed leaflets describing the barbarity of slaughtering the birds, and similar large posters were displayed on walls and hoardings throughout London and the country.[29]

The first official recognition of the necessity to curb the wholesale destruction of egrets came in 1899 when officers of the British Army were ordered to stop wearing osprey plumes. The government was sympathetic toward banning the traffic in feathers and skins, and, after several attempts, an Importation of Plumage (Prohibition) Act was passed in 1921, which banned the import of all plumage into Britain, except for the feathers of the African Ostrich and eider duck. Thereafter, the Society assisted in enforcing the Act and, in 1925, the Council of the Society decided 'that remonstrances should continue to be sent to Drapery firms, Millinery Establishments, and other shops which display and advertise Contraband Plumage, as well as to individuals seen wearing such feathers'.[30]

The single-mindedness of the Society gave it an easily recognised identity, but once established the strength of the Society lay in the fact that it broadened the scope of its work. It expanded from being simply an anti-plumage movement into an organisation working for the protection of wild birds in every way and by all available means. In this way, it secured the support of a wider section of the community, concerned with harmful developments in their own locality and in the country at large. This transition coincided with the granting of a royal charter to the Society in 1904, which became the Royal Society for the Protection of Birds (RSPB).

The Society was successful in attracting influential and expert patronage. Miss Poland secured the support of the Duchess of Portland who served as president of the Society until her death in 1954. Such public figures as Sir Edward Grey (later Lord Grey of Fallodon), Lord Lilford and the Poet Laureate, Alfred Austin, became members. Most of these people were already influential in older bodies, such as the RSPCA. Montagu Sharpe and F. E. Lemon were barristers with a keen interest in ornithology: they not only served as chairman and secretary of the Society respectively, but they played a leading role in formulating Wild Bird Protection Bills. The support of such ornithologists as W. H. Hudson and J. A. Harvie-Brown was of critical importance. By 1892, Hudson had written two of the five leaflets published by the Society: he was already well known and esteemed among naturalists and in the world of literature. By supporting the Society in such a direct and positive manner, he raised the standing of the Society and won it many distinguished members.[31]

For the first few years, the resources of the Society were extremely modest. A balance sheet was published in 1891 which recorded an income of £7. 13s. 8d. and outgoings of £6. 3s. 11¾d.: a weekly paper unkindly called this 'a sparrow's housekeeping book'. As the Society took on more commitments, so it needed a much larger annual income, and an associate membership was introduced for those contributing at least a shilling a year. Those who gave a guinea became life members and after 1897 they were called fellows of the Society. By the turn of the century, the Society had discovered the value of Christmas cards and calendars for publicising its work and raising funds. Six thousand cards were sold in 1899, with a cover-design by Archibald Thorburn and containing four stanzas written by Alfred Austin. But expenditure continued to outpace income, especially after the formation of a Watchers' Committee in 1902 to safeguard rare species (page 42). The Society resorted to special appeals for such ventures, but the results were often disappointing.[32]

The RSPB soon discovered the value of co-operating with organisations not specifically concerned with wildlife preservation. This may be illustrated by reference to lighthouses and the liaison established between the Society and the Elder Brethren of Trinity House. Wherever powerful beams were installed in lighthouses, ornithologists reported finding large numbers of migrant birds lying dead beneath the structures each morning. At first, it was thought the birds had crashed into the light, and one observer described how he had 'stood on the gallery of the Eddystone lighthouse and watched the migrants striking the great lantern and falling into the surf beneath for ten and a half hours without a break' during the height of migration.

J. P. Thijsse studied the problem at the Terschelling lighthouse on the Frisian Islands of Holland, where the strong light of 30 million candlepower caused havoc on one of the most important European migration routes. Thijsse believed that the birds flew around, rather than at the light, and eventually fell to the ground and death through sheer exhaustion. He, therefore, arranged for ladder-like perches to be provided for the birds on migration nights near the roof and light of the lighthouse, and he reported to the RSPB in 1913 that once this had been done, 'instead of thousands perishing in a single night . . . only a hundred died during the whole migration time'.[33]

Armed with this information, a deputation from the RSPB met the Elder Brethren of Trinity House to explain the success of the perches in Holland. The Elder Brethren agreed to instal similar perches at St Catherines Point in the Isle of Wight and at the Casquets near Alderney. The RSPB provided the necessary funds for the perches and erection work, and the project proved so successful that further perches were placed in position on the Spurn and the South Bishop lighthouses.

However, some ornithologists continued to insist that the birds died by crashing into the lighthouses, and they claimed the perches would simply provide another obstacle for the birds. Consequently, the towers of a number of lighthouses were floodlit in a series of experiments, so as to warn the birds of danger. The experiments proved so successful that the perches were later taken down. Dungeness was the first lighthouse in Britain to be floodlit and, by 1960, seven towers had been illuminated.[34]

The Oil Menace

The role of voluntary bodies in alerting public opinion to the dangers faced by wildlife may be illustrated by the example of the RSPB and its fight against aoil pollution. The Society acted as a very important pressure group in persuading the government to introduce legislation and to seek international co-operation in reducing the menace to all forms of marine life. The campaign also demonstrated the need for greater liaison between voluntary bodies concerned with nature preservation, both in Britain and overseas.

The invention of new processes often created new hazards for wildlife, and this was clearly seen with respect to the internal combustion engine and the use of oil. The people of the Scilly Isles were familiar with shipwrecks and made use of the objects washed up on the beaches, but in 1907 a new kind of wreck occurred. The ship *Thomas W. Lawson* sank and oil escaped into the sea as its tanks burst on the rocks. Many birds and rabbits on the island of Annet died on the beaches, killed by the oil. The islanders were terrified lest the oil caught fire and the smoke suffocated the community.[35]

The incidence of oil pollution increased, and the following report from a watcher employed by the RSPB was typical of many. He wrote, 'on the foreshore of Dungeness I have seen nine scoters with oil on their plumage, and many more seem to be making towards the shore. Several guillemots are completely covered; it is pitiful to see them trying to rid themselves of the terrible stuff; undoubtedly all must perish, even those with the least bit of oil on; in my experience none recover. I am taking on myself the painful duty of putting them out of misery in the most humane manner.'[36]

The RSPB publicised the effects of oil on seabirds, and received the support of such public figures as Lord Montagu who described in the House of Lords in 1922 how swans had died in the Solent and Beaulieu river from oil. Not only were birds directly killed by the oil, but their food supplies were contaminated. Whitebait were 'washed up in summer by the million, caught in the oil'. The fishing industry was menaced and holiday resorts complained that the thick, tarry oil washed onto the beaches deterred many holiday-makers from the seaside.[37]

Although some observers blamed the increased number of shipwrecks during the 1914–18 war, the rise in pollution clearly reflected the growing number of oil-fired vessels and oil tankers. In order to maintain their stability, the vessels replaced the oil in their tanks with sea-water: when they drew near or entered port, they simply emptied the bilge-water in readiness for filling the tanks with oil again. The bilge-water usually contained an oily sediment. Consequently, there was serious pollution off the Kent coast between Folkestone and Margate where many vessels pumped out their bilges before entering the Port of London.

The Board of Trade was the government department most directly responsible for curbing sea pollution since merchant vessels were the fundamental cause of the problem. It first became aware of the problem in 1918 and, spurred on by the agitation from the RSPB and elsewhere, it convened a conference in 1921 of representatives of harbour authorities, shipowners and oil companies. In 1922, Parliament passed the Oil in Navigable Waters Act, which levied fines of up to £100 for the discharge or escape of oil into navigable waters within three miles of the coast. The Act came into force on 1 January 1923, and replies to a questionnaire by local authorities, chambers of commerce, harbour authorities and coastguards in 1924 indicated that the Act had 'had undoubtedly a good effect, but that the nuisance was still serious'. The Board of Trade stressed the need to retain the goodwill of the shipping industry, especially as it was so hard to identify and prosecute any vessel causing pollution.[38]

Whilst the Act was a step in the right direction, both the voluntary bodies and government agreed that little could be achieved until every country took action, both in territorial waters and on the high seas. In 1925, the RSPB sent 1,232 circulars to the members of both the Houses of Commons and Lords, calling for an international conference to be convened on ways of curbing oil pollution. The circulars aroused widespread support, questions were asked in Parliament, and it was suggested that the matter should re raised at the League of Nations.[39]

Meanwhile, great concern was shown in the United States over the growing incidence of pollution, and an interdepartmental committee reviewed the problem throughout the world in 1926. It concluded that 'practically all agencies engaged in the production, transportation, handling or use of oil must be regarded as actual or potential sources of oil pollution of coastal territorial waters'. In June 1926, the American government invited foreign governments to send 'experts' for 'an exchange of views on technical matters and to consider the formulation of proposals for dealing with the problem of oil pollution of navigable waters through international agreement'.

The conference was duly held in Washington and was attended by 'experts' from thirteen nations. A draft convention was prepared which envisaged legislation against 'the discharge of crude fuel or diesel oil, or any mixture containing more than 0.05 per cent of such oil, or having a content of such oil sufficient to form a film on the surface of the sea visible to the naked eye in daylight in clear weather'. The British experts believed the most effective method of reducing pollution was to fit separators to ships, which would separate the oil from the bilge-water prior to discharge. Separators had been devised which were relatively efficient and cheap. The conference, however, failed to reach agreement on this question: some nations were afraid that the inspection for separators and an examination of their efficiency would be tantamount to spying and that military secrets might be revealed to potential enemies.

The conference recommended instead that each nation should have the right to ban the discharge of oil up to fifty nautical miles from its coasts and, in exceptional circumstances, the limit should be extended to 150 nautical miles. Account would have to be taken of the configuration of the coast, prevailing winds, currents and fishing grounds. Although the draft convention was only concerned with merchant vessels, it called upon every nation to ensure that war ships complied with any regulations and caused the minimum of pollution.

Although the British government regarded the draft convention as another step in the right direction, it believed the oil-free zones would be difficult to define and enforce. There were also misgivings lest the convention should give the French the right to legislate against oil pollution in British territorial waters, some of which were within fifty nautical miles of France. But, in the event, the convention was never adopted since Germany, Italy and Japan refused to give their support and the other nations believed it was futile to proceed without unanimous agreement. Furthermore, the stimulus for action died down in the late 1920s following reports of an improvement in oil pollution. The United States government claimed in 1929 that a convention had become unnecessary in view of the voluntary co-operation already given by the shipping industry.

The RSPB denied that there was any improvement in pollution and, having despaired temporarily of international action, the Society tried to persuade the British government to take unilateral action again. The government, however, refused to enforce the installation of separators since this would raise 'difficult diplomatic questions' and it would be unfair to expect British shipowners to fit separators while foreign operators were spared the cost and trouble. In any case, about

300 ships were already fitted with the devices and shipowners seemed to have voluntarily adopted the fifty-mile limit. The number of complaints of oil pollution in Britain had fallen from twenty-nine in 1926, to eleven in 1930, and the 1922 Act seemed to be effective. By 1933, twenty of the twenty-seven cases brought under the Act had been upheld in the courts.

Nevertheless, the agitation for further curbs on pollution continued. In 1929, the RSPB organised the printing of over 180,000 special stamps for use on envelopes. The stamps showed 'a suppliant bird', together with the words 'Urge Shipowners to install Oil-Separators and so Save the Seabirds'. They were printed in over six languages and were sold in Britain for three pence a dozen. Simultaneously, over 10,000 copies of an illustrated leaflet were sent to members of parliament and shareholders of shipping companies.[40]

Questions were again raised in Parliament and eventually the sustained agitation had its effect by spurring the British government into again trying to secure international co-operation. In 1934, it placed the issue on the agenda of the League of Nations, drawing attention to 'the great destruction of sea birds in circumstances involving much suffering, as well as of damage to inshore fisheries and to the amenities of seaside resorts and the beaches generally'. The League referred the question to its Communications and Transit Organisation which drew up a draft convention very similar to that produced at Washington in 1926. There were plans for another conference, but once again Germany and Italy refused to participate. Britain and the United States decided to resort to diplomatic pressure, but by this time there were growing fears of a second world war. With the threat of war, any hope of controlling the environmental hazard of oil pollution vanished, whether at the international or national level.

The British Correlating Committee

Stimulated by such problems as oil pollution, there were periodic attempts to strengthen liaison between the various voluntary bodies. This was especially important for the protection of birds which bred in one country, spent the winter in another, and passed through other countries on migration. In each, they might be slaughtered for food or their feathers, or captured alive and placed in cages. It was impossible to preserve them without international co-operation, and yet there was widespread ignorance as to what was happening in each country.

T. Gilbert Pearson, the President of the National Association of Audubon Societies in America, drew attention to the lack of liaison between countries, during a visit to Europe in 1922. At his instigation, a meeting was held in London to examine the idea of an international organisation; it was attended by such figures as Jean Delacour of France, P. G. van Tienhoven of Holland, and Lord Grey and P. R. Lowe of Britain. This meeting decided to form an International Council for Bird Preservation (ICBP), and every country would create a National Section which would act as a focal point for national opinion and information, and as a channel for international co-operation.[41]

These developments in the preservation of birds encouraged discussions as to whether an international organisation was required for preserving all forms of wildlife. The idea was advanced by van Tienhoven at a conference in 1923, and it initially won support from the various voluntary bodies and learned societies in Britain. A meeting of interested parties set up a Central Correlating Committee for the Protection of Nature in January 1924 to act as a 'telephone exchange' and co-ordinating body. Representatives of the ten constituent societies would meet once a year and discuss common problems and draw up common policies on a wide range of topics within the national and international fields.[42]

Although some of the early meetings of the Committee had a world-wide flavour and included discussions on the future of the Dik-dik in Africa, whales and various migratory species, the Committee remained a purely British affair, and it changed its name to the British Correlating Committee in order to avoid giving the impression that it was an international organisation. At the invitation of the CPRE, the Committee gave evidence on behalf of naturalists to the National Park Committee in 1929 (page 130), but otherwise it achieved comparatively little. This was because the constituent societies made so little use of the Committee for discussion and decision-making. There was no point in holding annual meetings after 1926 because there was simply nothing on the agenda to discuss, and the redundant Committee was finally wound up in 1936.[43]

The creation of an international, and indeed a national body in the 1920s may have been too ambitious, but the need for a central, co-ordinating body to protect wild plants remained. The several societies concerned with their protection were all too small and poor to make much impact on public opinion. According to a correspondent to *The Times* in 1931, there was need for a single large body which would provide the same resources and assistance as the Automobile Association in the motoring world. If a single wild plant society was established, it would soon become well known and the public would much more readily obey its notices and participate in its work.

In April 1931, C. S. Garnett proposed a new co-ordinating body, called the Wild Plant Conservation Board, which would advise on the formulation and implementation of legislation and by-laws for wild plant protection and provide an advisory service on such questions as re-introducing extinct species. The representatives of over twenty interested organisations discussed the idea during the conference of the British Association in 1931, and it was decided to set up a specialist committee within the CPRE, called the Wild Plant Conservation Board. This would ensure that the Board was well-known from the start and could speak with greater authority. The secretary and staff of the CPRE would provide administrative help: these were all advantages which the British Correlating Committee lacked.[44]

Herbert Smith was elected chairman and the Board initially met twice a year, but once again the constituent members largely ignored the opportunities offered by such a co-ordinating body. The Board achieved very little and gradually it was eclipsed by the activities of other bodies. For example, the Botanical Exchange Club and Society of the British Isles was renamed the Botanical Society of the British Isles (BSBI) in 1947 and soon afterwards formed a Threats Committee to recommend ways of averting or mitigating the loss of plant species. It compiled reports on areas of high botanical interest, and in 1950 the name of the committee was changed to Conservation Committee.

The growth of these various voluntary bodies, pledged to the preservation of wild plants and animals, provides an important case-study of how a number of people perceived a threat to the world in which they lived, and then took steps to offset the danger. Their immediate response was to form groups of like-thinking persons so as collectively to win public support for laws and propaganda campaigns. In order to achieve success, they had to ensure that their organisations were efficiently run and could compete with others for the public ear: they had to overcome hostility, incredulity and apathy in successfully promoting the preservation of wildlife from cruelty and over-collection.

Chapter Two

Resort to Legislation

There were three ways of preserving wildlife from cruelty and over-collecting: through legislation, educational work, and by creating nature reserves. The efficacy of each method was hotly debated, but most commentators rejected nature reserves as ineffective and costly. They were at best stop-gap measures when the other two methods failed. It was far more effective to pass legislation which would have an immediate effect on cruelty and over-collecting. In the longer term, education was equally important since it would ensure that adults and children came to support and respect the laws to protect wildlife.

As a result, the history of the nature preservation movement in the nineteenth century revolved around an endless succession of Parliamentary Bills and the organisation of public appeals and educational programmes.

The early promotion of legislation owed much to the RSPCA. The first measures were designed to prevent cruelty to domestic animals and they followed the pattern of most early nineteenth-century social legislation in so far as they were 'vaguely benevolent and general', and only later became more detailed and specific. In 1822, Richard Martin obtained an Act which made cruelty to cattle illegal, and thereby set a valuable precedent. Martin's Act was superceded and consolidated in 1835, and was used by the RSPCA in 1838 to stop bull-running in Stamford. The Act also forbade wanton cruelty to any animal, and imposed fines on those who kept places for 'running, baiting, or fighting any Bull, Bear, Badger, Dog, or other Animal (whether of domestic or wild Nature or Kind), or for Cock-fighting'.[1]

The Wild Birds Protection Acts

By the 1860s, there was mounting opposition to the indiscriminate slaughter of wild birds, which gave rise to demands for fresh legislation. In 1867, Canon H. B. Tristram gave a paper at the meeting of the British Association at Dundee, in which he described the role of birds of prey in reducing the incidence of disease among grouse. The predators removed infected birds which would otherwise spread the disease. At the following conference at Norwich in 1868, Professor Alfred Newton gave a paper on the zoological aspects of the Game Laws, in which he warned that the continued slaughter of wild birds during the breeding season would inevitably lead to their extinction.[2]

Newton was a founder member of the British Ornithologists Union (BOU), editor of its journal *Ibis*, and had been elected Professor of Comparative Anatomy at Cambridge in 1866. His widely-publicised lecture at Norwich was the first occasion when such an expert ornithologist and leading academic figure publicly supported wildlife protection. Having reviewed foreign experience, Newton went on to recommend the imposition of a statutory close-time which would coincide with the main breeding season of the endangered species.[3]

Newton's lecture stimulated the Biological Section of the British Association into setting up a committee to consider the 'possibility of establishing a close-time for the protection of indigenous animals'. It included such distinguished members as F. Buckland, H. B. Tristram and J. E. Harting, and the committee was frequently called upon to provide expert advice and evidence during the preparation of subsequent legislation.

During the various discussions of 1868, some commentators wrongly blamed the slaughter of the seabirds of Flamborough Head on the local Yorkshire population, and this prompted the vicar of the parish of nearby Bridlington, the Rev. H. F. Barnes-Lawrence, to make his own enquiries. Soon afterwards, he convened a meeting of local clergy to discuss ways of stopping the annual excursions of trippers and the battues (page 4). In October, a further meeting set up the East Riding Association for the Protection of Sea Birds. The Archbishop of York immediately donated £1 to the Association and allowed his name to be used in promoting any legislation. During the winter, circulars were printed and a form of petition to Parliament was drawn up.[4]

In 1869, the local member of Parliament, Christopher Sykes, and the Duke of Northumberland promoted a Sea Birds Protection Bill, which received the support of the RSPCA and the close-time committee of the British Association. Sykes justified the Bill in the House of Commons on humanitarian grounds and as a means of protecting those birds which helped the farmer and fisherman. He described how flocks of seabirds ventured as far as twenty miles inland, following the plough and eating the worms and harmful grubs in the turned-over soil. At sea, the cry of the birds on the cliffs warned mariners on foggy nights of the presence of rocks—the birds were called the Flamborough pilots.[5]

The Bill was passed in June 1869, and secured a close-time of 1 April until 1 August for thirty-three kinds of seabird (Table 1). Fines of £1, plus costs, would be levied on any person killing, injuring or having possession of one of these birds at that time of the year. To take account of local variations, justices at the Quarter Sessions, or the Lord Lieutenant in Ireland, could apply to the Home Office for orders to extend or vary the close-time. Unfortunately, some of the names used in the schedule to the Act were so vague or ambiguous that a great deal of confusion occurred as to which species were actually preserved.[6]

At first, it was intended that the Bill should ban the collecting of eggs, but it was soon found this would inflict great hardship on 'the poorer classes living on the coast'. At Flamborough Head, for instance, four gangs of local farm labourers, called climmers, traditionally descended the cliffs to collect up to 1,400 eggs a day for sale as food or for use in the manufacture of leather in the West Riding. Certain parts of the cliffs were left untouched so as to avoid any risk of over-collecting. These climmers had been badly affected by the increasing popularity of battues: the number of birds had fallen so sharply that it was only worth two gangs operating in the 1850s and 1860s.[7]

In order to help these local men and avoid controversy during the passage of the Bill, egg-collecting and the slaughter of young birds, unable to fly, were allowed to continue. The island of St Kilda was entirely excluded from the provisions of the Act: the inhabitants were heavily dependent on the bird colonies for sustenance, and sportsmen

Auk	Kittiwake	Sea Parrot
Bonxie	Loon	Sea Swallow
Cornish Chough	Marrot	Shearwater
Coulterneb	Merganser	Shelldrake
Diver	Murre	Skua
Eider Duck	Oyster Catcher	Smew
Fulmar	Petrel	Solan Goose
Gannet	Puffin	Tarrock
Grebe	Razor Bill	Tern
Guillemot	Scout	Tystey
Gull	Seamew	Willock

Table 1

Seabirds awarded protection under the Sea Birds Preservation Act of 1869

never ventured that far for their battues. The Act also contained a provision whereby an Order in Council could be issued for rescinding the close-time in other parts of the country, if this was in the interests of 'the inhabitants of the more remote parts of the sea coasts'.

As in the case of Martin's Act, the measure was an important precedent for further legislation. The close-time committee of the British Association instigated a further Bill in 1872, specifically for the protection of wildfowl which were shot and sold to poulterers' shops. The birds to be protected are identified in Table 2. Each year,

*Avocet	Nightjar	*Stonecurlew
Bittern	Nuthatch	Stonechat
Blackcap	Owl	*Stonehatch
Chiffchaff	Oxbird	*Summer Snipe
Coot	*Pewit	Swallow
Creeper	*Phalarope	Swan
Crossbill	Pipit	Swift
Cuckoo	*Plover	*Teal
*Curlew	*Ploverspage	*Thicknee
*Dotterel	*Pochard	Titmouse, Long-tailed
*Dunbird	*Purre	Titmouse, Bearded
*Dunlin	Quail	Wagtail
Flycatcher	Redpoll	Warbler, Dartford
*Godwit	*Redshank	Warbler, Reed
Golden-crested Wren	Redstart	Warbler, Sedge
Goldfinch	Robin Redbreast	*Whaup
*Greenshank	*Ruff & Reeve	Wheatear
Hawfinch	*Sanderling	Whinchat
Hedgesparrow	Sand Grouse	*Whimbrel
Kingfisher	*Sandpiper	*Widgeon
Landrail	*Sealark	*Woodcock
*Lapwing	*Shoveller	*Wild Duck
*Mallard	Siskin	Woodlark
Martin	*Snipe	Woodpecker
Moor Hen	*Spoonbill	Woodwren
Nightingale	*Stint	Wren
		Wryneck

Table 2

The birds awarded protection under the Wild Birds Protection Act of 1872. Those marked with an asterisk were identified in the earlier Bill, and were given special protection, together with the wild goose, in the Wild Fowl Protection Act of 1876.

thousands were killed in the breeding season, when they were unusually tame and easier to slaughter. Several species, which had once been abundant, were reduced to stray visitors to Britain. The Bill imposed a fine of £1, plus costs, on anyone who killed, took, or had in their possession any of the birds during the close-time. Again, orders could be obtained for amending the close season.[8]

In an almost deserted House, Auberon Herbert, described the Bill as too limited, and secured a motion which proposed extending protection to all wild birds. A House of Commons committee subsequently rejected this sweeping motion, and settled on a compromise whereby 79 birds were to be protected during a close-time from 14 March until 1 August (Table 2). There was, however, no provision for orders and many of the names on the schedule were once again either imprecise or ambiguous.[9]

Newton claimed the Act was useless in protecting wildfowl since the profit from selling the birds would outweigh the cost of the fine. This was because the Commons Committee had been obliged to reduce the penalties in order to avoid treating a boy, who killed a robin or hedge-sparrow, as a criminal. Instead of being fined £1, a first offender was simply reprimanded and fines of only five shillings, including costs, were to be levied on subsequent offences.

Consequently, a further Wild Fowl Protection Bill had to be introduced in 1876. This was successful and granted a close-season from 15 February until 10 July for the wildfowl identified in the original Bill of 1872, plus the wild goose. Fines of up to £1 could be levied, and provision was made for orders to be issued, amending the close-time.[10]

In 1880, the close-time committee helped to promote a further Wild Birds Protection Act, which granted all birds a close-season between 1 March and 1 August: any offender would be reprimanded and liable to costs for the first offence, and fined up to five shillings with costs for subsequent offences. Harsher penalties would be invoked for killing, taking or having possession of any birds identified on a schedule, namely a fine of up to £1 for each offence. Once again, orders could be obtained to take account of local variations. Although it was originally planned merely to extend earlier legislation, it was soon decided to repeal all earlier Acts in order to avoid even greater legislative confusion. The birds on the schedules of the 1869 and 1876 Acts were accordingly incorporated in the new schedules, with the exception of the black-headed gull and wild goose. There was at first no intention of adding further birds, but the House of Lords successfully moved amendments for the inclusion of the American quail, bittern, cuckoo, goldfinch, kingfisher, nightjar, nightingale, owl, oxbird, and woodpecker, which had been included in the schedule of the 1872 Act, and the bee-eater, colin, fern-owl, goatsucker, hoopoe, night-hawk, oriole and roller. The lark was given protection in the following year.[11]

Unfortunately, the measure was amended in two ways which made it harder to secure convictions. The original Bill allowed landowners and occupiers to authorise any person in writing to destroy birds causing damage to property, so long as the species was not identified in a schedule. But Sir William Harcourt claimed the need for written consent would be far too troublesome, and accordingly only the verbal authority of the owner or occupier was required. This had the effect of providing a loophole for the bird-catcher: it was much harder to prove that no verbal consent for bird destruction had been obtained.

Secondly, the Act of 1880 prohibited any person selling or possessing any wild bird between 15 March and 1 August that had recently been killed or taken 'unless such person shall prove that the said wild bird was either killed or taken or bought or received during the period in which such wild birds could be legally killed or taken, or from some person residing out of the United Kingdom'. Soon afterward, an action was brought against a poulterer who had bought wild duck at Leadenhall Market from a salesman who had in turn bought them from a person living outside the United Kingdom. The court found this to be illegal, and immediately poulterers agitated for a revision of the Act so as to overcome this technical difficulty.

The government conceded the point, and introduced a further Wild Birds Protection Bill in 1881, which stated that any person could sell or possess any wild bird if he satisfied the court that:

i) the killing of such wild bird, if in a place to which the said Act extends, was lawful at the time when and by the person by whom it was killed; or

ii) that the wild bird was killed in some place to which the said Act does not extend, and the fact that the wild bird was imported from some place to which the said Act does not extend shall until the contrary is proved, be evidence that the bird was killed in some place to which the said Act does not extend.

Although this amendment, which became law in 1881, was simply designed to clarify and thereby strengthen bird protection, it tended to have the opposite effect. It became much harder to secure convictions against illegal shooting, trapping and collecting under the 1880 Act.[12]

The inadequacy of the 1880 Act soon became clear. Whilst it provided a general scheme for the protection of birds, it failed to stop the collection of eggs which was, in the longer term, an equally serious threat to bird survival. Oology was becoming very highly organised, and a sense of urgency was introduced in 1891 when an organisation called the Naturalists Publishing Company advertised an expedition to some of the finest bird colonies in the Shetlands for the purpose of egg-collecting.

This stimulated Alfred Pease to introduce a Bill in 1891 which sought to protect birds' eggs by exploiting the opportunities provided by recent local government reforms. In 1888, county councils and county borough councils had been established, and Pease proposed granting them powers to make schedules of eggs most badly in need of protection in their respective areas. Any person taking or destroying such eggs would be fined five shillings per egg.[13]

Although the Bill failed, it formed the basis of a further measure, introduced by Sir Herbert Maxwell in 1893. This passed the House of Commons, but then became the centre of a great storm of controversy as to whether the councils should protect individual species or individual areas of land. In the House of Lords, Lords Walsingham attacked the Bill on the grounds that no council had the competence to decide which species required protection. He proposed an amendment which gave councils powers to designate sanctuaries where every bird would be protected. This would greatly facilitate the work of individuals and societies which were already trying to safeguard such areas.[14]

Maxwell refused to support the changeling Bill when it returned to the Commons, and the measure was dropped. He poured scorn on the proponents of sanctuaries, noting the absurdity of protecting the eggs of crows and other undesirable birds just because they happened to be laid among those of rare and beautiful birds requiring protection.

Eventually, a compromise was struck, and in 1894 Maxwell introduced a successful Bill which gave the councils the option of protecting specific birds and their eggs, or forming areas for the protection of all species. In the event, neither solution was ideal for it proved notoriously difficult to identify the eggs of protected species from the remainder, and the protection of areas simply attracted the attention of collectors. The councils generally preferred to issue orders to protect individual species and, by 1910, seventy authorities had issued schedules of protected species whereas only seventeen areas had been designated as sanctuaries, but these included such key localities as the Norfolk Broads, Brean Down, Dungeness, the Farne Islands and Skokholm.[15]

In 1896, there were attempts to improve law enforcement and protect selected species and areas throughout the year. Lord Stamford introduced a measure drafted by the RSPB in order to remove the defects of the 1880 Act, namely that bird-catchers had to be caught in the act of actually taking the birds and, secondly, that the courts had no powers to confiscate the equipment of the catchers. The Bill overcame these problems by treating the catchers as trespassers and allowed the nets and decoys to be seized. The government declined, however, to support the measure on the grounds that the proposed changes in the law of trespass were too radical.

The initiative then passed to the County Councils Association, which had recently appointed a committee of experts to enquire into the need for bird protection throughout the year. The committee included Lord Lilford, Sir Herbert Maxwell, W. H. Hudson and Montagu Sharpe, and their report formed the basis of a new Bill which became law in the same year. This gave councils the right to apply for orders to protect any bird or area throughout the entire year. Magistrates were empowered to confiscate traps and nets used by those convicted of offences under the Act. Unlike previous legislation, the measure did not apply to Ireland.[16]

There occurred in the early part of this century a further five Acts which extended existing legislation and tried to check some of the worst forms of cruelty toward birds. In 1902, Lord Jersey secured an Act which allowed birds or eggs taken illegally to be confiscated. This ended the anomaly of collectors selling the carcases, skins or eggs for amounts exceeding the fines imposed by the courts.[17]

St Kilda had been omitted from the provisions of the 1869 Act and subsequent legislation in order to avoid any possibility of dislocating the traditional collection of eggs. By 1900, however, collectors had 'discovered' the distinctive St Kilda wren and the forked-tailed petrel, and there was a real possibility of these birds becoming extinct. Sir Herbert Maxwell obtained an Act in 1904 which extended the provisions of earlier legislation to the island. The wren and petrel were included in the schedule of protected species, but the fulmar, gannet, guillemot, puffin and razorbill were excluded.[18]

In 1904, Sydney Buxton secured an Act which banned the use of the pole-trap, which was not only hideously cruel but also made a mockery of bird protection. According to W. H. Hudson, 'half-a-dozen pole-traps in use on one estate would keep down and even exterminate the owls inhabiting the country for many miles around'.[19]

In May 1908, Hudson published his book *The Land's End*, which contained a passage describing the use of the teagle in Cornwall (page 5). Sir Frederick Banbury was so appalled by the barbarity of the hooks and pieces of thread, as described by Hudson, that he secured an Act for the prohibition of their use, all within the space of three months.[20]

Finally, the Protection of Birds Act of 1925 placed a ban on the use of bird lime and the practice of using birds as decoys for others. It became illegal to keep a bird, other than poultry, in a cage which was so small that the bird could not stretch its wings.[21]

The relevant Wild Birds Protection Acts, passed by Westminster, remained in force in the Irish Free State until 1930 when they were replaced by fresh legislation. In that year, two measures were passed by the Dail Eireann, one for game and the other for wild birds. The Game Preservation Act related to the hare, pheasant, partridge, grouse, quail, land rail, plover, snipe, and woodcock, all kinds of wild duck, including mallard, teal and widgeon, and all kinds of geese, including brent and barnacle geese. A close-time was imposed, which varied according to species.[22]

The Protection of Wild Birds Act of 1930 was a private member's measure which received full government support. It related to all species not included in the provisions of the Game Preservation Act, and introduced a close-time from 1 March until 31 July, when it was illegal to kill or take birds. Landowners and occupiers, and persons authorised by them, were, however, allowed to kill any bird which damaged crops or property, with the exception of 70 species identified in a schedule to the Act. A fine of up to £1 per bird was imposed on any offence related to a scheduled species. For other birds, a first offender was simply reprimanded and discharged on payment of costs, and subsequent offences would be fined up to ten shillings per bird. Existing protective orders remained in force and new ones could be issued by the Minister of Justice, on receipt of an application from the local authorities.

The Act extended the ban on the pole-trap and teagle to include the use of bird lime and decoys. This aroused the greatest controversy during the passage of the measure through the Dail. Many deputies believed it would destroy the bird-catching trade, which employed an estimated 300 people. The deputy for Dublin Borough South, Sean F. Lemass, claimed it would bring even greater misery to those who 'make a precarious livelihood by catching and rearing song birds'. He continued, 'if conditions improve, and if the economic situation becomes better, so that there is a reasonable prospect for the persons finding employment in other spheres we can then afford to indulge in luxury legislation of this kind, but at present we cannot do so. We must put the necessities of human beings before those of wild birds'. Another deputy, F. Fahy, retorted that no one could justify cruelty, otherwise a case could be made for retaining torture in order to keep the torturer in employment.[23]

Finally, the Act forbade the export of the chough, crossbill, goldfinch, kingfisher, linnet, peregrine falcon, redpoll, siskin, skylark, twite and woodlark for sale as live birds. Traffic in these species had been increasing, and the deputy for Langford-Westmeath described during the debates how goldfinches were sent by the dozen from his constituency to Belfast, where they were shipped to England. Again there was opposition: one deputy asked why it should be illegal to export these birds when the import of caged canaries was allowed.

Since the Wild Birds Protection Act of 1896 had not applied to Ireland, it had been impossible to protect a bird species or area throughout the year. The Act of 1930 removed this anomaly, and a year later the Dublin Corporation obtained the first order for a sanctuary, at North Bull in Dublin Bay. For many years, P. G. Kennedy and the Irish Society for the Protection of Birds had advocated a sanctuary on this island, so close to the schools and colleges of Dublin.[24]

In spite of this range of legislation, the RSPB and its Irish counterpart regarded the measures as inadequate. Councils were not compelled to apply for orders, and Monmouth and Radnor in Wales, and Bute, Elgin and Linlithgow in Scotland, for example, took no action. This led to many anomalies along administrative boundaries: the Cheshire County Council made orders for their part of the Dee estuary, but the Flintshire County Council gave no protection. Thirty-nine borough councils were similarly apathetic, providing the bird-catcher with virtual immunity.[25]

But in many respects, the Act passed by the Dail in 1930 was the last of its generation: new ideas were abroad. In 1899 and 1900, J. Bigwood introduced two Bills in the Commons which were essentially designed to test public opinion. With the backing of the RSPB, he tried to reverse the principles of the Act of 1880 so as to protect all birds during the close-season, with the exception of the few which damaged crops. The councils would apply to the Home Secretary in the normal way for orders, but in this case to place birds on a Black List.[26]

Prompted by the inadequacy of the White List system and the potential of a Black List, the RSPB pressed for an official enquiry from 1903 onwards. The Home Office finally conceded a departmental committee of enquiry in 1913: the Hon. E. S. Montagu was chairman and Lord Lucas, Parliamentary Secretary to the Board of Agriculture, F. Elliott of the Home Office, E. G. B. Meade-Waldo of the RSPB, W. R. Ogilvie-Grant of the Natural History Museum, H. S. Gladstone, and W. Eagle Clarke of the Royal Scottish Museum served as members. A draft report was completed by the outbreak of war in August 1914, but no further progress was made until 1919 when a further three meetings were convened and the report was issued in August of that year.[27]

The committee had to decide whether to adopt an entirely new approach to legislation, or simply to consolidate and amend existing legislation. It was agreed that the Black List would provide the best means of protecting rare species, and accordingly the committee planned to adopt this new concept right up to the point when its draft report was being written. At this point, it changed its mind, owing to 'the difficulties which the committee experienced in attempting to draw up a detailed scheme of protection on these lines'.

This was largely due to the fact that the committee could not draw a clear distinction between harmful birds, worthy of a place on the Black List, and those which were beneficial or innocuous. Very few birds remained unswervingly in one class throughout the year and often the pests of one area were tolerated or even encouraged in another. Extremely little was known about the feeding habits and behavioural patterns of birds, and consequently the impact of individual species on agriculture, forestry, orchards, gardens and fisheries was imperfectly known (page 49).

In the light of these difficulties, the departmental committee finally decided to improve and extend existing legislation. It proposed extending the close-season from 1 March until 1 September, issuing a new set of schedules of protected birds, and suggested granting uniform protection to birds, nests and eggs. The local authorities should continue to propose and implement new and amended orders, but these should be arranged in 'ornithological groupings'. Instead of each council applying separately to the Home Office, common orders should be drawn up. The Home Office should have the right to intervene and issue or amend orders where one or more councils failed to take the initiative.

The committee thought these reforms would suffice if steps were taken to ensure that the law was administered on scientific criteria. Accordingly, the committee recommended appointing an Ornithological Advisory Committee which would, for example, collect and classify information, investigate the habits of birds, and thereby provide an expert advisory service to the Home Office and other interested parties. The Advisory Committee would consist of scientists, together with agriculturalists and field naturalists with expert local knowledge.

In 1921, the Home Office appointed a Wild Birds Advisory Committee for England and Wales, and another for Scotland. Lord Grey was the chairman of the former, which included a representative of the Ministry of Agriculture, P. R. Lowe of the British Museum, Montagu Sharpe of the RSPB, and E. C. Stuart Baker of the British Ornithologists Union, with Sir Eric Holderness as secretary. H. S. Gladstone was chairman of the Scottish committee, with J. Ritchie as secretary.[28]

Their most important task was to draw up a new Wild Birds Protection Bill which would improve and extend existing legislation, and in 1923 a government Bill was introduced by Lord Grey and passed the House of Lords. It was then dropped owing to the dissolution of Parliament and a general election. Further Bills of 1925 and 1926 failed to make any progress owing to the pressures on the Parliamentary timetable. Another attempt in 1927 was initially more successful: Sir

Clive Morrison-Bell succeeded in piloting the Bill through its second reading without a division being taken.

This Bill adopted four categories of protected birds, namely those protected irrespective of the wishes of landowners and occupiers throughout the year, or close-season, if the landowners and occupiers gave their consent. The close-season was defined as 1 March to 31 July. On the initiative of councils, the Home Office would issue orders modifying the schedules and length of the close-season to comply with local circumstances and needs. It would be illegal to sell or have in possession any birds, plumage, skins or eggs belonging to the protected species, and the onus of proof was placed on the defendent in proving his innocence.[29]

The Bill was referred to a House of Commons committee where the proponents of the Black List attacked the Bill for containing all the deficiencies of the White List system. They tabled so many amendments that the Bill made little progress and the sponsors finally decided to drop the measure. The government refused to contemplate any further moves: a member of the Home Office commented, 'up to the present, our efforts to put the protection of wild birds on a better footing have been defeated by the controversies between the different schools of would-be protectors ... it is no use the Home Office wasting any more time until the hot-heads have learned a lesson'.

The initiative now moved to the Stormont in North Ireland which followed the Dail in 1931 in trying to codify and extend earlier legislation passed at Westminster. The Ulster Society for the Protection of Birds was founded in 1927 and played a major role in formulating the new Act which, together with an amending Act of 1950, was based on the principles of the Black List. Every bird, egg and nest was protected throughout the year, with the exception of species placed in category I, namely the bullfinch, cormorant, great black-backed gull, hooded crow, house sparrow, Irish jay, jackdaw, lesser black-backed gull, magpie, rook, shag, sparrow hawk, starling, and wood pigeon. The eggs and nests of the blackbird, chaffinch and greenfinch (category II) were protected, but a landowner and occupier, or any person authorised by them in writing, were empowered to kill or take these birds 'for the purpose of protecting crops or property from damage'. The eggs and nests of the common curlew, common redshank, golden plover, grey plover, rock dove, stock dove, and whimbrel, and all species of ducks, geese and swans, were similarly protected, but the birds themselves (category III) could be killed, taken and sold outside a close-season which extended from 1 March until 12 August.[30]

With these exceptions, it was illegal to kill, injure or take any birds or take or knowingly and wilfully disturb any egg or nest, except 'in the ordinary course of farming and forestry work'. It was illegal to sell or even possess any of the protected birds, eggs or nests, and it became unlawful to kill, take or disturb any species during Sundays, except for the purpose of protecting property, crops, game or fisheries.

The Minister of Home Affairs was given powers to amend the schedules and modify the close period. Thus, the mute swan was outlawed in 1935 because of the supposed damage to duck grass, but the slaughter of so many birds during the war persuaded the Minister to restore full protection in 1946. The peregrine falcon was outlawed in 1940 to protect army carrier pigeons, but likewise was protected again after the war. The barnacle and brent geese, which were placed in category III in the Act, were transferred by the Minister to category II, but their numbers declined so rapidly that they were soon afterward restored to their former status.[31]

The Act of 1931 and its amending legislation made it illegal to purchase or sell birds and their eggs during periods when they were protected. A penalty of up to £25 or three months in jail was imposed on a first offence, and £100 and six months in prison on subsequent offences. Only licensed game dealers could undertake legal transactions, and a register of any purchase or sale had to be kept. Consignments of dead birds had to be clearly marked whilst in transit. The Minister was allowed to issue orders exempting traders from the regulations during the first fifteen days of a close-period, and to permit the import of birds and eggs from outside Northern Ireland.

As in the case of the Act passed by the Dail, the pole-trap and teagle remained illegal, and a ban was placed on the use of bird lime, decoys, and those cages which were too small for birds. In addition, a fine of £25 or imprisonment for up to three months was imposed on those who used motor boats or planes for taking birds, and on anyone who participated in shooting matches where captive wild birds were liberated for the purpose of being shot.

A Wild Birds Advisory Committee was established to advise the Minister, which played an important part in promoting the amending legislation of 1950. The Minister was empowered to grant licences for exempting research or educational workers from the provisions of the Act, and to grant orders for the designation of bird sanctuaries. In the case of the latter, the consent of the appropriate landowners and occupiers was required before an order became valid.

The Act of 1931 placed Northern Ireland far ahead of any other part of the British Isles in the protection of wild birds. After the debacle of 1927, Westminster resorted once again to piecemeal legislation. A Protection of Birds Act of 1933 made it illegal to capture any one of sixty-six resident or migrant species for sale, or to sell, offer for sale, or possess any of these species. The measure, which was introduced and secured as a private member's Bill, imposed a fine of up to

£2 for a first offence and up to £5 on subsequent offences. Three further measures secured protection for the lapwing, quail and water-fowl. The first, the Protection of Lapwings Act of 1928, made it illegal to sell or possess lapwings or their eggs for human consumption between 1 March and 31 August, on pain of a fine of up to £5. This had the full support of the Ministry of Agriculture on account of the way in which lapwings helped to keep down a wide range of farm pests.[32]

Whilst such legislation obtained widespread support, E. M. Nicholson was highly critical of this piecemeal approach to bird protection. It was, for example, naive to imagine the Protection of Lapwings Act would stop any further decline in the number of lap-wings, which faced not only human persecution but other kinds of enemy and handicap. Their food supplies were threatened by the increasing number of rooks, jackdaws and gulls which had become very common due to the elimination of their natural predators, the larger birds of prey. Far from being a substitute, the Acts on behalf of individual species emphasised the need for a comprehensive bird protection measure, based on scientific criteria.[33]

The search for an effective Bill, which would win unanimous support continued. In 1938, the County Councils Association and RSPB appealed for another departmental committee of enquiry, but mean-while the Wild Birds Advisory Committees were reviewing the various options and recommended a new Bill which adopted the concepts of both the White and Black Lists. All birds would be protected, except for a comparatively few species. There would in addition be a White List identifying particularly rare species which required special safe-guards. This would be achieved by imposing heavier penalties for taking such birds, eggs and nests.[34]

After the war, the resuscitated Wild Birds Advisory Committees made similar proposals, but there seemed little prospect of the govern-ment finding sufficient parliamentary time to secure the passage of such a Bill. In 1952, Lord Templewood proposed that the government should allow a private member to take it over. This was received with little favour, but in 1953 Lady Tweedsmuir drew a place in the ballot for private members' Bills, and chose to promote the Wild Birds Protection Bill. She quickly received the support of the government, and the measure became the longest and most complex Bill ever introduced by a private member. There was, however, a risk that arguments over the inclusion of individual species and the length of close-times might leave insufficient time for the passage of the measure but, with the aid of Lord Templewood and Lord Hurcomb, the Bill was piloted through Parliament and received the royal assent in 1954.[35]

The Protection of Birds Act of 1954 simplified the protection of birds by repealing fifteen previous Acts, including Game Laws dating back to 1772 and all the wild bird legislation since 1880. It attempted to protect every wild bird, egg and nest on the basis of both the Black and White Lists. It was, for example, legal for authorised persons to take or destroy both the birds and eggs of twenty species throughout the year, and to take or destroy a further thirty-three birds (not eggs) outside a close-season. On the other hand, special protection was given to forty-nine species throughout the year, and the brambling, black-tailed godwit, whimbrel, greylag goose and six types of duck during the close-season. Any person taking or destroying these prescribed birds, eggs and nests would be liable to special penalties.

The Minister retained powers to amend schedules and the length of the close-season, but the Act gave him powers to take the initiative in issuing new orders. A new Advisory Committee was set up, one for England and Wales, and another for Scotland.

The measure rationalised the situation with regard to sanctuaries. Previously every bird was protected, which Lord Grey had described as 'a fatal limitation' since it meant that even the one or two harmful species had to be preserved. The new Act introduced special penalties for anyone taking or destroying a bird, egg or nest, or committing trespass, on the sanctuaries, but made it legal for an authorised person to take or destroy the birds identified on the Black List in the Act.

The protection of eggs raised special problems. There was an obvious reluctance to prosecute schoolboys, caught stealing sparrows' eggs, and accordingly it remained legal for anyone to take the eggs of twenty-two of the most common species, and further birds could be added to the schedule by the Secretary of State. In addition, the eggs of the black-headed gull or common gull could be taken for consumption and, by an amendment passed in the House of Lords, the eggs of the lapwing could be taken before 15 April in each year. It was argued that most of these early clutches were unsuccessful and their loss would stimulate the birds into laying successful clutches later in the season, thereby helping to sustain and increase the population.

These sections of the Act were opposed by bird protectionists and, following the heavy bird mortality in the hard winter of 1962–3, Lord Hurcomb asked the government on St Valentine's Day to withdraw the orders allowing the eggs of common species to be taken. This was granted, and in 1967 a further Protection of Birds Act was passed which removed the concessions made on egg-collecting in 1954. The Secretary of State was deprived of powers to issue orders permitting the collection of eggs, and it became illegal to sell or import the eggs of the lapwing without a licence. Other sections of the amending Act dealt with sanctuaries and such activities as ringing.[36]

The Grey Seals Protection Acts

Mammals have received comparatively little support from legislation. The most notable instance was the Grey Seals (Protection) Act of 1914 which imposed a statutory close-time between 1 October and 15 December each year, which coincided with the breeding season of the animals.[37]

The grey seal *Halichoerus grypus* spends most of the year at sea, but during the breeding season the animals congregate in large numbers on a few well-defined breeding grounds, called rookeries. Although it was very difficult for sealers and fishermen to land on these rookeries, except in very calm conditions, once on the islands or rocky promontories large numbers of pups and females were clubbed to death within a few hours. The young cannot swim for the first two or three weeks, and the females refuse to desert them. Since the female grey seal produces only one pup a year, there was a serious risk of the seals being exterminated, and the preamble to the Act noted that their number had fallen in Scottish waters to less than 500, and there were even fewer on the Farne and Scilly Isles, and around the coast of Ireland.

Lord Charnwood, who introduced the measure in the House of Lords, described the raids on the rookeries as an 'unquestionably dirty business'. There was a risk of the raids becoming more frequent owing to the increasing popularity of sealskins as motoring jackets. The government decided not to oppose the Bill since no livelihood was immediately threatened, and the measure could be easily enforced since the grey seal was easy to distinguish from the smaller common seal which also had a different breeding season. The Fishery Board for Scotland remarked that 'the Bill does not seem to have much concern with fishing interests but more with natural history'. There were, however, fears of a dramatic rise in the number of grey seals, once protection had been secured, and of serious damage to salmon fisheries. To guard against this possibility, the Act was introduced for a trial period of only five years. In the event, it remained in force on an annual basis throughout the 1920s, under the Expiring Laws Continuance Act.

Although comparatively little publicity was given to the Act, there were few reports of further raids. The constabulary at Port of Ness claimed no boats had left for Rona or Sula Sgeir since 1914, and although some grey seal skins were sold in Glasgow and Edinburgh there was no organised traffic. During the 1920s, the replacement of the traditional fishing boats by small motor boats may have indirectly facilitated protection. The new motor boats were quite unfitted for crossing the intervening forty-five miles of open Atlantic waters to some of the rookeries.

In 1926, the Fishery Board issued a memorandum drawing attention to the damage caused by seals to salmon gear and the fish themselves. Although the bulk of the damage was caused by the common seal, some was attributed to the rising population of grey seals. The Irish Free State had dropped the Act from its own Expiring Laws Continuance Act in 1923, and the Scottish Secretary ordered a review of the Scottish position in 1926. The Fisheries Board made arrangements for a census of the main rookeries by W. L. Calderwood and J. Ritchie in 1926, but the prohibitive cost of coal after the General Strike made it impossible to provide a boat. In spite of rough seas, successful surveys were made in the breeding seasons of 1927 and 1928.

The surveys indicated that there were 1,003 pups, and therefore at least as many female adults in the rookeries, which had mated with at least 330 males. Since seals do not breed until their fifth year, it was assumed 2,000 non-breeding seals, allowing for normal mortality, must have been in the open seas, and accordingly Calderwood and Ritchie estimated that the grey seal population had risen to at least 4,300. They concluded that the Act might be dropped since there was no longer any risk of the seal becoming extinct.

On the other hand, the repeal of the measure was bound to arouse opposition from naturalists and would probably bring no benefits to local fishermen since even the greater population of grey seals appeared to cause little harm to fishing. Calderwood and Ritchie also warned that if the Act was dropped, Norwegian whalers might be encouraged to raid the rookeries. The whalers had already largely exterminated the species in Norway and were frequent visitors to the waters around Rona. In these circumstances, the Act would have to be re-introduced.

The Scottish Secretary, therefore, decided to give the grey seal permanent protection, and a Grey Seals Protection Act was passed in 1932, with a similar measure for Northern Ireland soon afterward. Both extended the close-season to include the entire breeding season, namely 1 September to 31 December, with a maximum penalty of £10 for each offence. The appropriate Minister could issue orders for withdrawing or modifying the length of the close-season where there was evidence of damage to salmon fisheries.

Naturalists wanted the new Act to give complete protection to the most famous seal colonies of Haskeir Mor and Haskeir Beig in the Outer Hebrides through the designation of a sanctuary. Drafting considerations made this impossible, and so a group of members of parliament secured an amendment which prevented the Minister from withdrawing or reducing the length of the close-season for these islands.[38]

By 1947, Ritchie and Calderwood estimated that the number of grey seals in Scotland had risen even higher and, by the 1960s, there was evidence that the population was doubling every nine years, causing serious malnutrition in some rookeries, upsetting the 'balance of nature' and leading, for example, to a decline in puffins which shared the same breeding grounds. The seals were also blamed for serious losses of fish. Accordingly, the Scottish Secretary authorised an annual cull of 800 in Orkney. In contrast, the common seal *Phoca vitulina* had experienced a dramatic decline: at Fitful Head in the Shetland Isles, for example, the population of 300 adults and ninety-one pups in 1954 had fallen to thirty-eight adults and two pups in 1968. A close-season for this species was urgently needed, and yet numbers had to be carefully regulated since each seal ate an estimated two tons of fish per annum.

Accordingly, parliament approved a Conservation of Seals Act in 1970, which sought to strike a delicate balance between a viable breeding population and one that would cause minimum damage to fishing interests. The close-season of the grey seal remained unchanged, and a three-month close-season was introduced for the common seal. The Ministers were given reserve powers to protect an area throughout the year, and could issue licences for the slaughter of seals, even in the close-season, for research purposes, conservation, and for the protection of fisheries. Before doing so, the Ministers had to take account of scientific data on the current size and distribution of the population.[39]

From the 1950s, parliament gave some legislative protection to other mammals. In many respects, it adopted a similar procedure to that used for recent bird protection. The Deer (Scotland) Act of 1959 prescribed measures to prevent poaching and introduced a close-season for red deer *Cervus elaphus*. A Red Deer Commission was appointed to advise on the conservation and control of the animals. In 1963, protection was given to red, fallow, roe and sika deer in England and Wales, and an order extended protection to all species in Scotland in 1966. The badger *Meles meles* was given protection under the Badgers Act of 1973, which prohibited the casual slaughter of the animals, badger-digging, the use of badger-tongs, the possession of the corpse or pelt of a freshly-killed badger, and the sale, offer for sale, or possession of a live animal.[40]

By-laws and the Protection of Plants

Under the Local Government Act of 1888, county and borough councils were allowed to make by-laws for the maintenance of good behaviour and suppression of nuisances not punishable under any other Act.[41] Although there was no specific reference to by-laws for the protection of wild plants, most councils introduced them for this purpose. The by-law obtained by the Leicestershire County Council in 1913 may be

cited: it stipulated that 'no person shall (unless authorised by the owner
or occupier, if any, or by Law so to do) uproot or destroy any ferns
or other wild plants growing in any road, lane, roadside waste, wayside
bank or hedge, common, or other public place, in such manner or in
such quantities as to damage or disfigure any such road, lane, roadside
waste, wayside bank or hedge, common, or other public place.'
Offenders would be fined up to £5 for each offence.

Such by-laws had very little effect: they proved both inadequate and
difficult to enforce, and in 1928 the County Councils Association,
spurred on by various natural history societies, persuaded the Home
Secretary to convene a conference to draw up a new model by-law.
The conference proposed the following by-law, which was subsequently
adopted by twenty-five counties. This stipulated that 'no person shall
(unless authorised by the owner or occupier if any or by Law so to do)
uproot any ferns or wild plants growing in any road, lane, roadside
bank or hedge, common or other place to which the public has access'.

Such organisations as the Society for the Promotion of Nature
Reserves (page 60) and British Ecological Society were still not
satisfied: they wanted the by-law to apply to both private and public
land, and a schedule of protected plants to be appended to each by-law.
In 1933, a deputation from the Wild Plant Conservation Board asked
the Home Office for the following model by-law: 'no person shall
(without lawful authority, the burden of proving which shall be on
the defendent) uproot any ferns, flowers or other plants or take away
mushrooms or cut any trees or remove from trees ivy mistletoe or
other plants attached thereto and growing either in any land privately
owned or in any road, lane, roadside waste, roadside bank or hedge,
common or other place to which the public has access'.[42]

The Home Office pointed out that by-laws could only apply to public
land and that it was impracticable to append lists of specially protected
plants. But in 1934 it agreed to issue a new model by-law which was
subsequently adopted in twenty-four counties. This stated that 'no
person shall, without lawful authority, uproot any ferns, primroses or
other plants, growing in any road, lane, roadside waste, roadside bank
or hedge, common or other place to which the public have access'.

Although the councils were under no obligation to introduce by-laws,
only eight counties in England and Wales failed to do so by 1940. In a
survey of each county conducted by the CPRE, it was discovered that a
copy of the by-law was given to each policeman in Nottinghamshire,
and that the by-law was displayed at every popular picnic spot in Kent.
But most councils regarded the by-laws as a waste of effort since few
people were aware of their existence and even fewer were prepared to
act as 'common informers'. Only the police took the initiative in
implementing them, and the Flintshire County Council commented

'it is extremely unlikely that any person is going to be so stupid as to begin rooting up wild plants with a police constable looking on, and the fact that a constable sees a fern in somebody's car would not justify his making a charge against the owner unless the latter was foolish enough to admit that he had recently dug up the fern unlawfully'.

With respect to private land, a close study was made of the Malicious Damage Act of 1861 and the Larceny Acts of 1861 and 1916 to see whether they could be used or adapted to protect wild plants. Generally, the measures were of little use since it was difficult to prove malice on the part of the defendent, and it was hard to prove the landowner had incurred a financial loss due to the removal of the wild plants.[43]

It was clearly unnecessary and impracticable to prevent everyone taking wild plants, and the voluntary bodies concentrated their attention on trying to eradicate commercial picking and uprooting, since this caused the most extensive damage. Likewise, it was unnecessary to safeguard every plant: no-one wanted to stop children making daisy chains! Several councils had asked for expert help in deciding which plant species required special protection and, in response, H. W. Pugsley drew up schedules on behalf of the Wild Plant Conservation Board in 1934 for nearly thirty counties, which identified both rare species and those picked in very large numbers which required special protection. Copies of each schedule were sent to the councils, magistrates, policemen and teachers in the respective counties for information and guidance.[44]

The Selborne Society drafted several Wild Plant Protection Bills, and the Wild Plant Conservation Board debated the value of a Bill in the early 1930s, which would entirely ban the uprooting of a small number of plants identified in a schedule, and forbid the picking, uprooting and possession of any wild plants for sale without the landowner's consent. These proposed measures, however, never reached parliament. There were, for example, grave doubts over the Bill of the Wild Plant Conservation Board since it allegedly created a legal precedent by placing the onus of proving innocence on the defendant.

The first significant attempt to secure legislation did not occur until 1967 when the Botanical Society of the British Isles, Council for Nature and SPNR sponsored a Bill which similarly made it illegal to pick, uproot or offer for sale any species identified in a schedule to the Bill, and forbade the uprooting of any other plant, except a noxious weed, without the permission of the landowner or lessee. The Bill failed to make any progress, and there was further delay until 1974 when another, and eventually successful Bill, was introduced (page 242).[45]

The Enforcement of the Law

There were only 284 convictions under the Wild Birds Protection Acts between 1896 and 1900, 440 between 1901 and 1905, 314 between 1906 and 1910, 202 between 1911 and 1915, and 96 between 1916 and 1920. The RSPB believed these low figures reflected the failure of the authorities to publicise the legislation and orders, and the police to enforce them. Indeed, many constables were uncertain as to their powers and duties, and magistrates were apathetic and even hostile to attempts to enforce the laws.

The RSPB was, therefore, obliged to play a major role in publicising and enforcing the Acts. It published the terms of the 1904 Act prohibiting pole-traps in 250 newspapers in 1930, and it organised a display of posters in the hop-gardens of Kent, warning the-Cockney hop-pickers of the penalties of taking birds illegally. It was common practice for pickers to catch linnets and take them back to London at the end of the season.[46]

A generation or so earlier, the RSPCA had faced similar problems in trying to enforce legislation, and it had decided to employ its own police force. By 1897, the Society employed 120 private constables, respected men dedicated to eradicating cruelty toward animals. In spite of its meagre resources, the RSPB decided to follow a similar course, and a Watchers' Committee was formed in 1902 to provide the necessary expertise and organisation. E. G. B. Meade-Waldo served as chairman until his death in 1933. The work fell into two broad divisions, namely the general protection of birds and secondly the strict preservation of areas designated as bird sanctuaries.[47]

A relatively small number of ex-police inspectors was employed 'to track bird-catchers, make tours of inspection of bird shops, to call on Police Stations, and to distribute notices and pamphlets respecting the law'. During October and November 1912, for example, Inspector Moxey visited the bird-shops, open markets and Club Row in London, giving cautions and getting police assistance in some cases where it seemed likely that a prosecution would be needed. In a Walworth shop, a very wild blackbird was found in a small and dirty cage, with a broken wing and tail feathers. At Leytonstone, several trap-cages on piles were found in back gardens, intended for catching birds on the edge of Epping Forest. Moxey succeeded in getting six birds liberated and two cages destroyed. At Club Row, he reported seeing a man selling starlings: there were thirty in a small box and the man was carrying three by their necks in his hand.

Inspectors also toured the countryside, trying to discover where the birds were caught and eggs collected illegally. It was extremely difficult and frustrating work because of vested interests and apathy. Perhaps the hardest task was tracking down pole-traps set in such remote parts as the grouse moors of Wales. An inspector's report of 1909 makes this abundantly clear: he wrote, 'very little English is spoken by the class from whom I want information. The hills are terrible, and the thick growth of foliage renders it most difficult to see to advantage at a distance. Yesterday I got within a short distance of a place where I have reason to believe there are traps set, when a heavy mist suddenly began to fall, and I was obliged to make a hasty retreat, as the mountains are full of ravines'.[48]

The RSPB drew some consolation from the fact that cruelty, bird-catching and egg-collecting seemed to decline wherever placards were displayed, police and plain-clothes men became active, and magistrates ordered the seizure of nets and decoys. But there was a growing sense of frustration at the high cost and general futility of enforcing fundamentally inadequate laws. Various courses of action were suggested: R. H. Garnett proposed the compilation of a Black List of egg-collectors for the confidential use of watchers, and in the same columns of *The Field* P. H. Manson-Bahr suggested the formation of 'a society for the extermination of the egg-collector'.

The ideas aroused sufficient enthusiasm to warrant the formation of an Association of Bird-watchers and Wardens in 1936, with Manson-Bahr as chairman and N. Tracy as its industrious secretary. It was essentially a ginger group to the Watchers' Committee of the RSPB, trying to arouse the public conscience and promote more effective action against collectors.

One of its first ventures was to adopt a scheme devised by Geoffrey Dent, which had previously been rejected by the RSPB as too expensive. This was to reward gamekeepers and foresters for every nest where birds of the Falconidae family and short-eared owl were successfully reared. Members of the Association would adopt the nests and pay the rewards when due. In 1938, the nests of nine hobbys and three marsh-harriers were safeguarded in this way, and twenty-one and nine birds respectively were reared.[49]

Meanwhile, a printed Black List was sent to members of the Association, providing the names, addresses and a thumb-nail sketch of over 150 reputed collectors. Guards were mounted over nests, and in this way over eight raids by collectors were frustrated in 1937.

During 1939, visits were made to the Spey Valley in Scotland where systematic collecting was taking place. This provided an opportunity for contacts to be made with the British Oological Association, and in 1940 an agreement was proposed between the Association of Bird-watchers and Wardens and the British Oological Association whereby oologists agreed not to take the eggs of protected birds on the condition that permits were issued for the collection of limited numbers to 'accredited' collectors. In the course of these discussions, three schedules were drawn up, identifying those eggs which should never be taken, those which could be collected in limited quantities under licence, and those which could be taken, except in specified areas. Although this agreement was never implemented owing to the war, the prospect of such an arrangement stimulated the RSPB into assessing which species and areas required special protection (page 94). After the war, the RSPB itself began making payments to farmers and others who assisted in the protection of rare birds, and the Association was merged with the Society in 1947.

This general enforcement of the law had to be complemented by a special watch being kept on leading bird sanctuaries. As the *Daily News* pointed out in 1908, the determined collector would risk large fines to secure his eggs, and 'it becomes absolutely necessary to appoint special watchers to keep the birds under observation all through the nesting season'. By 1920, the RSPB employed twenty-nine watchers in thirteen areas during the nesting season for £405. By 1937, the number of paid and voluntary watchers had risen to sixty-eight. The biennial reports of the Watchers' Committee indicated some of the practical problems encountered by these men. In the Orkneys, the Committee had to make a large grant to the watcher in 1918 so that he could buy a motor cycle: he had a beat of 40 miles and it was especially important to travel the full distance after the arrival of the steamer which frequently brought collectors to the islands.[50]

By 1923, Meade-Waldo claimed that the Society had saved the Kentish plover, Cornish chough, roseate tern, and the raven and peregrine falcon of southern England, from extinction. In addition, the phalarope, eider duck, grebe, shellduck, gannet, diver, fulmar, petrel, tern, kite, skua, harrier, buzzard, merlin, heron, stone curlew, whimbrel and rock pipit had benefited from protection. Ironically, the scale of success in the Shetlands created fresh problems: the great skua, once threatened with extinction, became so abundant that all protection had to be withdrawn, except on Hermaness. Meade-Waldo hoped natural factors would soon bring the population into balance.[51]

From the 1930s, the question of employing watchers on sanctuaries became merged with the more general difficulties of managing both people and the wildlife communities on nature reserves actually owned by the RSPB and other voluntary bodies. This will be discussed in detail in chapter 7. Meanwhile, the search for more effective ways of policing wildlife in the countryside at large continued.

During the early 1940s, Geoffrey Dent proposed the employment of a biological policeman with the rank of inspector in each county. If a salary of £400 per annum was paid, the post would probably attract the right type of trained biologist, and his sole job would be the enforcement of the protective laws, keeping any sanctuaries under surveillance, and generally providing courses on nature preservation for his fellow police-officers and the public.[52]

The Huxley Committee was asked in 1945 to examine the efficacy of legislation on wildlife (page 111). It lacked time to carry out an exhaustive survey, and recommended that a special wildlife committee should be appointed for examining ways of safeguarding wildlife outside the proposed nature reserves, and that its recommendations should be incorporated in a Wild Life Protection Bill. It was essential that the terms of the Bill should be easily enforced, which meant that the public had to understand, support and obey the measure. This could only be achieved if the objectives of the Bill were clearly defined and sensible. Every effort had to be made to advertise and explain its provisions, and this was a considerable educational challenge.[53]

The Role of Education

The protection of wildlife ultimately depended on every person having a love and understanding of wild plants and animals. Without this, every Act of Parliament, order and by-law was a paper-tiger. The voluntary bodies had to create a climate of opinion whereby it was unfashionable and even contemptible to pick flowers or hunt down animals.

This was a tremendous assignment for it meant breaking down long established customs and prejudice. The close-time committee, set up by the British Association in 1868 (page 23), remarked, 'our British agriculturalist is in general no naturalist, and takes it for granted that every grain-eating bird must do him harm. He accordingly does his best to exterminate sparrows and other small birds, little thinking of the benefit they render him in destroying insects'. Likewise, game preservers and their keepers continued to wage war on birds of prey, oblivious to the fact that these birds were 'the sanitary police of nature, removing the diseased birds before they infected healthy stock'.[54]

This ignorance and bias, complained of by the close-time committee, were shared by the public at large. W. H. Hudson was amazed at how little contact people had with wildlife. He visited the Booth collection of stuffed birds at Brighton, to find both adults and children admiring the lifeless, crude exhibits. He wrote, 'the obvious explanation is that they know no better'. They had not seen the birds at first hand, in the real living work. They had no standards of comparison.[55]

There was no alternative but to mount a tremendous educational programme, and in this respect popular writers played an important part in first capturing the interest of the public. Perhaps the most prolific writer was the Reverend Francis O. Morris who published the first part of his popular account of ornithology *A history of British birds* in 1850. Although coloured plates were included, almost everyone could afford to buy the instalments, which were followed in 1852 by two new series, *A natural history of nests and eggs of British birds* and *A history of butterflies*. Morris also wrote hundreds of letters to newspapers and journals extolling the need for wildlife protection: he wrote a letter or article for every issue of *The Animal World* between 1869 and 1872.[56]

Later in the nineteenth century, Eliza Brightwen aroused sympathy for wildlife in her books *Wild nature won by kindness* and *Inmates of my house and garden*, but the most outstanding propagandist was W. H. Hudson. Whilst his books were only read by a minority, his readers were influential and vocal members of society. Although few of them wanted to read about the cruelty and selfishness of Man, they encountered such passages interspersed with the many other topics which characterised Hudson's volumes. According to Nicholson, 'they read him for himself rather than for his birds but, like the Ancient Mariner, he refused to let them go without hearing his tale to the end'.[57]

The voluntary bodies produced a wide variety of leaflets: the Society for the Protection of Birds produced fifty titles by 1904, in addition to a series of educational pamphlets, each devoted to a different bird species. Articles were prepared for magazines, such as the *Ramblers Yearbook*, the *Morris Owner* and *Austin Magazine*, and every opportunity was seized to write to the press: in 1932, for instance, the Wild Plant Conservation Board protested in the columns of the *News Chronicle* at the publication of a photograph of a girl holding an enormous bunch of bluebells. In general, the press and especially *The Times* and *Daily Mail* gave valuable support, and published appeals for the protection of plants and animals during the spring and especially before Bank Holidays.

Considerable use was made of posters. In 1925, the Society for the Promotion of Nature Reserves issued a poster which asked people to pick flowers 'sparingly' and not to dig up the roots. As with many posters, there was a great debate over the poster's style and wording. One critic found the poster too negative and hostile: instead of discouraging visitors to the countryside, they should be encouraged to look at wild plants and animals. By winning their confidence, the visitors would be much more likely to obey the notices. But other critics attacked the poster for not entirely banning the picking of flowers. In 1932, a landowner in Teesdale asked the Society to take its poster down because he was erecting a new poster which completely forbade the picking of flowers. He believed this was the only way of saving the few remaining blue gentians growing near the roadside.[58]

The voluntary societies had to use every technique available to discipline and educate the public. In an address to the Museums Association in 1925, F. R. Rowley called upon curators to orientate their displays toward the need for wildlife preservation. Visitors to herbaria in museums should be reminded of the damage caused by uprooting plants in the countryside, and they should be shown exhibits of seabirds with their plumage clogged with oil. The RSPB itself mounted a display at the International Horticultural Exhibition at Chelsea in 1912 in order to remind horticulturalists and gardeners of the need to safeguard bird life. The display was especially important, following reports of thrushes and other birds being killed by arsenical weed-killers and solutions of copper salts applied to kill worms.[59]

The value of broadcasting was soon realised: reasoned talks on the wireless made a far greater impact than leaflets and posters. Well-known authorities gave occasional talks, which were neither sentimental nor sensational. Announcers made brief appeals for the protection of wild plants and animals before news bulletins during spring and at weekends, and in 1929 the BBC suggested making appeals between lighter programmes in order to reach those people who rarely listened to the news and serious programmes.[60]

It was very difficult to gauge the success of these campaigns, and many societies came near to despair. The Society for the Protection of Wild Flowers commented that 'to educate the adult is sometimes impossible. One has to contend with thoughtlessness, stupidity, habit and selfishness.' On the other hand, it was much easier to influence children through their lessons at school. Lord Lilford was very optimistic that schoolboys, once they had learnt the rudiments of ornithology, would turn from bird-nesting to studying the ways and behaviour of the various types of birds.[61]

But lessons in nature study could take an unexpected turn. A member of the Cotteswold Naturalists' Field Club was horrified to see the winner of a competition at the Cheltenham Floral Fete in 1933 holding twenty-two specimens of *Epipactis palustris*. The plant was only found in Gloucestershire on Sevenhampton Common, in a bog of three acres, which was remote and had previously been little disturbed by the public. Now it seemed the school-girls of the Cheltenham district had discovered the bog and its flowers, and it was likely the plant would soon become extinct.[62]

A. B. Rendle and F. J. Chittenden tried to resolve this kind of problem by drawing up a simple list of rules for the organisers of wild flower competitions. These were that (i) the exhibit should consist of 'say' twelve different specimens, (ii) the specimens must not include the root and should if possible show leaf as well as flowers, and (iii) plants that are known to be uncommon locally should be forbidden. But the Wild Plant Conservation Board was not impressed by this compromise. Nature study and wild flower competitions stimulated children to travel further afield, using public transport, bicycles and cars, and they had a natural desire to take whatever they discovered. It was a waste of time to ask them not to pick a rare plant because few children could distinguish a rare from a common plant, and 'their teachers were often as ignorant as the children'.[63]

The Board called for a fundamental reappraisal of the purpose and content of lessons in nature study at school. Surely, the lessons were not designed to teach children how to hunt and collect rare species: it was far more important to teach every child to recognise and understand plants and animals living near their homes. Wherever possible every school should have its own wild flower garden, where children could study the life histories of the more common plants. They could grow the plants from seed, and discover for themselves the differences between the foliage of young and old dandelions, and the way the sunshine affected the fronds of bracken and the leaves of the Yorkshire fog.[64]

Although not specifically concerned with wildlife or nature preservation, the scout and guide movements played an important role in introducing many children to the countryside. Baden-Powell realised, however, that most children, brought up and living in towns, would soon become bored with the unfamiliar surroundings of the countryside unless they understood what they saw. Scoutmasters were, therefore, told to instruct their troops in 'the calls and customs of birds and animals, the wonders of the stars, the beauties of the flowers, of the hills, of the sunsets, the wonderful mechanism of the individual specimen whether of plant or mammal, insect or reptile, and its exact reproduction in millions of the same species'. Through guidance and instruction, the boys and their parents would soon come to treat the landscape and its wildlife with respect and sympathy.[65]

The RSPB was particularly successful in establishing liaison with schools and education authorities. In 1903, it initiated the Bird and Tree Challenge Shield Competition, whereby children in elementary schools wrote essays on a bird and tree, largely based on their own outdoor observations during the previous year. The six best essays of each school were submitted to the Society for assessment, and a shield, medals, certificates and books were awarded as prizes. The scheme was supported by nine county educational authorities in the 1920s, and an average of twenty-two schools in each county took part. W. H. Hudson contributed £1,000 to the cost of the scheme just before his death in 1922. In his will, he left the residue of his estate to the education account of the RSPB, which amounted to £5,800. This was invested, and the annual revenue was used to expand further the Bird and Tree Competition.[66]

The Contribution of Research

The various voluntary bodies quickly discovered the frustrations of preserving wildlife because so little was known of the behaviour and requirements of individual plant and animal species. Accordingly, they looked to research for clear-cut, objective evidence to support their contentions. In this, they were frequently disappointed for the results of research simply underlined the complex behaviour and inter-relationships of species.

The Society for the Promotion of Nature Reserves first encountered this problem in 1922 when it sent a circular to the owners of each deer forest in Scotland, appealing for the preservation of the pine marten and wild cat. The circular was signed by three well-known and distinguished public figures, Lord Ullswater, Lord Grey and Lord Rothschild. It met with a mixed reception. Although some estate owners claimed they protected both species, many were critical of attempts to preserve the wild cat. The owner of the Airlee estate reported that he left the cat unmolested on its 'natural grounds', but he had to stop the animals invading his grouse moors and causing serious damage. Lord Lovat censured the 'bracketing' of the pine marten with the wild cat. The former was rare and caused little damage, whereas the cat was 'a definite scourge' which was so common as to be a serious menace to game birds and lambs.[67]

This kind of reaction stimulated the search for more objective information on the distribution, abundance and behaviour of such alleged vermin as the wild cat. Were naturalists correct in regarding the wild cat as a species facing extinction? Could the allegations of the estate owners and their keepers be substantiated? The voluntary bodies could not be effective until they had found the answers to such fundamental questions.

Perhaps the utility and harmful effects of individual bird species aroused the greatest controversy, especially during the debates over the relative merits of the White and Black Lists (page 32). The RSPB noted 'Great Britain has not distinguished itself in the study of economic ornithology, which is a difficult and tedious business involving long, detailed, and extraordinarily complex investigations. Of pronouncements positive and airy there have always been more than plenty; but the wide area of research essential, with consideration to crops, soil, natural foods and food supply, weather seasons, decrease or increase in numbers, competition species, and all the matters included in ecological investigation, is another thing'.[68]

Not surprisingly, most controversy surrounded the protection of predatory species. There were many debates as to whether the peregrine falcon *Falco peregrinus* should be included on the various county schedules of protected birds, and in 1925 the National Homing Pigeon Society issued a circular appealing for the removal of all protection and indeed for the extermination of the peregrine falcon because of the large number of homing pigeons it destroyed. The Society described how 2,660 pigeons' legs with 1,028 metal rings were found in the nests of the peregrine falcons on the Great Orme in 1923 and 1924.

The RSPB accused the Society of being extremely narrow in its outlook. The peregrine falcon took over a hundred wood pigeons for every homing pigeon killed: since four to five million pigeons were bred each year, the losses were in any case negligible. The RSPB drew a distinction between birds reared in completely artificial conditions and capable of being bred in unlimited numbers, and the peregrine falcon which was extremely rare and threatened with extinction. Whereas homing pigeons belonged to only one man, the peregrine falcon was owned by everyone.

The Home Office asked the Wild Birds Advisory Committees to review the question and, after a long debate, the Minister was informed, 'it is clearly impossible for the Home Office to assent to a policy which deliberately aims at the total extermination of the peregrine falcon which is commonly regarded as one of the finest of the surviving British birds of prey'. The Committees believed the bird should continue to be protected, except in those areas where there was positive proof of it causing serious losses among homing pigeons.[69]

Perhaps the most controversial bird was the little owl *Athene noctua vidalii* which was not only a bird of prey but an alien, introduced in the nineteenth century. Together with other owls, it was given some protection under the various county orders, but the little owl spread so rapidly that there were soon reports of its taking large numbers of chicks from game and poultry runs. Accordingly, some counties removed it from their schedules of protected species, and in 1935 the British Field Sports Society sent circulars to the remaining forty-seven counties where the owl was protected, appealing to them to withdraw all protection. This stimulated fourteen councils immediately to ask the Home Office to rescind their orders, and the whole question was referred to the Wild Bird Advisory Committees. A split soon developed on the committees: P. R. Lowe supported the requests for outlawry since the birds were 'becoming rather a pest and may very probably develop into a serious one', whereas Montagu Sharpe claimed the little owl caused comparatively little damage. It was finally decided to support all applications for outlawry for an experimental period of five years. By 1940, the bird had been removed from the schedules of thirty counties.[70]

The debates over the peregrine falcon and little owl underlined the need for more research on the diet and behaviour of the birds. Fortunately, there had been a revival of interest in field research, stimulated by the research of J. S. Huxley on the courtship habits of the great crested grebe. In a seminal paper to the Zoological Society of London in 1914, Huxley had demonstrated the vital need to understand animal behaviour, and consequently to study the species in its natural habitat rather than in the laboratory.[71] Huxley himself played a leading part in founding the British Trust for Ornithology in 1933 specifically to undertake this kind of research on British birds. A network of watchers was organised to provide data, collected simultaneously over the greater part of a bird's range, for correlation and synthesis in resolving questions related to the bird's movements, diet, life expectancy and general behaviour.

The research of W. E. Collinges was usually taken as a model of the kind of research required in assessing the damage caused by birds. His papers on the food and feeding habits of the little owl were published in the *Journal of the Ministry of Agriculture* in 1922, based on the analysis of stomach contents of a large number of birds, taken in various areas at different times of the year. Following the outlawry of the little owl in 1935, A. Hibbert-Ware undertook a more detailed study on behalf of the British Trust for Ornithology, and the results were published in 1938. These indicated a 'remarkable absence of chick remains (poultry or game) in pellets' obtained during the summers of 1936–7. Insects and rodents made up the bulk of the diet, except in times of stress, and accordingly there was no justification for any persecution of the little owl.[72]

Whilst such research was a step in the right direction, it rarely changed people's views. Opponents of the little owl claimed the surveys undertaken on behalf of the British Trust for Ornithology coincided with a period when the population of owls was abnormally low and that once the number of birds increased a much larger number of native birds, game and chicken would be eaten. In this complex situation, the Wild Bird Advisory Committees decided to allow the experimental period of outlawry to run its full course. In 1940–1, when the question came up for review, eleven counties decided to rehabilitate the little owl.

Research was required not only to identify pests but also to assess the impact of man on wildlife. F. Fraser Darling emphasised this point in 1938 when he described how human activities could unwittingly disrupt the social behaviour of wild animals. Unless the species could adapt their feeding and breeding habits to changes in land use and management, there was a risk of their becoming locally extinct.[73]

Many naturalists and societies were specifically interested in the tolerance of individual plant species to picking and trampling. Experiments were undertaken to discover their tolerance in a range of conditions, for there was some evidence that plants occupying favourable conditions could withstand far more picking than those growing in unsuitable places. Thus the primroses of Devon could endure much more damage than those of the east of England.

A great deal of interest was shown in one experiment conducted at the Royal Botanic Gardens at Kew in order to assess the impact of picking on bluebells. Four plots were set out. On one, the bluebells were cut to the ground, and on another they were pulled up. On the third plot, the bluebells were trampled on, and the fourth plot was left untouched as a control. At the end of five years, there was no marked change in the number of bluebells on the plots which had been cut or pulled, but there was a striking diminution of plants where the bluebells had been trampled. On the basis of this kind of evidence, it was suggested that plants could be picked in moderation as long as there was no damage to the leaves through trampling.[74]

Clearly, many more studies of this kind were required, and in 1928 E. J. Salisbury launched a *Biological Flora of Britain*, which was designed to collate and provide information on native and naturalised species and their ecological relationships, including details of any field trials and experiments which had been carried out. Salisbury noted that 'much relevant information is to be found scattered through the multitude of botanical journals but it is difficult of access. A great deal is known to field-naturalists but has never been published, and is likely to be lost with the death of the individuals.' Whilst no reference was made to nature preservation, the production of the *Flora* would clearly be useful to the various voluntary bodies. The British Ecological Society supported the idea, but no progress was made until 1941 when plans for a *Flora* were revived and the *Journal of Ecology* published the first studies of individual species in that year.[75]

The need for autecological studies was underlined by the various attempts to save species threatened with extinction. The Llandudno Field Club warned, for example, that the Ormes Head cotoneaster *Cotoneaster integerrimus* would soon be extinct unless 'something is done to prevent it'. Although the bush was abundant in the 1830s, it had become rare by the 1880s owing to the 'rapacity of collectors'. Only nine bushes survived in 1908, confined to 'bleak and out of the way crags'. The Field Club warned that even if the nine bushes survived the collector, 'the species runs a risk of dying out in time of its own accord from exposure and for want of cross-fertilisation'. Although each of the bushes had blossomed in 1909, only five ripe berries were produced.[76]

Fortunately, a number of bushes from the original stock had been planted in various gardens in the Llandudno district, and these were 'visited' by large numbers of wasps *Vespa vulgaris* and *V. germanica*, bumble bees *Bombus terrestris*, and flies of the genus *Musca*. The Field Club wanted to use the seeds and layers from these bushes to establish new sanctuaries in private gardens and in the public gardens of the Happy Valley. 'Then, when strong colonies have in course of time, been established in this way, seeds from them might be sown ... in suitable places upon the cliffs of the headland.' Gradually, the bush would be reintroduced to each part of its only British habitat, before it was too late.

In 1925, the Council of the Royal Entomological Society formed a committee specifically for the preservation of British Lepidoptera. The members of the new committee included Lord Rothschild, H. M. Edelsten, J. C. F. Fryer, N. D. Riley and W. G. Sheldon. It was intended to protect rare and distinctive species in their existing haunts and to introduce butterflies 'into suitable areas where they are at present absent, and where they will be protected by the owners, or occupiers, or by a local committee consisting of naturalists and others who sympathize with the protection of Nature'.[77]

Attempts to introduce species to areas where they had previously been absent aroused a great deal of controversy. Several writers advocated the scattering of wild plant seed during walks, and from car and railway carriage windows so as to enhance the appearance of the countryside. But this was generally condemned by botanists. A. B. Rendle pointed out that most of the seed would be wasted since it would not germinate and most plants would fail to compete with the existing flora. The few species which flourished would probably become agricultural pests. There were also fears that transplanting and the scattering of seed would obscure the natural distribution of species, and prevent future generations of botanists from studying the processes of natural change in the countryside.[78]

Transplanting was only justified in two circumstances. The first was where the plant or animal had become locally extinct. It was essential, however, to know the source of the new stock and to record the introduction in a reputable scientific journal. The second occasion was where a rare species was threatened with extinction due to the destruction of its habitat. Thus, plans were laid in the late 1940s for transplanting specimens of the sedge *Schoenus ferrugineus* from its only station in the British Isles, on the banks of Loch Tummel. It was proposed to raise the level of the loch by fifteen feet as part of a hydro-electric power scheme. G. Taylor suggested replanting the sedge on other sites in the vice-county and, at a later date, re-introducing the plant to the sides of the loch at the new and higher level.[79]

Clearly the protection and enhancement of wildlife had to be founded on scientific principles, and during discussions in the 1940s great stress was laid on the need for a government biological service which could undertake research and experiments on the management of wildlife (see page 206). Information was needed on the long-term effects of killing species for food, sport and as a form of pest control. Help was required in assessing the consequences of picking flowers and introducing aliens. Objective data on these subjects would help the various societies and organisations to become much more efficient and effective in protecting wildlife and educating public opinion.

Chapter Three

Environmental Changes and Wildlife

Every effort was made to enforce the various Acts, orders and by-laws, and to educate the public in the ways of the countryside, but it soon became clear that public behaviour would not improve overnight. Public access had to be restricted on sites of high biological interest, wherever practicable, and the most effective way to achieve this was to acquire the land and control its use.

This was the conclusion of the Farne Islands Association, a voluntary body of naturalists which managed the Farne Islands on behalf of their two owners in the early 1900s. Over 1,000 people visited the islands in 1922: some were keen ornithologists, but many were 'simply trippers who have really no love of birds, but simply go to the islands for a day's holiday and think nothing of destroying the birds' eggs or young—either accidentally or intentionally'. In 1923, the Association decided to prohibit visits to twelve of the fifteen islands during the nesting season, and no-one was allowed to stay more than fifteen minutes on Staple Island. In order to secure greater control over public access, the Association launched a public appeal for the purchase of the islands and eventually the money was raised, and the islands were handed over to the National Trust for safe-keeping.[1]

The more responsible clubs and societies tried to persuade collectors to pick flowers sparingly and not to disturb rare species, but the Society for the Promotion of Nature Reserves commented in 1928 that 'far stronger deterrents are required to restrain the unscrupulous collecting hog from uprooting all the rare plants within his reach'. It concluded that the answer was to buy the property affected and manage it as a nature sanctuary or reserve. In 1910, the Hon. N. C. Rothschild bought 300 acres of Woodwalton Fen, Huntingdonshire, in order to safeguard its wildlife from collectors. The reserve comprised the largest tract of surviving fenland in Huntingdonshire, and contained several species which were rare or absent elsewhere. The fen violet *Viola stagnina* was abundant, and *Viola montana* and *Luzula pallescens* had recently been discovered on the site. Their survival was attributed to the remoteness of the fen from the nearest railway station and the fact that a boat was needed to explore the area thoroughly. This had previously deterred all but the most determined collectors.[2]

But other naturalists were sceptical of the value of such sanctuaries. They believed the cost of acquiring and guarding the land would be prohibitive, and the very act of making a sanctuary would attract the attention of collectors. The creation of reserves would simply be an excuse for not tackling the much harder task of eradicating collecting and bird-catching.[3]

In the face of such arguments, many naturalists simply kept the location of rare species a closely guarded secret. The National Trust struck a compromise, acquiring areas of natural history interest but giving little publicity to any rare species present. No reference was made to the preservation of the Cornish chough on one of the Trust's Cornish properties. No publicity was given to the efforts of a local committee in protecting a rare plant and butterfly on another site in Gloucestershire. It was much more prudent to advertise the superb scenery and fine walking country of these protected properties.[4]

In this climate of opinion, it is likely that the number of sanctuaries would have remained small. The first priority was to introduce and enforce legislation to stop cruelty and over-collecting. A vigorous educational campaign would play a major role in enforcing the various Acts, orders and by-laws. Convictions and stringent penalties would soon make watchers redundant and sanctuaries irrelevant to wildlife protection. From thenceforth, naturalists would only interfere with wildlife during a natural disaster, such as following a severe winter or devastating floods.

This view prevailed throughout the first part of the present century: sanctuaries were subsidiary to the need for legislation, merely a stop-gap measure. In this sense, the creation of the Society for the Promotion of Nature Reserves (page 60) and the activities of the watchers of the RSPB were a very minor component of the nature preservation movement until the 1940s. The drafting of Wild Birds Protection Bills and local by-laws was regarded as being much more important. But a profound change in the value of sanctuaries began to occur during the inter-war period, stimulated by the destruction of the habitat through changes in land use and management.

Changes in Land Use and Management

Between the wars, there was increasing alarm at the scale of changes in land use and management. J. C. F. Fryer and H. M. Edelsten described the destruction of food plants and breeding areas as the greatest threat to insect life. Geoffrey Dent of the RSPB remarked that legislation to protect wild birds, even if enforced, was useless 'if the means of subsistence are taken away' from the birds.

Previously, many important sites for wildlife had survived because they had no commercial value, either for agriculture or forestry, or for building and industrial development. This situation began to change. In 1937, for example, the RSPB was horrified to learn of the destruction of the heronry at Islington in Norfolk, which was the second largest heronry in the county and seventh in Britain. The landowner had decided to fell the trees in order to grow potatoes.[5]

Even the more extensive 'wastelands' were being exploited for new purposes. The sand dunes of Braunton Burrows, Devon, had been traditionally regarded as a refuge for wildlife, with a rich insect fauna and such plants as the round-headed club rush *Scirpus holoschoenus* and the water germander *Teucrium scordium*. But gradually, the situation changed. A golf course and huts for holiday-makers were constructed on part of the dunes, and a local bulb grower began dumping rubbish on another part. During the Second World War, the dunes were used for military training and the situation became so serious that botanists debated whether to transplant several of the rare plants to 'safer sites' as a last resort.[6]

The most dramatic form of change was building development. In 1932, there were fears that the snakes-tongue buttercup *Ranunculus ophioglossifolius* would become extinct at Badgeworth Marsh, Gloucestershire, because the owner wanted to sell the land for building development. He filled half the marsh with rubbish and clinker in order to increase its potential value and, in order to prevent the destruction of the entire site, the Cotteswold Naturalists' Field Club bought the remaining area of marsh, about one-fifth of an acre, for £53.[7]

By the late 1930s, several naturalists began to discern a change in the relationship between nature preservation and agriculture. Traditionally, farmers were regarded as the custodians of the countryside, protecting amenity and sustaining wildlife as a by-product of their husbandry of the land. For this reason, the National Trust deplored the depression in farming which characterised the late 1920s and early 1930s. It considered neglected pastures and woodlands, ill-kept hedges and farm buildings, just as harmful to the amenity of the countryside as ill-placed buildings and industrial development. The Trust rejected any idea of a clash between progressive and prosperous farming and the naturalist.

But changes in farming practice were beginning to have far-reaching effects: many wetland sites were being drained and subsequently cultivated, and grasslands were being ploughed up and managed as part of the rotational system of farm crops. According to E. J. Salisbury in 1929, one-sixth of all the plants recorded in England had become rare or extinct in one or more counties, largely due to the impact of land drainage.[8]

There was a serious risk that all the old pastures and meadows would disappear, together with their characteristic plants and animals. In 1938, one of the last remaining fritillary meadows in Mickfield, Suffolk, was roughly ploughed and drainage began. In addition to the fritillary, the meadow contained the green-winged orchid *Orchis morio*, spotted orchid *Orchis fuchsii*, dyers greenwood *Genista tinctoria*, creeping jenny *Lysimachia nummalaria*, twayblade *Listera ovata*, and adders-tongue fern *Ophioglossum vulgatum*. A local naturalist wrote to the *East Anglian Times* and warned, 'the countryside is rapidly becoming less floriferous in this mechanical and destructive age, and naturalists must defend the heritage of beautiful wild flowers unless our future flora is to comprise only aliens and weeds'. In time, every ancient pasture would disappear unless a conscious effort was made to save it. An appeal for the acquisition of Mickfield Meadow was launched, and eventually £75 was collected.[9]

The threat to old established grasslands, marshes and fens increased during the Second World War as a result of efforts to increase food production. Herbert Smith, as chairman of the Wild Plant Conservation Board, admitted that some loss of wildlife was inevitable, but he appealed to the Ministry of Agriculture and the county War Agricultural Executive Committees to seek the advice of botanists when selecting areas for reclamation. He wrote 'where land has never been cultivated or at least not since the critical days of the Napoleonic Wars it may be the habitat of rare British plants, and if it be ploughed up such plants may be exterminated to the grave detriment of botanical science'.

On the instructions of the Ministry, a few county War Agricultural Executive Committees sought help in discovering whether a requisitioned area had any biological interest. At Farnham Mires, in the West Riding of Yorkshire, G. Taylor succeeded in persuading the county committee to spare over twenty-five acres of pasture, containing the birds-eye primrose *Primula farinosa* and autumn crocus *Colchicum autumnale*. He convinced the committee 'that it would be a catastrophe to disturb an area so rich and on which plants are still to be found in the same place as they were recorded 300 years ago'.[10]

But elsewhere, the picture was generally more gloomy. In May 1944, the Wild Plant Conservation Board wrote to the Hertfordshire county committee asking for the protection of a series of meadows, only to discover that almost all the grasslands had been ploughed up in the preceding week. Similar losses were reported from the Lake District, where the mosses were being excavated for peat for horticultural use and complete stands of spruce and larch were felled to meet the wartime shortages of fuel and timber. A local entomologist described the extinction of *Tortrix eucosma pygamaeana* (Hubn) and *T. eucosma ratzeburgiana* (Ratz) in a woodland of the parish of Witherslack, where spruce of up to sixty feet had been felled in 1941. He commented that 'had they left only a few trees, this would not have occurred'.[11]

At the same time as these striking changes in land use and management were being reported, biologists were beginning to demonstrate through their research the increasing capacity of man to change the distribution and abundance of plant and animal species. In 1920, James Ritchie published a book describing man's impact on the wild animals of Scotland in the past. The most profound changes had been stimulated by the spread of cultivation and introduction of domestic livestock. The natural environment had been transformed: according to Ritchie, prehistoric Scotland comprised fifty-four per cent of woodland, forty per cent mountain and moorland, and six per cent meadowland. By the twentieth century, forty-eight per cent of the surface was covered by mountain and heath pasture, twenty-five per cent by arable land, twenty-two per cent was wild mountain and moorland, and only five per cent was wooded. These changes had caused some species to become rare or extinct, and a few to become more abundant and widespread, sharing the new 'man-made environment' with aliens introduced by man, both deliberately and by accident.[12]

Such research emphasised the cumulative effects of the relatively slow changes of land use and management in the past. The accelerated rate of these trends in the mid-twentieth century promised to bring further dramatic changes in the distribution and abundance of species. Urgent steps had to be taken to preserve their habitat, namely their living space or feeding grounds. The harmful effects of building and industrial development, afforestation and agricultural changes, had to be averted or minimised, and this was most successfully achieved through acquiring the land occupied by the species and managing it as a nature reserve.

The National Trust and Society for the Promotion of Nature Reserves

Once naturalists had perceived the effects of changes in land use and management, and the consequent need for nature reserves, they began to draw on the experience and achievements of those organisations which had already acquired land for non-commercial reasons. The most important of these bodies was the National Trust, and it is necessary to briefly outline the origins and early development of the

National Trust in order to illustrate its contribution to preserving wildlife.

The people living in the centres of cities in the nineteenth century spent more and more time working indoors and walking on 'macadam-ized roads and stone-laid footways'. The poorer people especially had little opportunity to penetrate the countryside and, consequently, they took their exercise on the nearby urban commons. These commons were originally intensively used for grazing livestock and other purposes, but gradually the common rights fell into disuse and several lords of the manor tried to enclose part or all of the commons for cultivation or building development. Either way, public access would have been severely curtailed, and accordingly the commoners and local residents challenged the legality of these moves in a series of famous legal battles. Outside the courts, the debate ranged over a wider field. Attention was drawn to 'the supreme necessity of preserving all that still remained open, for the health and recreation of the people'. The Commons Preservation Society played an important role in safeguarding the commons. Founded in 1865, it co-ordinated and led the opposition to the enclosure and development of such commons as Hampstead Heath and Epping Forest.[13]

This Society met with sufficient success to prove that a public pressure group could be effective, if well directed and co-ordinated. Nevertheless, it operated within a necessarily restricted field and could not buy land or common rights since it had no corporate status. Robert Hunter, the Society's honorary solicitor, became convinced of the need for a statutory body which would acquire and hold land, and take a wider interest in the environment. In a speech in 1884, he advocated the creation of a Land Company to buy and accept gifts of land, buildings and common rights for the benefit of the nation. His proposal won the support of the extremely energetic social worker, Octavia Hill, and, by the end of 1885, they had agreed to call such a body the National Trust.[14]

But little happened until 1893 when they were joined by Canon Hardwicke Rawnsley, the leading defender of the Lake District. In that year, several estates in the Lakes had come onto the market and Rawnsley realised that even if they could be bought by public subscrip-tion, there would be no body capable of administering and managing them for the benefit of the nation. The National Trust would be ideal for the purpose. A meeting in the autumn of 1893 decided that a 'National Trust for Historic Sites and Natural Scenery' should be set up to act as a perpetual custodian for property given to the nation.

In drawing up a constitution, detailed reference was made to the constitution of the Trustees of Public Reservations in Massachusetts, which was founded in 1891 similarly to hold land in the public interest.

Hunter drew up the final Memorandum and Articles of Association, and one of the nine signatories was James Bryce, who was then President of the Board of Trade. These Articles were approved with little amendment by the Board of Trade, and the new body, now called the National Trust for Places of Historic Interest or Natural Beauty, was registered as a charitable body under the Companies Act of 1894. Its objects were 'to promote the permanent preservation, for the benefit of the Nation, of lands and tenements (including buildings) of beauty or historic interest; and as regards land, to preserve (so far as practicable) their natural aspect, features, and animal and plant life'.

Hunter stressed right from the start the value of securing special legislation or a royal charter for the National Trust. By 1906, the Trust had acquired twenty-four properties and there was an urgent need to regulate public access to them. Hunter drafted a private Bill, which was largely based on the original Articles of Association, but which gave the Trust the right to formulate by-laws. Perhaps the most important part was the clause which enabled the Trust to declare its land and buildings inalienable, which meant that they could not be sold or given away. This was an important safeguard to those who were thinking of giving the Trust their land or buildings. The Bill was passed without opposition in 1907.

Despite numerous efforts, no formal organisation was established in Scotland, nor any property acquired, until 1931 when a National Trust for Scotland was established, at the instigation of the Association for the Preservation of Rural Scotland (page 72). An Act of 1938 granted the Scottish Trust similar powers to those held by its sister body south of the border.[15]

By 1910, the National Trust owned thirteen sites of special interest to the naturalist, including parts of Wicken Fen and the Ruskin Reserve at Cothill in Berkshire. However, several naturalists were impatient at at the rate of progress: the National Trust was always short of capital and it was concerned not only with wild plants and animals, but also with sites of architectural and archaeological interest. Naturalists were worried at the almost random way in which potential nature reserves were acquired, with apparently little regard for the national significance of their plants and animals.

In May 1912, a group of four men met to discuss ways of promoting nature preservation on more rational lines. They were N. C. Rothschild, W. R. Ogilvie-Grant, F. R. Henley and C. E. Fagan, and they decided to form a new body, called the Society for the Promotion of Nature Reserves (SPNR). They took the word promotion very literally: the Society would simply stimulate the National Trust and other bodies and individuals to create nature reserves. There were no plans for the Society itself to own or manage land.[16]

The SPNR expected to promote reserves in two ways. First, it would undertake a survey of each part of the country and then draw up a list of areas 'worthy of protection'. Secondly, it would canvas support for the acquisition of these areas of land. All too often, naturalists first learned of an important site when a builder had bought the land for development. Then a public appeal was launched and the ground was purchased at a wildly inflated price. The Society hoped that its members, naturalists and the general public would keep a watchful eye on important areas, report any threats to wildlife, and help to persuade landowners to give or sell land on favourable terms for nature reserves.

The first formal meeting of the SPNR was held in the precincts of the British Museum (Natural History) on 26 July 1912, when the objectives of the Society were formally defined. These were:

i) to collect and collate information as to areas of land in the United Kingdom which retain primitive conditions and contain rare and local species liable to extinction owing to building, drainage, disafforestation, or in consequence of the cupidity of collectors;

ii) to prepare schemes, showing which areas should be secured as nature reserves;

iii) to obtain such areas and, if thought desirable, to hand them over to the National Trust for Places of Historic Interest or Natural Beauty under such conditions as may be necessary;

iv) to preserve for posterity as a national possession some part at least of our native land, its faunal, floral and geographical features;

v) to encourage the love of Nature, and to educate public opinion to a better knowledge of Nature Study.

In a somewhat philosophical leader, *The Times* applauded the creation of the SPNR. The pressures on the countryside had changed. In the nineteenth century, there had been a rapid growth in towns and drift from the countryside: in the early 1900s, the trend was reversed, and people began to leave the towns. There was a risk of the entire countryside being covered by 'a sort of universal suburb'. The leader writer continued, 'it was no use regreting this tendency: in many ways it is full of health and hope; but it is certain that lovers of nature will have to act resolutely and quickly if the last unspoilt relics of wild nature in Britain are to be preserved for the interest and inspiration of generations to come.'[17]

As soon as the Society was founded, Rothschild wrote to many potential benefactors, asking them to join the Society and perhaps donate land. Rothschild asked Lord Brownlow in 1912 whether he would lease Inchcombe Hollow in Buckinghamshire for a nominal sum. On learning that Sir Arthur Lee had given the Chequers Estate in

Buckinghamshire to the nation as a country residence for the Prime Minister, Rothschild wrote to Lee, stressing the tremendous importance of the Box Woods on the estate. They were in many respects better than those on Box Hill in Surrey. Lee promised to do his utmost to ensure the trustees of the estate protected the trees and bushes from destruction.[18]

During the first few years of the Society's existence, many members provided information on important areas, which were threatened by destruction. One correspondent, for example, described the decline of the nightingale and other species in the grounds of the Lodge at Sandy in Bedfordshire. Following the death of Viscount Peel, parts of the woodland and heath had been reclaimed for market-gardening and, whilst the correspondent wrote his letter, 'bonfires of heather and undergrowth were burning vigorously'. The writer hoped the Society would be able to persuade the new owner to spare the areas most frequented by the nightingale and other important species.[19]

At first, most of the energies of the Society were spent in completing a survey of areas worthy of preservation. There was a general feeling of optimism, although a few correspondents sounded a note of caution. T. A. Coward, for example, was afraid the Society might upset those landowners who were already protecting wildlife on their estates: he warned the Society not to interfere with the management of Rostherne Mere, Cheshire, which was already treated by its owner as a reserve. Another correspondent, Arthur Acton, was afraid the Society would waste its resources in areas where wildlife was in no danger of extinction. He suggested the Society should concentrate on England and especially the Midlands where the threat to wildlife was greatest: there was, for example, no need to establish nature reserves in north Wales. He commented that 'mining is decaying and districts which twenty years ago were spoiled are going back into most interesting wild nature. The flora of a disused lime quarry or an old colliery tip heap is vastly more interesting than the natural flora of the site'.[20]

Soon after the formation of the SPNR, war broke out and severely curtailed activities. A large proportion of the executive committee and active members of the Society was absorbed into the armed services and essential civilian work. Nevertheless, the Society looked forward to a rapid recovery after the war, when extensive areas of land would change hands and every effort would be made to reclaim areas for food production. The Society would play a vital role in this work, acquiring and preserving those sites which were marginal to agriculture but important to the naturalist. The nature reserves would be 'handed down to posterity for the enjoyment of lovers of wild nature, the pursuit of scientific knowledge, and the well-being of the community in general'.[21]

Unfortunately, these aspirations remained a pious hope after the war. At first, the Society offered several pieces of land to the National Trust, in accordance with its charter, and made grants for the maintenance of other sites of natural history interest (page 173), but thereafter the Society and the National Trust seem to have provided one another with comparatively little practical help. The Trust rejected the idea of a formal joint committee since several people were serving simultaneously on the executive committees of each organisation. For example, Sir Robert Hunter, a founder member of the National Trust, served on the executive committee of the SPNR and, on his death in 1913, F. W. Oliver succeeded him as the Trust's representative.[22]

The relative impotence of the SPNR in protecting important sites between the wars was demonstrated in 1927 when the owner of St Kilda offered to sell the island for £3,000. The small human population had recently abandoned the island, which had, therefore, become an ideal nature reserve. The scenery and colonies of seabirds were outstanding, the island contained a distinctive breed of Soay sheep and a unique variety of mouse *Mus sylvaticus hortensis*. But the purchase price was far too high for the Society, which simply referred the question to the National Trust and promised some measure of help in the event of acquisition. As it happened, the island was eventually bought by the Earl of Dumfries who managed it as a reserve.[23]

During the first twenty or thirty years of its existence the SPNR and its concept of nature reserves were outside the mainstream of the nature preservation movement, which was primarily concerned with crushing cruelty towards animals and such practices as bird-catching and egg-collecting. Nature reserves were regarded by most people as a subsidiary and very expensive means of supplementing legislation. In a sense, the SPNR was premature: its achievements were accordingly very modest. It was not until the 1940s that the potential of the Society was fully realised, when naturalists began to recognise changes in land use and management as the main threat to wildlife, when they realised that the acquisition and management of nature reserves, rather than legislation, would be the most effective way of making the world safe for wild plants and animals.

In view of this lack of enthusiasm for nature reserves between the wars, the SPNR was even more heavily dependent on dynamic leadership, strong regional and local support, and large financial resources. In common with most voluntary bodies interested in the environment, the Society lacked all three assets, and consequently languished throughout the inter-war period.

Whereas the RSPB tried to secure as many members as possible, the SPNR was primarily interested in obtaining the patronage of public figures and expert naturalists. This was made clear in its royal charter, granted in 1916, which established a two-tier structure of associates and members of council. The associates had no powers and could not even elect council members or any officers. They were not invited to any meetings unless fifteen members of the council or its executive committee wanted them to be present. They could not vote at any meeting unless the privilege was granted by two-thirds of the council.

Not surprisingly, the number of associate members remained low, rising from 241 in 1923 to 292 in 1935, and 298 members in 1942. By comparison, the RSPB had 975 fellows and 3,339 members in 1933. At first, associate members received no information as to what the SPNR was doing. As early as 1914, P. Chalmers-Mitchell complained that he did 'not know if the Society has any meetings, if it does any work, by whom it is actually managed, or in fact anything about it'. The situation was to some extent improved in 1923 when the first *Annual Handbook* was published, which included a membership list, brief details of nature reserves, and a summary of the previous year's activities. But it was a very inferior publication, compared with *Bird Notes and News* of the RSPB. Some improvements were made in 1935 when the *Handbook* was printed on glossy paper and included photographs and more detailed reports.[24]

The founders of the SPNR never intended it to be 'democratic': power was deliberately placed in the hands of the council, limited by the royal charter to fifty members. These included such distinguished biologists as G. C. Druce, E. J. Salisbury and A. G. Tansley, and some of the most influential figures in the political and social world. Such men as Lord Grey of Fallodon brought both prestige and the experience of other societies to the SPNR. Lord Ullswater was the first president of the Society, between 1912 and 1931. As James W. Lowther, he was Speaker of the House of Commons for several years and, according to the Society's *Handbook*, 'it was of immense advantage to the new organisation to have as president so influential a man'.[25]

It was expected that the council, with such strong powers and composed of such influential figures, would soon become a powerful force in promoting the acquisition and well-being of reserves. But the Society was extremely dependent on N. C. Rothschild, who alone had the resources and stature to recruit further outstanding figures to the council and win the necessary patronage. Accordingly, the early promise of the Society was blighted by his bad health and then his tragic death in 1923. From 1918, ill-health prevented his attending any meetings and, according to the Annual Report of 1920, it was an 'absence which seriously militated against the full activities of the Society'.[26]

Without the stimulus of Rothschild, the SPNR achieved very little. The members of the SPNR Council were elected for life, and although each grew older and many developed other interests, very few resigned. This meant that it was impossible to recruit the necessary fresh talent, with new ideas. By 1940, the Society amounted to little more than twenty active people, who were all members of the executive committee of the Council. Lord Rothschild became president in 1931: he was the brother of N. C. Rothschild and founder of the natural history museum at Tring, Hertfordshire. Lord Onslow succeeded him in 1937 and was simultaneously president of the SPNR, the Zoological Society of London and the Society for the Preservation of the Fauna of the Empire.

The Society would probably have become completely moribund in the 1930s if it had not been for the contribution of its honorary secretary, Herbert Smith, who served from 1921 to his death in 1953. Smith was a leading authority on gemstones and became secretary of the central office of the Natural History Museum of the British Museum in 1921. Soon after his appointment, Lord Ullswater persuaded him to replace W. R. Ogilvie-Grant as secretary of the SPNR so as to ensure the continuance of the link between the Society and the Museum. Smith agreed, and continued to use a room at the Museum even after his retirement in 1937.

Beside dynamic leadership, the SPNR needed lots of local support, and at first there was an encouraging response. The Cumberland Nature Reserves Association, for example, pledged its full support. The Association had been founded in 1914 and Lord Ullswater was its first president. Wardens were appointed for several eyries of peregrine falcons, buzzards and ravens, and funds were raised for wardening the Kingsmoor nature reserve near Carlisle. A survey was undertaken of the wild plants on this 'small but rich area of common land'.[27]

The Association soon became defunct, but a County Naturalists' Trust was founded in Norfolk in 1926, which acquired seven reserves by the 1940s. A detailed examination of the Trust's growth is made on page 226. But this kind of local development was exceptional, and the SPNR received very little practical aid from regional and local clubs and societies.

The work of the Society was also limited by its very small annual income. Soon after its foundation, Rothschild learned that Andrew Carnegie had established a trust of £25 million, with an annual income of about £2 million. The SPNR noted that if a quarter of one year's income was invested on behalf of the Society, it would be able 'to purchase and maintain all the Nature Reserves they desired to acquire in the British Isles *for all time*'. In spite of approaches from Lord Grey and others, Carnegie refused to provide any assistance.[28]

The refusal of Carnegie and other potential benefactors to make a grant to the Society was a heavy blow. The charter prevented the

SPNR from levying an annual subscription on its members. In any case, the Society could hardly raise a subscription from its associate members who had no control over policy or the expenditure of funds. In the event, most members were a liability rather than an asset since they received a free copy of the *Annual Handbook*, without giving anything in return. In one year, Smith appealed for a gift of ten shillings from every member, but only £21 was received from an aggregate of eight people.

Although there was a high proportion of wealthy persons in the membership list, the Society relied heavily on the generosity of its founder, N. C. Rothschild, throughout the inter-war period. On his death in 1923, the president, Lord Ullswater, warned 'our financial position will I fear be seriously if not vitally affected by the death of our chief benefactor', but Rothschild made a bequest of £5,000 to the Society in his will, together with Ray Island in Essex. The capital was invested and initially yielded an annual income of £255. The Society sold Ray Island in 1925, because it thought the island had little wildlife interest and extra funds were badly needed for managing the reserve at Woodwalton Fen.[29]

At first, some members of the executive committee were tempted to use the bequest for acquiring sites which would otherwise be destroyed. In 1925, Lord Ullswater proposed spending £1,000 to purchase Hawksmoor, Staffordshire, but Sir Sidney Harmer warned that once the entire bequest was spent the Society would be bankrupt. Instead, the Society simply spent the annual income from its investments. These amounted to £500 in 1928, of which £300 was spent 'on running commitments', principally at Woodwalton Fen.

In 1932, the famous botanist, G. C. Druce, died and bequeathed the residue of his estate equally between the SPNR and the University of Oxford. This was contested, but in 1939 the Society received its share. It was invested, and the annual income of the Society trebled to £1,500. Lord Onslow wanted the money to be used to acquire a large nature reserve, instead of being frittered away on 'numerous small objects', but H. M. Edelsten was quick to point out that some of the extra income was badly needed for managing the Woodwalton Fen nature reserve, which had just been enlarged (page 174). The steep rise in costs during the war also made inroads, but nevertheless the Society had an overall surplus of £530 in 1947.[30]

From 1939 onwards, Herbert Smith began to reap the rewards of keeping the Society alive during the critical years of the 1930s. The Society was for the first time 'pretty well off', and looked forward to playing a more positive role in the future. At first, the outbreak of war threatened to end this rennaissance, but by 1942 Smith remarked that 'the Society is surprisingly busy, not only in spite of the war but possibly also because of it'.[31] Whereas the Society had failed to influence government thinking on nature preservation in the 1914–18 war, it was to have a profound influence in the Second World War. But before tracing the steps by which the government became involved in nature preservation, it is first necessary to review the various attempts to preserve amenity and promote outdoor recreation during the inter-war period. Developments in these two fields were to have important repercussions for nature conservation.

Chapter Four

Wildlife and Concern for the Countryside

The SPNR took the word 'promotion' in its title very literally: it promoted nature reserves, and left the actual purchase and management of the reserves to other organisations. It believed one effective way of stimulating interest in reserves and raising funds was to hold meetings of representatives from all the interested bodies so as to work out a common policy on all aspects of nature preservation.

But even when a consensus of opinion had been worked out, naturalists were a comparatively small and weak pressure group, and the SPNR realised between the wars that the only way to become effective was to work closely with those organisations concerned with amenity and outdoor recreation. By joining forces, naturalists obtained far greater opportunities for publicising the needs of wildlife and the benefits of nature preservation.

In order to understand the growing liaison between nature preservation, the preservation of amenity, and the provision of recreational opportunities, it is necessary to describe the problems faced by the advocates of amenity and recreation, and the attempts made to resolve them through such concepts as national parks.

From the 1890s, there was a great increase in the number of people visiting the countryside for leisure and recreation. This was largely due to the shortening of the working week and the growing popularity of the bicycle and motor-car. Whereas trains tended to concentrate trippers in recognised holiday-resorts, the owner of a bicycle or car could choose to visit wherever he pleased. The cover design of the Ordnance Survey maps for Eastbourne, Hastings and Bournemouth, published in 1928, illustrated this new found freedom. The cover design showed a rambler exploring the countryside, map in hand, with cyclists and a car passing on the nearby road. By the 1920s, special tourist maps had been published for Snowdonia, the New Forest, Lake District and Deeside.

As long ago as 1884, James Bryce had introduced a Bill to allow any person to walk over mountains and moorland for recreation, scientific and artistic study, irrespective of the wishes of the land owner and occupier. The measure failed, as did many further attempts to secure an Access to Mountains Bill in, for example, 1908, 1926, 1927 and 1931. Meanwhile, attempts were made to establish long-distance pathways. There was already an 'unofficial' South Downs Way along the crest of the South Downs over the short downland turf, traditionally grazed by sheep. The Commons, Open Spaces and Footpaths Preservation Society fought to stop fences being erected and the grasslands being ploughed up during and immediately after the First World War, when beef and grain prices were relatively high. It wanted the government to purchase the crest of the Downs 'so as to preserve for ever the public right to wander over the turf and enjoy the famous views'.[1]

The number of people venturing into the countryside for a day, weekend and even longer, was increasing. The Federation of Rambling Clubs was founded in 1905 and had 40,000 members by 1931. The Ramblers Association was formed in 1935. The Co-operative Holidays Association was created in 1891, and the Holiday Fellowship was established in 1913. Although the Youth Hostels Association was only founded in 1930, it had nearly 300 hostels and over 83,000 members by 1939.

Coinciding with this increasing interest in outdoor recreation, there was, paradoxically, an increasing threat to areas of outstanding scenery and wildlife interest. This threat was often the result of a change in the pattern of land ownership. Previously, many important areas had been protected by large landowners who could afford the financial sacrifice which the preservation of amenity and wildlife often entailed, but for a variety of reasons these men were now being obliged to sell their estates. Areas which had been protected were being sold, often for housing development.

A wide variety of uses was found for previously rural land. Lord Gage received offers to buy parts of his Sussex estate for a light railway and workshops in the Cuckmere Valley; the War Office asked for a lease of the downland parts of his estate for military training; a syndicate wanted to develop his land in the Pevensey Levels for testing and racing motor cars. Such proposals frequently aroused a great deal of local opposition, expressed in the form of local meetings, petitions and pamphlets. In 1934, plans were announced for the reclamation of the coastal saltings to the west of West Wittering in Sussex. There were proposals to turn the area into a golf course, mooring basin and grounds for a hotel. A group of local people launched a petition, and a pamphlet was published, which pointed out that the saltings were 'one of the few unspoilt, natural areas of coastal scenery that remain in the south of England' and that there was no local demand for a golf course or hotel. Whilst the scheme might provide work for the unemployed of the district, the pamphlet remarked, rather acidly, that the pulling down of Chichester Cathedral would also provide work.[2]

There was a need for a watchdog over the landscape. This was, perhaps, most clearly demonstrated in the Lake District where many projects had been proposed, including a plan to build a railway along the shore of Lake Windermere and a road over Styhead Pass. These plans were defeated, but Lord Bryce of Borrowdale, in a letter to *The Times* in 1919, described the increasing difficulties of safeguarding 'the wild sublimity of the landscape'. Individual persons and local societies generally lacked the resources and expertise to fend off all the threats to the Lake District. Lord Bryce stressed the urgent need for a commission 'to be set up charged with the duty of preventing the construction of any work calculated to inflict grave injury upon natural beauties which we owe it to posterity to preserve'.[3]

The National Trust could not undertake this role. Although the founders expected the Trust to wage battles for the protection of amenity, wildlife and important buildings, its resources were soon overstretched. By the 1940s, the Trust owned over 100 farms and 480 cottages, in addition to open spaces, amenity woodlands and ancient buildings. The founders of the movement had not forseen such developments and their associated land agency problems: the Trust simply had to concentrate on its own properties and role as landowner and manager, leaving the broader environmental issues to others.

No other body had the same stature and broad appeal to act as an environmental watchdog, and so a new organisation was proposed to co-ordinate the activities of all the existing voluntary bodies. There had been one previous attempt to achieve this, in 1898, when SCAPA (Society for Checking the Abuses of Public Advertising) set up an organisation, representing about ten voluntary bodies, which would cover all aspects and parts of the countryside.

Nothing came of this venture, but during the 1920s a number of civic societies were founded in London, Birmingham and other towns which kept urban developments under surveillance. The President of the Royal Institute of British Architects (RIBA), Guy Dawber, referred to these new bodies in 1926 as a model of a larger organisation to keep changes throughout the entire country under review. In the same year, L. P. Abercrombie, the distinguished planner, wrote a book which suggested how the activities of these civic societies and other organisations might be co-ordinated under a National League for the Preservation of Rural England. The League would make a single, simple and direct appeal to everyone concerned with the preservation of the countryside.[4]

The idea met with widespread approval, and the Council for the Preservation of Rural England (CPRE) was founded in the same year, to co-ordinate the activities of the various voluntary bodies and learned societies, promote legislation, keep planning schemes under surveillance, and provide an advisory service to every landowner and occupier seeking to preserve and enhance the amenity of their property. Twenty-two bodies became constituent members of the Council, and a larger number was affiliated in order to ensure the closest liaison between all those interested in preserving the countryside.

There was an urgent need for funds to cover the cost of vital secretarial assistance, postage, printing, travel and the organisation of meetings and exhibitions. The constituent and affiliated bodies were generally too poor to contribute adequate assistance, and so the Council decided to enrol private persons as Associate Members for a subscription of one guinea a year. This provided a valuable source of revenue and gave individuals the feeling that they were contributing in a tangible manner to the work of the new organisation.[5]

Almost immediately, several branches of the CPRE commissioned studies of their respective regions. A report on the Thames Valley from Cricklade to Staines was published in 1929, compiled by 'three experts acting in an honorary capacity'. It frequently criticised existing forms of land use in the Valley and recommended ways of preserving the more attractive parts of the area. For example, the report described how the views from Bablock Hythe had been ruined by the erection of ten railway carriages on brick piers. It urged the restriction of housing development on Wytham Hill, near Oxford, which was part of the city's green belt.[6]

The Concept of National Parks

The growing popularity of rambling, and the increasing threats to amenity and wildlife, stimulated interest in the concept of national parks which had been introduced to America and Africa in the late nineteenth century. Such parks were composed of virgin territory and owned by the federal or state governments. The 600 state parks in America covered 2.75 million acres by 1930. Lord Bledisloe, the Parliamentary Secretary to the Ministry of Agriculture, made a private visit to the Jasper and Banff Parks in Canada, and the Yellowstone Park of the United States, in 1925, and he described how 'they not only provided beautiful sanctuaries for wild animals and birds, as well as for the wild flowers and ferns of endless variety and beauty, but, in particular, they constitute a most perfect holiday resort for persons of all classes engaged normally in strenuous work'.[7]

Such glowing reports stimulated discussions as to whether similar parks should be established in Britain for the provision of facilities for outdoor recreation and for the preservation of amenity and wildlife. In 1928, Lord Bledisloe wrote to the Prime Minister and Office of Works, stressing the value of converting the Forest of Dean into a national park. He even offered part of his estate in the Forest for this purpose.

Nothing came of this suggestion, but in 1929 the CPRE submitted a memorandum to the new Prime Minister, J. Ramsay MacDonald, asking for an enquiry into the need for a series of national parks in Britain. The CPRE was supported by the Association for the Preservation of Rural Scotland (APRS), which was founded in 1927, and the Council for the Preservation of Rural Wales (CPRW), founded in 1928.

The Prime Minister referred the question to the First Commissioner of Works, G. Lansbury, and the Minister of Agriculture, N. Buxton, who suggested that an inter-departmental committee should be set up, composed of representatives from the Office of Works, Ministries of Agriculture and Health, Scottish Office, Commission of Crown Lands, and Forestry Commission. They proposed appointing a junior minister as chairman 'in order to avoid the possible criticism that the report (produced by the committee) was the work of unsympathetic bureaucrats'.[8] The following terms of reference were suggested:

> ... the committee would consider and report if it is desirable and feasible to establish one or more National Parks in Great Britain with a view to the preservation of the natural characteristics, including flora and fauna, and to the improvement of recreational facilities for the people; and to advise generally, and in particular as to the areas, if any, that are most suitable for the purpose.

Ramsay MacDonald agreed, and nominated the Parliamentary Secretary to the Ministry of Agriculture, Christopher Addison, as chairman. The committee began work in September 1929 and completed its report in 1931. It advocated the establishment of a series of parks with three objectives, namely (i) to safeguard areas of exceptional natural interest against disorderly development and spoliation, (ii) to improve the means of access for pedestrians to areas of natural beauty, and (iii) to promote measures for the protection of flora and fauna. The parks should be administered by a statutory authority for England and Wales, and another for Scotland.[9]

As witnesses to the Addison Committee, the advocates of outdoor recreation described how the national parks would promote the 'open air habit', providing camping sites and cheap accommodation for ramblers, scouts and guides, and even for the 'city dweller of small means' who wanted to spend a weekend or even his annual holiday in the countryside. The parks would become essential features of a 'national health service' at a time when the government was trying to improve the general standard of health of the nation. Advocates of such parks noted that the Treasury already provided more than £200,000 each year on the upkeep of the Crown Parks of London. Expenditure on town football and cricket grounds was increasing. Surely, the provision of outdoor recreational facilities in tracts of unspoilt countryside was just as important for the 'national health scheme'.[10]

For other commentators, national parks were a device for protecting the wilder stretches of countryside and coastline, composed of rough land and rock, rather than fields of grain and sown grass. In this way, George Bernard Shaw urged the government in 1929 to make the Malvern Hills a national park, so as to prevent further quarrying.[11] In a letter to *The Times*, he wrote:

> ...visitors from Worcester, coming through Malvern Wells, used to see the unspoilt northern hills with an indescribable pleasure. They now see it hideously disfigured by three gigantic scoops, reaching so nearly to the top of the ridge that they bring home with a shock the appalling conviction that before very long the scoops will go right through, leaving between them a couple of enormous jagged teeth of hill, which will presumably be blasted away in their turn, changing the Malvern Hills into the Malvern Flats.

The parks would also be a means of safeguarding wildlife, perhaps smaller versions of those in America and South Africa. As long ago as 1909, Charles Stewart had advocated the creation of a Scottish national park in order to preserve both the wild scenery and indigenous animals of the Highlands. He thought the islands of Jura and Rhum would be ideal for the purpose. It was not necessary to preserve large herds of animals, such as were required for sporting purposes, but merely sufficient specimens to ensure 'careful breeding'.

Stewart estimated that a grant of £50,000 would be required from the Treasury for buying the sheep farms and deer forests falling within the national park. Some of this revenue would be recouped from selling improved stags to sportsmen, breeding and hatching salmon and trout, and from the sale of seedlings and saplings of both conifer and hardwood species growing in the park. But Stewart emphasised that the real value of the park would be in preserving the land from speculators, and in making it more accessible to naturalists and tourists. The former gillies, farm hands and crofters would find more regular and profitable employment from wardening the park and looking after the wild animals.[12]

A Conflict in Objectives

Although there was widespread support for the concept of national parks, there were many debates as to the actual use and administration of individual parks. Some observers challenged the wisdom of spending public money on creating parks in such remote areas as the Cairngorms. If the area was visited by a small number of people, would it be right to provide them with facilities at the taxpayers' expense? If the parks authority tried to justify expenditure by encouraging large numbers of people to visit the park areas, surely the essential character of the Cairngorms and similar areas would be destroyed?

The Addison Committee highlighted a potential conflict between the various proponents of national parks. The representatives of the National Trust claimed that preservation was the primary objective in setting up parks and that access, however important, only came second. It should only be permitted where the public could not damage the amenity of the areas. In contrast, L. P. Abercrombie stated that the parks should be used primarily for recreation, and that for this reason they should be situated near the chief centres of population. One witness to the Committee suggested that small parks should be created in twelve areas which were accessible by bicycle and train from towns, and each should be equipped with weekend camps. The Automobile Association, in its evidence, stressed the need for plenty of hostels, camps, parking places and service stations, and 'in view of the rapidly growing number of aircraft owners, suitable ground should be cleared to serve as an aerodrome, with protection against wind and cattle'.[13]

It was soon clear that analogies with the national parks of America was misleading. These parks were so immense that they could accommodate 'palatial hotels with jazz bands', and yet provide refuge for the shyest animals. But the British national parks would be necessarily much smaller, and *The Times* warned of the almost inevitable clash between the lovers of the countryside and those who demanded camping sites, swimming pools, amusement centres and car parks.[14]

In trying to resolve this potential conflict, the Addison Committee tried to assess the ways in which visitors to the parks would adversely affect amenity and wildlife. Would the parks precipitate a mass invasion? Lord Bledisloe drew attention to the large number of people already visiting the park areas. The creation of a series of parks, far from making the situation worse, might help to reduce the incidence of trespassing and vandalism. In the case of the Forest of Dean, people camped where they pleased, and there was, as a result, 'no bird life apart from magpies, although the neighbouring estates harboured an exceptional number of types'. If such areas as the Forest of Dean were designated national parks, people would take a greater pride and, therefore, greater care in the appearance of the woodlands. It would be easier to formulate by-laws and warden the Forest: a camp site for 500 people could be provided on the edge of the woodlands, thereby making it possible to prohibit camping elsewhere in the Forest.[15]

Perhaps the most intractacable problem was how to preserve wildlife from the disturbance of visitors. The British Correlating Committee, in its evidence to the Addison Committee, described how the provision of recreational facilities and preservation of wildlife were two irreconcilable objectives. The parks would soon attract large numbers of people, and C. J. Wainwright described what had happened at Sutton Park, a popular open space near Birmingham, where the 'natural flora was gradually being replaced by newspapers and its fauna by lovers from the City!' Obviously by-laws could be introduced by the national parks authority, but the laws, even if enforced and observed, could not preserve the balance of nature. The more vulnerable and shy species were bound to disappear, whilst others, for example the grey squirrel, would become more numerous.[16]

The British Correlating Committee felt there were only two ways of resolving this conflict in demand. Small enclosures should be erected within the national parks where wildlife could be protected from disturbance from visitors. The parks authority would make by-laws and employ watchers for this purpose. Secondly, and much more important, the Committee recommended that a series of national nature reserves should be established outside the parks, where the land would be used entirely for wildlife preservation.

In its report, the Addison Committee recommended two kinds of park. One would serve as *national reserves*, designated for the preservation of scenery and wildlife, and include such areas as the Lake District, Snowdonia, the Pembrokeshire coast and South Downs. The other would be *regional reserves*, primarily designated for outdoor recreation and accordingly situated near urban centres. The High Peak District would be an ideal choice for a regional reserve, since half the population of England lived within sixty miles of its probable boundaries.

The debate over the functions and administration of national parks continued throughout the 1930s. One of the leading advocates of national parks, John Dower, accepted the scope for conflict but rejected the notion of two kinds of park. In a speech in 1937, he claimed that one kind of demand justified and supported the other. Large numbers of people had to be admitted to the parks in order to justify the expense of protecting their beauty and wildlife: at the same time, public access and recreational activities had to be carefully regulated, otherwise the parks would become 'neglected, blotched and evanescent', and this would ultimately be to the detriment of everyone.[17]

A National Parks Authority

In order to satisfy the various demands and avoid conflict, the use of each area within the parks had to be carefully regulated. The most effective way was to acquire the land. This would clearly be expensive, but Lord Onslow commented 'people are apt to be frightened at the cost of buying a large area of land and maintaining it, but in the first place private individuals acquire deer forests and what is possible for a private individual should not be impossible for the public generally either under the Government or by means of public subscription'.

Nevertheless, witnesses to the Addison Committee warned of great opposition to any increase in rates or taxation. The Convention of Scottish Burghs noted that £1,600,000 were already spent on public parks in towns and that it would be prohibitively expensive to purchase and maintain large areas of land in such remote parts as the Cairngorms. Many commentators, therefore, turned their attention to the acquisition of smaller parks, but this was not an entirely satisfactory solution. The amenity of small areas could be so easily ruined or harmed by developments on neighbouring land over which the parks authority had no control.[18]

The Addison Committee believed the problem could be overcome through a judicious combination of regional planning and land acquisition. It recommended that local authorities should set up a Regional Committee, with executive powers, for each 'geographical unit' in the country. Each national park area would be automatically administered as a single unit: the Lake District would, for example, be under one planning body as opposed to the three existing advisory committees. The Regional Committees would draw up plans for the optimum development of the national parks, scheduling tracts of land containing outstanding scenery or wildlife. They would be able to enter into agreements with landowners for the preservation of natural features, with the power to award compensation for any restrictions imposed on land use. If necessary, the Committees could acquire land by compulsory purchase.

In order to select the national park areas and stimulate the Regional Committees appointed by the local authorities, the Addison Committee recommended the establishment of a national parks authority. This would obviously be an expensive step, and the Committee was well aware of the world monetary crisis of 1930–1. The Addison Committee accordingly proposed two alternative ways of constituting the national parks authority, depending on the amount of money available.

If at least £100,000 were provided annually for at least five years, a national parks authority could be set up for England and Wales, and another for Scotland. The authorities would select the park areas, make grants and provide expert guidance. It was suggested that each authority should consist of up to five members, chosen by virtue of their experience of public service rather than as representatives of interested organisations. Liaison would be maintained through a Central Co-ordinating Committee, made up of three members of the English and Welsh authority, two members of the Scottish authority, and a member of parliament nominated by the government. Each authority would be supported by a consultative committee made up of representatives of voluntary bodies and experts in the fields of planning, law and estate agency work.

In the event of the government providing less than £100,000 per annum, but not less than £10,000, an alternative kind of authority would have to be found. In such a situation, the Addison Committee suggested that the Ministry of Health, and the Department of Health for Scotland, should choose the parks and provide guidance to local authorities. Each Ministry should appoint an advisory committee, analogous to the Royal Fine Arts Commission.

The Prime Minister referred the report of the Addison Committee to the Minister of Health, Arthur Greenwood, who was responsible for the government's involvement in town planning issues. Greenwood was keen to implement the proposals for the establishment of a national parks authority, and agreed with the Prime Minister that the Treasury should be asked for £100,000 per annum for five years, in spite of the recent publication of a report which emphasised the serious financial state of the country. Once the Treasury agreed, Greenwood and the Scottish Secretary would make a joint approach to the Cabinet.[19]

But first, Greenwood wanted to secure the enactment of his Town and Country Planning Bill, which would, in some respects, prepare the way for legislation on national parks. Under the Town Planning Acts of 1919 and 1925, local authorities could draw up planning schemes wherever development was proposed or taking place. But the imple-mentation of effective schemes to regulate building development was slow, and there were soon demands for rural areas also to be subject to some kind of planning control. A private member's Bill, introduced by E. Hilton Young, brought matters to a head in 1929. His Rural Amenities Bill tried to extend planning schemes to all parts of the country, and it was given an unopposed second reading in the House of Commons. It was only withdrawn when Greenwood announced the government's intention of bringing forward its own Bill.[20]

Greenwood's Bill repealed and consolidated previous legislation, and allowed district councils, or joint planning committees acting on their behalf, to introduce planning schemes for any kind of land, whether urban or rural. The Bill had almost completed its progress through parliament when the government fell, and a general election ensued. A generally weaker Town and Country Planning Bill was passed in 1932, which neverless gave local authorities powers to control rural land use and to 'preserve existing buildings and other objects of architectural, historic or artistic interest, and places of natural interest or beauty'.[21]

This delay in implementing the recommendations of the Addison Committee, caused by the Town and Country Planning Bills, had far-reaching consequences for national parks. By the end of 1932, the financial situation had grown so serious that any enthusiasm on the part of the government for a national parks authority had vanished, and the new Minister of Health, paradoxically E. Hilton Young, refused to ask the Treasury for a grant of either £100,000 or £10,000 per annum. The voluntary bodies appealed for the implementation of those recommendations which incurred no additional expenditure, and in particular the appointment of an advisory committee to help safe-guard the amenity of potential national parks. The government claimed this was unnecessary since the Royal Fine Arts Commission itself had powers to inquire into any question affecting public amenities, although it admittedly had no expert on rural planning among its membership and had confined its attention to buildings and monuments.

But in any case the government was sceptical of the value of *ad hoc* committees, which simply encouraged a polarisation of viewpoints. Hilton Young claimed that 'what is wanted for preserving amenities is not so much a central body . . . but more active propaganda, and not least important, informed propaganda'. Instead of creating committees which would cut right across the planning powers of local authorities, the voluntary bodies should help the local authorities in reconciling land-use changes with the preservation of amenity. If they failed, 'amenity would be the one to suffer in the long run'.[22]

Piecemeal Achievements

Instead of creating a national parks authority, the government allowed a curious collection of bodies to become responsible for preserving the countryside and providing opportunities for outdoor recreation. Local authorities continued to control changes in land use, albeit under greater surveillance from the Ministry of Health. The Forestry Commission became the only official body which actually extended facilities for rambling and trekking, through the creation of National Forest Parks. The task of implementing the Access to Mountains Act of 1939, which defined public rights of access to open land more rigorously, was given to the Ministry of Agriculture.

In view of this diffusion of responsibility, it was more than ever necessary for the advocates of amenity, wildlife and recreation to combine and formulate common policies, for the voluntary bodies alone provided an overall view of this sector of the environmental field. The Association for the Preservation of Rural Scotland (APRS) set up a National Parks Committee in 1934, and the CPRE and CPRW convened a conference at the Central Hall, Westminster, in November 1934 which formed a Standing Committee on National Parks, under the chairmanship of Norman Birkett. This Committee agitated not only for the establishment of a series of parks, but also for a general improvement in public access to the countryside.

The voluntary organisations seized every opportunity to influence planning policies. When a Commissioner was appointed to recommend ways of stimulating employment and improving the standard of living of people in south Wales in 1934, under the Special Areas (Development and Improvement) Act, the voluntary bodies recommended the establishment of a national park in the Vale of Neath, close to the Brecon Beacons and Black Mountains. This would generate some employment and, more especially, provide the opportunity for cheap and healthy holidays for the inhabitants of the depressed industrial areas of Monmouth, Glamorgan, Brecknock and Pembrokeshire. The Commissioner, P. M. Stewart, accepted the suggestion and commented in his report that 'I am convinced such a Park would appeal to the imagination and would prove to be increasingly attractive to a growing number of persons who are taking open-air holidays.'[23]

The concept of national parks was accepted by the influential Next Five Years Group, which referred in its publications to the need for parks and the preservation of 'those stretches of country which the nation should safeguard as a national inheritance'. During a debate in parliament on the value of public works in offsetting unemployment, Harold Macmillan stressed the benefits not only of road-building and industrial schemes, but also of the establishment of national parks and other facilities for outdoor recreation.[24]

In spite of such proposals, the government steadfastly refused to set up a national parks authority, even when the economy revived. By that time, schemes were being prepared under the 1932 Town and Country Planning Act for most parts of the proposed parks. Under Section 34 of the Act, planning authorities were making agreements with many landowners for the restriction of building development on their land: the most famous example occurred on the South Downs where 10,000 acres were voluntarily preserved from building development on the basis of agreements with twenty-five landowners.[25]

79

Whilst welcoming these ventures, the voluntary bodies vigorously denied that they provided adequate substitutes for the creation of national parks. The schemes devised by local authorities would inevitably be local and piecemeal in character. According to John Dower, 'the essential elements of national decision, choice, and national responsibility would be lacking'. By means of deputations and memoranda, the Standing Committee on National Parks made a series of detailed criticisms of the provisions of the 1932 Act.

There were four serious omissions from the measure. First, the local planning authorities were not obliged to draw up planning schemes: it was completely left to the discretion of the 1,441 borough, urban and rural district councils. Neither were these bodies compelled to liaise with neighbouring councils in drawing up schemes: although the various Acts encouraged them to participate in joint planning committees and seek the guidance of county councils, many schemes were devised in isolation, creating a fragmented and piecemeal approach to planning. The Lake District, for example, was subdivided between three planning authorities which continued to act independently on many important planning matters. For its part, the Ministry of Health admitted these defects in the Act, but claimed they were being overcome. Local authorities were voluntarily joining with one another in drawing up schemes. Even in the Lake District, an advisory joint committee had been set up to co-ordinate the work of the three planning authorities. The Ministry was exerting considerable pressure on individual councils to participate in such regional schemes. The Chief Town Planning Inspector, G. L. Pepler, was continuously visiting councils, cajoling them into action.

Secondly, the Standing Committee noted that the authorities were not compelled to employ qualified, full-time planning officers or seek the aid of planning consultants: consequently, many major decisions were taken on a piecemeal basis by untrained part-time staff. Again, the Ministry admitted initial deficiencies, but stressed that increasingly the authorities were employing qualified planners and, as a further safeguard, each scheme had to receive the approval of the Minister before being implemented.

Thirdly, it was claimed that the poorer local authorities were afraid to ban building development or embark on ambitious planning schemes because of the inevitable claims for heavy compensation from those landowners adversely affected. A one penny rate in Westmorland raised only £1,600, and that for Cumberland yielded only £3,100. The Act of 1932 tried to overcome this difficulty by allowing local authorities to levy a betterment charge on those who benefited from planning decisions, but the powers were so circumscribed that there were only three instances where a betterment levy was raised between 1932 and 1943.[26]

Fourthly, the Town and Country Planning Act was criticised for failing to give the planning authorities any control over the activities of government departments and statutory undertakings, which were often responsible for the most striking changes in the landscape. This had been very clearly demonstrated in 1929 when the Electricity Commission announced plans to erect pylons over the South Downs in order to include Brighton in the national grid. The opposition was so intense that the Prime Minister, J. Ramsay MacDonald, intervened and instructed the Commission to do their utmost to avoid damaging such areas as the South Downs. He stressed that it was just as important to safeguard the beauty and peace of the countryside for future generations as it was to provide extra electricity. The erection of the pylons required the consent of the Minister of Transport, Herbert Morrison, who confessed that 'it was the duty of all concerned, whether as Ministers or as persons engaged in industry, to have regard to the healthily increasing insistence that material need should not ride rough-shod over "England's green and pleasant land".'

In spite of this assertion, Morrison felt compelled to give his consent to the erection of the pylons. He pointed out that the Electricity Commission was responsible for creating a national electricity grid in order to reduce 'the tragic wastage of capital which was involved in each undertaking generating its own peak load'. If this was to be achieved, such towns as Brighton had to be included in the grid and there was no alternative but to erect pylons over some part of the Downs. Suggestions that the cables should be buried underground were rejected: the work would cost at least seven times as much and, in any case, it was technically impossible to bury 132,000-volt cables underground.[27]

The CPRE fully appreciated the dilemma faced by individual ministries and statutory undertakings, and it welcomed the various gestures made toward amenity. But it condemned the *ad hoc* arrangements whereby the individual departments and undertakings reached their planning decisions. Each was necessarily biased toward its sectional interests. It was essential that regional planners and a central planning authority should have the last word. They alone could 'consider the geographical aspects of the locality and their bearing on the amenities and on the rational development of all the natural possibilities of the locality'. The same central planning authority would also meet the three other objections to the 1932 Act by providing local authorities with the requisite guidance and financial support in drawing up and implementing planning schemes.

Matters came to a head in 1937, largely due to the success of the voluntary bodies in arousing public interest. Whilst the preparation and implementation of planning schemes proceeded in areas with a high population, and therefore high rateable value, there was growing concern in the potential national parks where 'the local authorities have slender resources, preservation is required more in the national than the local interest, the proportion of land needing control or reservation is unusually high, and the attractiveness of the districts make the early possibility of sporadic development a particularly real danger'.

Since the protection of such key areas was a national concern, it seemed only appropriate that the government should give direct assistance. An internal memorandum of the Ministry of Health admitted, 'the course of events has led to the conclusion that the Government will be exposed to serious criticism and discredit if a purely negative reply continues to be given to the large body of opinion in favour of definite action for the preservation of the country-side. The National Parks appear to provide the best opportunity of making a gesture to indicate the reality of the Government's interest in the problem of preservation, applied to that portion of the problem in which the national interest is greatest and the opportunity of finding an alternative solution the most remote'.

Nothing could be achieved without financial assistance from the Exchequer. In this context, events took a somewhat dramatic turn in May 1937 when the Amenity Group of the House of Commons met the Chancellor of the Exchequer, Neville Chamberlain, primarily to discuss ways in which landowners might make gifts of land and buildings to such bodies as the National Trust in return for an exemption from death duties. The Group also stressed the need for the Treasury to assist voluntary bodies by providing funds to preserve outstanding scenery and buildings. Chamberlain, as 'a friend rather than as Chancellor', suggested the voluntary bodies should submit a formal request for a grant toward a specific project.

On hearing about this meeting, the Minister of Health decided that his 'Bill' to the Treasury for the coming year should 'include an item in respect of the National Parks Organisation for which the Council for the Preservation of Rural England and so many other idealists are pressing'. As an experiment, the Ministry would ask the Treasury for £15,000, spread over three years, for helping to establish two or three national parks. The money would be used to 'match' any contributions made by local authorities and voluntary bodies.

But enthusiasm for the experiment waned once the Ministry tried to decide which areas should receive this aid. Many of the planning schemes devised by local authorities for potential parks were well advanced, and the Ministry feared that any announcement of Exchequer aid might throw them 'back into the melting pot'. Instead of landowners freely entering into agreements without any question of payment, they would begin to demand heavy compensation, and 'a quite substantial amount of Exchequer money might find its way into the pockets of landowners without any appreciable result in securing *further* preservation'.[28]

In the light of these fears and serious misgivings on the part of the Treasury, it was decided to delay the experiment for at least a year, by which time several major planning schemes should have been submitted to the Minister under the terms of the 1932 Act. This would finally indicate the effectiveness of planning by local authorities, the extent to which the Minister could take a strict line in preserving the amenity of the countryside, and accordingly whether an Exchequer grant would be necessary in national park areas. By 1939, however, the experiment was forgotten: the cost of rearmaments and the imminence of war seemed much more important.

One of the most important tasks of the 'guardians of the countryside' between the wars was to keep major changes in land use under surveillance. In this context, the relationship between the voluntary bodies and the Forestry Commission was of critical importance. There had been relatively little planting during the nineteenth century, and Britain had become very dependent on overseas timber merchants. The danger of this heavy reliance on foreign supplies was demonstrated in the 1914–18 war, and the Forestry Commission was established by parliament in 1919 with the urgent task of promoting forestry, undertaking afforestation, and generally improving the production and supply of timber throughout the United Kingdom. In spite of chronic, and often severe economies imposed by the Treasury, the Commission owned 715,000 acres by 1939, of which 428,000 acres were under a forest crop.[29]

There was a mixed reaction to this successful, single-minded policy, but those concerned with outdoor recreation and amenity were generally hostile to the physical enclosure of open grass-heaths and moorland, and the replacement of oak and beech woods with an almost impenetrable stand of conifers. The greatest clash occurred in the Lake District where the Commission, for example, wanted to afforest 740 acres of upper Eskdale. This was opposed by a new society, called the Friends of the Lake District, which proposed alternative sites for afforestation and even offered to buy Upper Eskdale from the Commission at the original purchase price. The Commission refused to sell the land, but offered a compromise whereby it would leave 440 acres unplanted if the voluntary bodies compensated the Commission at the rate of £2 per acre, namely the difference between the revenue from forested and open ground. The remainder of the estate would be planted as a 'model forest'.[30]

The Friends rejected the compromise. Whilst accepting the Commission's capacity to plant a model forest, the real issue was the preservation of open moorland, and the society launched a petition against afforestation in the entire Lake District. This obtained 13,000 signatures, including many public figures. In 1936, H. H. Symonds published a book called *Afforestation in the Lake District* which censured the Commission for being so single-minded in pursuing its planting programme and in ignoring public opinion. Debates were initiated in Parliament calling for a Select Committee on the work of the Commission.[31]

The government rejected such an enquiry, but the Commission urgently debated whether it would be prudent to 'withdraw' from the Lake District. The Director-General, Sir Roy Robinson, argued that the Commission had reached a critical point in its growth when it 'must not merely be reasonable, but must demonstrate the fact'. He, therefore, proposed withdrawing from Eskdale, subject to compensation of £2 per acre. There followed a long period of negotiation, during which time the voluntary bodies launched an appeal for £1,480. Finally, the National Trust accepted custody of the property in 1943.[32]

During the 1930s, the Commission became increasingly aware of the need to improve its public image, and accordingly Robinson suggested in 1935 that a small joint informal committee should be formed with the CPRE to examine the various complaints levelled at the Commission and to suggest ways of 'making plantations more acceptable from the point of view of amenity'. The CPRE accepted the invitation, and thereafter the Commission referred every criticism to the representatives of both organisations on the joint informal committee. It described the committee in 1943 as both a vital channel of communication and 'the ultimate Court of Appeal' for questions of amenity. The CPRE for its part found the joint committee useful in providing an opportunity of discovering the Commission's plans and for influencing the location and layout of plantations.[33]

Robinson was keen that the joint committee should examine specific issues so as to avert such battles as those being fought over Eskdale, and in March 1935 the committee started to discuss the extent of afforestation in the Lake District. John Dower prepared a map which indicated where the CPRE wanted to ban planting (Figure 1). The Commission responded by proposing a much smaller area of 220 square miles. After prolonged debate, both parties agreed to exclude afforestation from a central zone of 300 square miles. The CPRE also wanted to ban planting from a 'special area' but the Commission refused, although agreeing to seek alternative land where possible. This agreement was published in 1936. The Commission stressed its voluntary nature, noting 'it is necessary to make the position clear because it has been suggested that something analogous to *country planning* has been accomplished'. In spite of its limitations, the agreement was highly

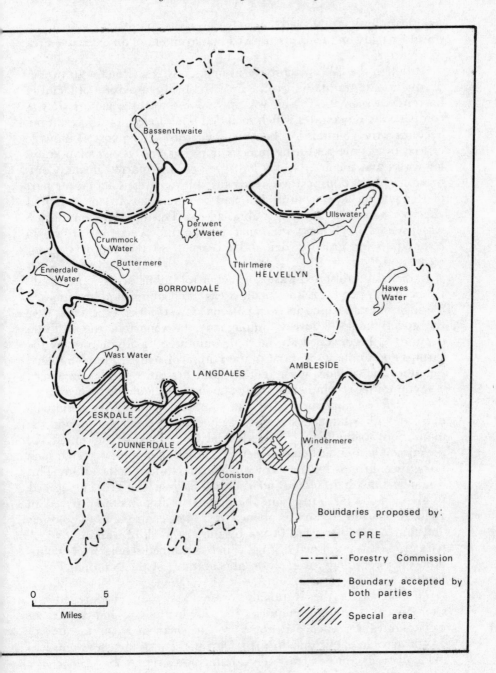

Figure 1
The restriction of afforestation in the Lake District

significant for it established liaison between the voluntary bodies and a statutory body on the future use and management of an extensive area of countryside.

Although the Commission was at first solely concerned with timber production, it gradually became involved in the provision of facilities for outdoor recreation. This was in response to three factors. It was compelled to buy estates which included land useless for afforestation. Secondly, the Commission became concerned at the cost of damage caused by people venturing into its nurseries and young plantations for walks and picnics. Nearly half the 400 fires started in the Commission's plantations in 1929 were caused by a careless act on the part of the public. The Commission had to appoint wardens and find effective ways of controlling public access. Thirdly, the Commission was accused, together with other major landowners, of failing to respond to the growing demand for access to the countryside for recreation.[34]

In order to utilise its 'wasteland', control public access, and satisfy the need for open trails and picnic areas, the Commission investigated the idea of establishing its own national forest parks, especially after the government's failure to implement the report of the Addison committee. It convened an internal committee 'to advise on how the surplus and unplantable land in the Forests of Ardgarten, Glenfinart, Benmore and Glenbranter might be put to a use of a public character'. The committee recommended that 35,000 acres should be turned into a national forest park for hiking and rambling. Routeways should be marked with whitened stones so as to guide walkers through the plantations to the higher ground. The Commissioners accepted the recommendations, although rejecting a proposal to limit access to such recognised groups as the Scottish Youth Hostels Association. This would be difficult to enforce and lead to ill-feeling. The Treasury agreed to give £5,000 for 'fitting out the park', the first visitors arrived in 1936, Ardgarten House was opened as a park centre, and five hostels and four camp sites were in use by the outbreak of war in 1939. A park guide was published in 1938 which contained scholarly contributions on the geology, vegetation and animals of the National Forest Park.[35]

The success of the National Forest Park soon encouraged the Commission to initiate enquiries into further parks, and a park of 23,000 acres was opened in the Forest of Dean in 1939, and one of 20,500 acres in Snowdonia in 1940. During the war, an assessment was made of twelve more areas: the Commission's report *Post-war forestry policy*, published in 1943, claimed that 'one new Park might be established every year for the next ten years, at a capital outlay not exceeding £50,000. If, on the other hand, it is desired to make a special feature of National Forest Parks, the provision of a further £100,000—making £150,000 in all—should enable the establishment of twenty Parks in all by the end of the first post-war decade.'[36]

During the first twenty years of its existence, the Forestry Commission was not only compelled to broaden its simple objective of timber production to take account of outdoor recreation and amenity, but it had entered into direct liaison with such bodies as the CPRE through the joint informal committee. By creating the National Forest Parks, the Commission had become the most important organisation in Britain for the provision of facilities for outdoor recreation. The voluntary bodies could take some of the credit for promoting these changes in outlook and land use.

Just before the outbreak of the Second World War, the voluntary bodies secured the first Act entirely devoted to furthering outdoor recreation. As already noted, there had been many unsuccessful attempts to improve public access to the countryside (page 69). But each Access to Mountains Bill failed, largely because the areas to be opened to the public were so ill-defined and a landowner was unable to obtain recompense for damage unless he prosecuted each visitor and could prove 'malicious intent'.

In spite of these setbacks, there was general agreement that the laws on trespassing should be modernised, and in 1938 discussions were initiated between the Commons, Open Spaces and Footpaths Preservation Society and the Land Union and Country Landowners Association. Whilst these talks were taking place, Arthur Creech Jones rather precipitately introduced another Access to Mountains Bill. In order to satisfy landowners, the new Bill made a wide range of abuses, including damage to crops or farmstock, an offence. Nevertheless, the Home Office condemned the measure as ill-timed and badly drafted, and the Cabinet agreed that the Bill should be blocked. During the second reading, however, 'the feeling of the House was overwhelmingly in favour of the principle of the Bill', and the government had no alternative but to withdraw its opposition. Creech Jones agreed to postpone sending the Bill to the committee stage until the talks between the Commons, Open Spaces and Footpaths Preservation Society and the landowners' organisations had been completed.[37]

By 1939, they had resulted in the formulation of a revised Bill, which was very much longer and retained only a very small part of the original measure. The list of offences was greatly extended, and walkers were required to give their names and addresses to any person authorised by the landowner or occupier. The areas covered by the measure were defined much more rigorously. Landowners, local authorities or voluntary bodies could apply to the Ministry of Agriculture for an order to bring land under the jurisdiction of the Act, and on the basis of this formula, the landowners withdrew their opposition, and the Bill was passed. Scotland was excluded since the law of trespass was different north of the Border and agreement between the various parties had not been reached.[38]

Although the Access to Mountains Bill was passed, the sponsors of the original measure were bitterly disappointed over its emasculated powers. Furthermore, the Act was never implemented: the need for orders threw a heavy administrative burden on the Ministry of Agriculture, and little was achieved before the outbreak of war when preparations for issuing orders were suspended. Nevertheless, the Act was a valuable precedent for those concerned with the countryside: Parliament had at last passed a measure exclusively designed for promoting the public enjoyment of the countryside.

By the outbreak of war in 1939, the voluntary bodies were increasingly optimistic of securing wider support for measures to preserve the countryside and expand opportunities for recreation. But their achievements during the 1930s had been piecemeal, limited to certain parts of the countryside or types of land use. There was a growing need for a national policy, which could only be formulated and initiated by the government itself, acting on the expert advice of local authorities and the appropriate voluntary bodies.

Chapter Five

Wildlife and Post-war Reconstruction

The attempts to set up machinery to improve opportunities for outdoor recreation and for the preservation of amenity and wildlife were themselves part of a wider, contemporary demand for the more rational use of the nation's resources. In order to understand how the naturalist, working in concert with the advocates of recreation and amenity, achieved government support for nature preservation, it is necessary to make detailed reference to the growing interest in land-use controls and planning during the late 1930s and war years.

The First World War of 1914–18 had shown the scope of planning for increasing efficiency and productivity. In the subsequent decade, there had been piecemeal attempts to place some industries on a more rational basis. A national electricity grid was finally established, a single broadcasting service was introduced, and the multiplicity of transport bodies in London was brought under a single body, the London Transport Executive.

The economic and political crises of 1929–31 focussed attention still more sharply on the wastage of manpower, natural resources, capital and enterprise in Britain. In 1931, over three million men were unemployed and much industrial plant was idle or under-used. In that year, E. M. Nicholson and G. Barry wrote a supplement to the *Weekend Review* stressing the need for a national plan for Britain, which would replace piecemeal development with long-term planning. The article stimulated the formation of a non-party research organisation called PEP (Political and Economic Planning), which undertook a series of surveys and in-depth studies of the more pressing economic and social problems of the 1930s. The results were intended to form the basis of fresh policies in 'a period of reconstruction'. In 1934, C. H. Allen and Harold Macmillan convened a group of public figures, similarly drawn from all political parties and professions, to produce a document called *The Next Five Years*, setting out an agreed policy on economic and foreign affairs. In the various discussions, the role of science received special attention. Greater use had to be made of the techniques and results of research in the formulation of public policies.[1]

One of the most pressing problems was the relative decline in the importance of heavy industries based on the coalfields, and the concentration of new industries in a broad belt extending from metropolitan London to Lancashire and the West Riding, facilitated by the increasing availability of electricity and the use of the motor lorry. This unevenness of regional development, with its adverse social and strategic implications, aroused much public disquiet and strengthened demands for the central co-ordination and guidance of land use throughout the country.

The Prime Minister, Neville Chamberlain, responded to these demands in 1937 by appointing a Royal Commission on the Distribution of the Industrial Population, under the chairmanship of Sir Montague Barlow. The members, who included L. P. Abercrombie, expressed profound concern at the creation of a 'great industrial axial belt in the centre of England', and recommended the appointment of a central planning board. A minority report suggested that a Ministry should be specifically appointed to take charge of land-use planning. Whether a Board or a Ministry, steps should be taken to redevelop congested areas and redistribute industry and the industrial population. There should be a reasonable balance in the location of industry throughout the country, so as to reduce the drift to London and the Home Counties. The Commission's report was completed in August 1939 but was not presented to Parliament until January 1940. Although it aroused widespread interest, the government made no attempt to implement any part of its recommendations: this was shelved until after the war.[2]

Planning for Post-war Reconstruction

With the outbreak of war, the optimism of the voluntary bodies gave way to pessimism. Following the precedent of the 1914–18 war, all legislation was dropped unless it was directly related to the war effort. There seemed no hope of any further progress in the provision of outdoor recreation or preservation of amenity and wildlife until the war was over.

The ensuing period of inactivity came to an end quite unexpectedly in October 1940, when the Prime Minister, Winston S. Churchill, established a new Ministry of Works and Buildings, primarily to co-ordinate and increase the efficiency of the various wartime government building programmes. He invited Sir John Reith, the famous former manager of the BBC, to become the new Minister. During the previous five months, Reith had been Minister of Transport and, in that time, he had developed a personal interest in the question of post-war reconstruction. He insisted that his new Ministry should be given the responsibility of planning for the post-war period. He was immediately opposed by the Minister of Health, who was traditionally responsible for town and country planning. The Lord Privy Seal, Clement Attlee, eventually produced a compromise whereby Reith would initiate and co-ordinate the planning of 'the physical environment' of post-war Britain.[3]

Within a month, Reith submitted a detailed memorandum to the Cabinet, which described the existing disorder in land-use planning. There was no national plan for the development of land and no co-ordination of information or research. Only five per cent of England and one per cent of Wales were covered by operative planning schemes. In spite of joint planning committees, most planning continued to be on a piecemeal basis without central direction. The provision of compensation deterred authorities from embarking on effective schemes. The chronic problems of industrial location and the existence of slum properties were being exacerbated by the lack of investment and the anomalies which had arisen during the war. Reith warned that the situation would reach crisis point by the end of the war unless the government formulated and implemented an effective national land-use plan with the minimum of delay.[4]

Reith set out in his memorandum the basic objectives of such a national plan, namely the optimum use of all land and the preservation of fertile areas for agriculture and market gardening, the creation and maintenance 'of a reasonable balance of industrial development and diversification of industry in areas', setting a limit to urban growth and redeveloping the congested centres of towns, the co-ordination of transport and utility services, and finally the preservation of areas of natural or historic interest and the reservation of national parks and coastal areas.

To achieve these aims, he proposed the creation of a central planning authority to lay down the general principles and supervise schemes in consultation with other government departments, statutory undertakings and local authorities. It would be assisted by an Advisory Council of experienced persons, and would create a research council. Regional officers and advisory committees would be appointed to ensure close liaison with local requirements and aspirations. Local authorities would continue to be responsible for detailed local planning, but strengthened by fully qualified staff and receiving more generous financial support from the Exchequer.

At first, Reith's personal initiative aroused little response. Churchill read the memorandum 'with great interest', but stressed the need to concentrate on more pressing tasks. But soon the War Cabinet became much more interested in longer-term planning, prompted by the need to reconstruct the blitzed centres of the cities and curb the alleged activities of land speculators. It also realised that planning and the promise of greater prosperity, security and happiness after the war could play a major role in stimulating the war effort.[5]

On the last day of 1940, Reith's memorandum was considered by a committee under the chairmanship of the Lord President of the Council, Sir John Anderson. The committee endorsed the memorandum and gave its consent to the appointment of an expert committee to investigate the most fundamental and complex planning question, namely the impact of planning on land values. Under the chairmanship of Mr Justice Uthwatt, an analysis was to be made of the payment of compensation and the levy of betterment charges, the stabilisation of land values, and the acquisition of land for public use.

On the other hand, several ministers were highly indignant at the way in which Reith was trying to poach on their 'estates'. In a personal letter to Churchill, the Minister of Agriculture, R. S. Hudson, accused Reith of trying to set up a Ministry of Cranks who would duplicate the work of half the departments in Whitehall. He wrote, 'My fear is that while we are busily engaged in trying to win the war these cranks will be concocting all sorts of schemes, and when the war is over and we have the job of putting a sane agricultural policy into operation we shall be faced with a whole series of theoretical plans and vested interests which will make our task quite impossible'.

At Churchill's behest, Hudson submitted a critical paper to Anderson's committee which illustrated the great difficulty of one department setting priorities in the planning field which inevitably encroached on the sectional interests of other ministries. Hudson insisted that the use and extent of agricultural land was purely a matter for his Ministry: in the event of a dispute as to how much farmland should be converted to industrial or urban use, such ministers as the Lord Privy Seal or Lord President should act as arbiters since they had no departmental responsibilities. Reith's Ministry would be quite inappropriate since it was primarily concerned with building development.[6]

In view of these misgivings, there was a double significance in Churchill's appointment of the Minister without Portfolio, Arthur Greenwood, as Minister with over-all responsibility for post-war reconstruction. First, this underlined the government's determination to 'plan for peace'. The War Aims Committee, which had previously met under Greenwood's chairmanship, was replaced by a Committee on Reconstruction Problems which was to prepare practical schemes for reconstruction so as to 'secure equality of opportunity and service among all classes of the community'.[7]

Secondly, the appointment of the Minister averted the risk of clashes between departments as forewarned by Hudson. Greenwood had no sectional interests: he would simply set the framework for post-war reconstruction, any Ministers worried over the implications of Reith's plans for the physical environment could appeal to the Committee on Reconstruction Problems, of which Greenwood was chairman. In a further attempt to ensure liaison between departments, an interdepartmental Advisory Committee was set up under Lord Reith, composed of senior officials representing the Minister without Portfolio, Treasury, Board of Trade, Ministries of Agriculture, Health and Transport, and the Scottish Home Department and Department of Health.[8]

A principal assistant secretary, H. G. Vincent, took charge of planning in Reith's Ministry, and Reith later wrote in his autobiography that 'no one could have shown greater assiduity and devotion . . . the credit for what was accomplished was in large measure Vincent's'. A small survey and research team of civil servants was assembled under Vincent's direction, and included John Dower, H. C. Bradshaw of the Royal Fine Arts Commission, and W. G. Holford who was Professor of Town Planning at Liverpool. G. L. Pepler, the town planning officer of the Ministry of Health, was later transferred to Reith's Ministry. In addition, a consultative panel of about twenty experts was appointed to provide information and ideas on specific issues. Drawn from local government, university departments and professional bodies, the experts included Sir Montague Barlow, L. P. Abercrombie, and three other members of the earlier Royal Commission.

This growing interest in land-use planning transformed the situation for the voluntary bodies. In spite of the war effort, it was an opportune time to urge the creation of national parks and nature reserves. The involvement of the government in land use and management was more readily accepted. The Minister without Portfolio, Arthur Greenwood, told the House of Commons that planning meant 'the pooling of our knowledge and experience so as to concert measures which will ensure that the limited land of our small islands is used to the best in the national interest', and he laid particular stress on the preservation of 'those beauties which, once gone, could never be restored'. There was a greater chance of the government actually taking a positive role in establishing and administering national parks and nature reserves. The war had created so much devastation that their creation would be a positive step and some compensation for the losses that had been sustained.[9]

The Commons, Open Spaces and Footpaths Preservation Society was the first voluntary body to take the initiative in lobbying the government, and it submitted a memorandum in October 1941, stressing the need to provide greater facilities for outdoor recreation. It recommended improvements in the preservation and upkeep of commons, footpaths and bridleways. In January 1942, the Association for the Preservation of Rural Scotland (APRS) convened a conference of representatives from thirty organisations which set up a new Scottish Council on National Parks in order to exert pressure on the government. In England and Wales, a deputation from the Standing Committee on National Parks met Lord Reith on 6 January 1942, and once again emphasised the need for a series of national parks and a national parks authority.[10]

During this period, Geoffrey Dent played an important part in encouraging naturalists to take the initiative in publicising the need for nature preservation in post-war planning. In 1940, the Association of Bird-watchers and Wardens negotiated an agreement with the British Oological Association, whereby the collection of rare birds and their eggs would be regulated by a licensing system (page 43). Although the war prevented the agreement being implemented, Dent urged the RSPB to undertake immediately a survey to discover which species and areas required special protection. This would help to ensure a rational preservation policy after the war. He emphasised the value of devising a scheme which would win government support.

At the same time as the survey was being carried out, Dent suggested that the RSPB should convene a series of meetings of interested persons to work out a commonly agreed nature preservation policy. He warned in May 1940 that 'if the Societies interested do not get together, and form a common policy of their own, no government is likely to do much, or listen to them, and we shall lose several more breeding species in the next twenty years'. The Council of the RSPB readily accepted the idea, and a small committee under the chairmanship of Dent was formed to undertake the survey and make other preparations for the post-war years.

This committee soon produced a memorandum setting out the functions of bird sanctuaries and the need for the government to give them additional protection. The memorandum described how:

America, our Dominions, and most advanced European countries have long since adopted the principle, that the State should take responsibility for the preservation of some part of its native wild life for the benefit of future generations. It has proved that the only way to do this effectively is to supplement the preservation laws by the provision of national parks or reserves to act as breeding reservoirs for those species which might otherwise be threatened with extermination. This country alone has left this task to chance and the initiative of private individuals and societies.

The memorandum was supplemented by lists of rare birds and areas where greater protection was urgently required.[11]

Although the surveys of species and sanctuaries were soon carried out, Dent failed to secure a meeting of interested parties until 1941, when the secretary of the RSPB, R. Preston Donaldson, discussed the idea of such a meeting with Herbert Smith, the secretary of the SPNR. Smith immediately supported the idea, and persuaded the SPNR itself to organise the conference, which would draw up a memorandum for presentation to the government, setting out the objectives and organisation necessary for the preservation of wildlife after the war. Two representatives from over thirty organisations were invited, including representatives from the various associations of local authorities.[12]

The Conference on Nature Preservation in Post-war Reconstruction

The Conference met on 5 June 1941, and most of the time was spent in discussing the memorandum on bird sanctuaries which had been prepared for the RSPB. In addition, two other memoranda were submitted: one by E. J. Salisbury on botanical aspects of nature preservation, and the other by J. C. F. Fryer and H. M. Edelsten, representing the entomologist's point of view. All emphasised the need to include as wide a variety of habitat as possible in any series of reserves.[13]

The Conference set up a drafting committee to compile a memorandum for submission to the government. This consisted of Sir Lawrence Chubb, G. Dent, P. Chalmers-Mitchell, W. L. Platts and E. J. Salisbury, and the secretary was Herbert Smith. There was agreement that whilst the concept of national parks had received much attention, little thought had been given to the creation of nature reserves. This should be quickly remedied (i) by ensuring that the principle of establishing nature reserves was incorporated in any national planning scheme, (ii) by creating an official body, representative of scientific interests, to draw up detailed proposals, and (iii) by ensuring that the management of these reserves was placed in the hands of persons with expertise and experience of wildlife management.

These recommendations were readily accepted by the Conference, although there was considerable controversy as to whether the Conference memorandum should make detailed reference to the question of selecting and administering national parks. Many of the proposed parks were extremely important for their wildlife. The representative of the County Councils Association, W. L. Platts, drafted a fresh memorandum which contained a detailed discussion of the relative powers of the local authorities and the proposed national parks authority. This proved so controversial that the Standing Committee on National Parks threatened to withdraw from the Conference. The remaining members thereupon decided to devote far greater attention to 'the scientific aspects of nature preservation'.[14] C. Diver and J. Ramsbottom were added to the drafting committee for this purpose, and they played a major role in drawing up a fresh document, which was accepted by the Conference on 6 October 1941. About 500 copies of this memorandum were printed, and copies were sent to the Prime Minister, various Ministers, and appropriate organisations and individuals.[15]

In spite of the war situation, the memorandum won considerable publicity for nature preservation and the concept of national nature reserves. *The Times*, in a leader devoted to 'Wild life in Trust', described how the various natural history societies and associations of local authorities had co-operated in providing a memorandum which set out their collective views on nature preservation after the war. It added 'this is a hopeful sign in the discussion of projects that seem at first sight to involve an acute conflict of interests'.

Soon afterward, the Standing Committee on National Parks invited the Conference to participate in a deputation to Lord Reith. On 6 January 1942, Sir Norman Birkett led the deputation: L. P. Abercrombie and H. H. Symonds represented the Standing Committee and stressed the need for national parks, and Lord Onslow, W. L. Platts and Herbert Smith represented the Conference and described the potential role of nature reserves in post-war reconstruction. Reith accepted the concepts of national parks and national nature reserves, and proposed as a first step the establishment of a small informal committee to consider the many points of detail. This would consist of Abercrombie, Symonds, Platts, and two members of his own Ministry, H. G. Vincent and G. L. Pepler.[16]

This committee, however, never met owing to a change in government departments and Ministers. During 1941, Reith had begun his most urgent tasks of creating a central planning authority and bringing the entire country under interim planning control. At first, it was widely assumed that government departments would retain their existing planning powers and simply consult the central planning body before implementing them. But Reith insisted that all planning powers should be transferred to this central body, which should be given the status of a planning Ministry. This met with a mixed response and the Chancellor of the Exchequer, Sir Kingsley Wood, opposed such a concept. But the Minister without Portfolio, Arthur Greenwood, supported the proposal, and submitted a memorandum to the War Cabinet advocating the transfer of all the planning powers of the Ministry of Health and other departments to Reith's Ministry, which would be renamed the Ministry of Works and Planning. The War Cabinet gave its approval on 9 February 1942: as before, the Minister without Portfolio would continue to act as arbiter in any dispute over departmental responsibilities.[17]

Soon afterward, Churchill asked Reith to resign, and Lord Portal became the new Minister of Works and Planning. In March 1942, Sir William Jowitt became Paymaster-General, and replaced Greenwood as chairman of the Committee on Reconstruction Problems. Within a few days, Sir Norman Birkett sent Jowitt a detailed memorandum setting out the views of the Standing Committee, and a deputation made up of Birkett, Abercrombie, Symonds and R. S. Chorley met Jowitt on 8 April. At the meeting, Jowitt expressed great interest in the concept of national parks and asked for more detailed plans and estimates of the cost of setting up the parks and the necessary administrative machinery.

On 4 May 1942, the drafting committee of the Conference on nature preservation also met Jowitt, and stressed the need for government aid in establishing nature reserves, which 'should be earmarked as soon as possible so that they could be fitted into post-war planning schemes'. C. Diver, a member of the deputation, proposed the appointment of a scientific body to draw up detailed proposals on nature conservation and to select a series of national nature reserves. Jowitt agreed on the need to incorporate nature reserves in any post-war planning scheme, but admitted that nature conservation was very low on the government's list of priorities, and that it was very unlikely that the government would be able to set up an official enquiry into the subject. He, therefore, suggested that the Conference itself should set up an enquiry and provide the government with the necessary data.[18]

These two meetings with the representatives of the Standing Committee and the Conference provided the occasion for Jowitt and the Minister of Works and Planning, Lord Portal, to discuss their respective responsibilities for outdoor recreation and the preservation of amenity and wildlife. They agreed to co-operate in drawing up joint proposals for submission to the Cabinet Committee on Reconstruction Problems.

From this time onwards, the Ministers began to make references in Parliament and in public to the need to facilitate outdoor recreation and preserve amenity and wildlife. Lord Portal referred to this during a debate of April 1942 when he said 'it is clear that no national planning of the use of land would satisfy the country if it did not provide for the preservation of extensive areas of great natural beauty and of the coast line. The question of National Parks and of the protection of our coast from ill-considered building development will be carefully examined and we fully realize the importance of this.' A few days later in the House of Commons, Sir William Jowitt spoke of the great value of the Lake District as a potential national park, provided with such facilities as youth hostels 'to give our young people a chance to roam about and get their exercise'. The Joint Parliamentary Secretary, H. G. Strauss, was of course quick to point out that little action could be taken until the war was won.[19]

The Chancellor of the Exchequer, Sir Kingsley Wood, struck an even more pessimistic note when asked by Jowitt for his views. He claimed that the government would lack both the administrative capacity and the necessary funds to set up a series of national parks until many years had elapsed in the post-war period. Instead, every effort should be made to protect amenity and facilitate outdoor recreation within the limits of existing resources and legislation. He suggested appointing two or three people to investigate how this might be achieved in such areas as the Lake District and Dovedale.[20]

Both Jowitt and Lord Portal disagreed with this view and they soon obtained support from an unexpected quarter, namely from a committee appointed by Reith in October 1941 to advise on the impact of building and industrial development on the countryside. In drawing up plans for re-building the blitzed and run-down parts of towns in post-war Britain, it was soon recognised that housing schemes, wider streets and more urban gardens would force many people to move to a new home in the countryside. Likewise, many industries would have to leave the city centres for new sites on the edge of the cities or further afield. Reith and his Ministry realised that 'all urban plans must be related to those of the surrounding country'. A fresh review of the recommendations of the Barlow report was urgently needed and, as part of this re-appraisal, Reith appointed a committee under Lord Justice Scott to assess the impact of these urban and industrial changes on the countryside.

The report of the Scott Committee was published in August 1942 and reaffirmed the need to secure a carefully controlled balance between agriculture and the use of land for residential and industrial development. It also contained detailed references to the question of amenity and outdoor recreation. The report considered that the creation of a series of national parks was long overdue, and recommended the establishment of a national parks authority within one year of peace.[21]

The Scott Committee also gave support to the notion of national nature reserves. On behalf of the County Councils Association, W. L. Platts gave evidence to the Committee and mentioned the need for nature preservation and the work of the Conference on nature preservation, and the Scott Committee thereupon requested copies of the Conference's memorandum. It commented on the value of national nature reserves in its report, stressing:

> . . . while some of the larger National Parks will naturally form or contain *nature reserves* and it may be possible to set aside portions of them specifically for the purpose, it is essential in other cases that prohibition of access shall be a first consideration, and for this reason nature reserves should also be established separately from national parks.

The Scott Committee recommended that the Ministry of Works and Planning, in liaison with the appropriate scientific societies, should select areas for national nature reserves and 'geological parks' and take the necessary steps to ensure their preservation and control.[22]

The momentum in devising a national plan for land use, which incorporated national parks and nature reserves, was maintained. In March 1943, the Ministry of Works and Planning was replaced by a Ministry of Town and Country Planning, which had the responsibility of securing 'consistency and continuity in the framing and execution of a national policy with respect to the use and development of land throughout England and Wales'. W. S. Morrison became the new Minister, and H. G. Strauss was appointed to a new post of Parliamentary Secretary for Planning. The Scottish Secretary, Thomas Johnston, obtained similar planning powers for Scotland.[23]

In its Interim Report of July 1941, the Uthwatt Committee (page 92) recommended that every part of the country should be subject to interim planning control so as to prevent any development taking place which would prejudice post-war reconstruction. By this time, only seventy-eight per cent of England and thirty-seven per cent of Wales were covered by operative or interim planning controls. This recommendation was adopted in the Town and Country Planning (Interim Development) Act of July 1943, which also increased the influence of county councils in the planning field, and allowed the Minister to appoint ten regional planning officers. Whilst these measures were primarily designed to facilitate the reconstruction of town centres affected by the blitz and urban blight, they were also an important step in protecting amenity and wildlife. The government had demonstrated its willingness to implement a national plan for the optimum use of land: now the voluntary bodies had to take the initiative in providing the data to support the establishment of national parks and nature reserves.[24]

The Nature Reserves Investigation Committee

When representatives of the Conference on nature preservation met Sir William Jowitt on 4 May 1942, Jowitt suggested that the Conference itself should carry out an enquiry on the need for nature preservation after the war. With some reluctance, the Conference agreed to accept this assignment, and a Nature Reserves Investigation Committee (NRIC) was formally constituted on 24 June 1942. It would first of all identify those plants and animals which were in danger of becoming extinct, and then recommend where national nature reserves should be established and how they should be managed.[25]

The NRIC effectively took over: the drafting committee was no longer needed and the Conference met only once more. The members of the NRIC were Sir Lawrence Chubb, G. Dent, C. Diver, J. C. F. Fryer, N. B. Kinnear, W. H. Pearsall, J. Ramsbottom, J. Ritchie, E. J. Salisbury and Herbert Smith as secretary. The membership was a clear indication of the growing influence of ecologists and the waning influence of the representatives of local authorities. There were objections to the appointment of a 'scientist' as chairman because he might not be sufficiently impartial, and Smith succeeded in persuading Sir Lawrence Chubb to take the chair. On learning of the formation of the committee, Sir Roy Robinson wrote to Sir William Jowitt suggesting that a representative of the Forestry Commission should become a member. The idea was passed onto the NRIC which accepted the proposal as a means of improving liaison with the Commission, and W. L. Taylor, the Chief Executive Officer, was subsequently co-opted in August 1942.[26]

The SPNR had defrayed the cost of the Conference, but was reluctant to meet the much heavier expenses of the NRIC. Lord Macmillan, the new president of the SPNR, therefore applied to the Pilgrim Trust for help, and secured a grant of £200 to cover expenses. In 1943, the Pilgrim Trust made a further grant of £250. The expenses of the NRIC were, nevertheless, modest: it spent less than £250 and recouped most of its outlay from the sale of memoranda. Herbert Smith proudly pointed out in 1945 that 'no call had been made on public funds. Had the Ministry of Town and Country Planning . . . undertaken it, the cost to date must have run to at least £10,000, and I wonder whether local naturalists would have so readily worked for a Government Department without any remuneration'.[27]

The NRIC immediately began work on a general report for submission to Sir William Jowitt by the end of 1942, which would set out the reasons for conserving sites and areas of key importance for their 'biology, zoology, geology, mineralogy and ecology'. There was at first no intention of publishing the report: it was to be purely for the guidance of Ministers responsible for town and country planning. But soon the objectives widened and the NRIC compiled a memorandum for both the government and general public, which was called *Nature conservation in Great Britain*. It was published in March 1943: the NRIC did not expect the government to make nature conservation its first priority, but conservation was something no government could afford to neglect. Once the natural heritage had been destroyed, it could never be replaced.[28]

Meanwhile, national parks had become the subject of a separate enquiry. Following the support given to national parks by Lord Portal and Sir William Jowitt in parliament (page 97), H. G. Vincent decided that the Ministry of Works and Planning itself should investigate 'the practical needs in certain potential areas' for national parks. For this task, he nominated John Dower, a leading architect and drafting secretary of the Standing Committee on National Parks. Instead of simply sifting through reports and papers in committee rooms, Dower would undertake field-work and 'on the spot, enquiries in the potential parks.[29]

It was decided to start with surveys of the Lake District, Peak District, Snowdonia and Dartmoor, which contained a wide variety of conditions and could 'be regarded as certain selections in any final scheme'. Dower was appointed as a research officer in the Ministry and began work in August 1942. He was instructed to prepare a purely 'factual report' on the Lake District in two months, recommending the optimum extent of the park, its 'conservation and development', and the provision of public access.[30]

Soon after the appointment of Dower, the Scott Report was published and, in view of its favourable reception and its references to national parks, Vincent asked Dower to widen his terms of reference so as to include 'a report on the general issues backed by the specific information he had obtained'. In spite of poor health, Dower accepted this larger task and completed a much longer report on the whole question of national parks by November 1943.

In this report, Dower defined the kind of national park required in Britain 'as an extensive area of beautiful and relatively wild country in which for the nation's benefit and by appropriate national decision and action, (i) the characteristic landscape beauty is strictly preserved, (ii) access and facilities for public open-air enjoyment, including particularly cross-country and foot-path walking, are amply provided, and (iii) wild life and places and buildings of historic, architectural or scientific interest are suitably protected'.[31]

Both Vincent and Dower were keen to ensure that adequate attention was paid to wildlife preservation in the proposed national parks. In September 1942, Vincent asked the NRIC to provide lists of areas which should be protected as nature reserves in the four potential parks of the Lake District, Peak District, Snowdonia and Dartmoor, which were being investigated by Dower. The NRIC decided to appoint sub-committees to the four areas, and their work is described on page 138. A memorandum based on their reports was submitted to the Ministry of Town and Country Planning in August 1943.[32]

Shortly after the presentation of the memorandum, the Ministry asked for the same kind of detailed information for each part of England and Wales and, accordingly, the NRIC decided to set up a sub-committee in each part of the country. In addition, it asked for the specialist help of the British Ecological Society, the RSPB and the Royal Entomological Society.

The British Ecological Society had already set up its own special enquiry in May 1943 to investigate the need for nature reserves. The chairman was A. G. Tansley, and the members were A. W. Boyd, C. S. Elton, E. W. Jones, O. W. Richards, together with C. Diver, W. H. Pearsall, J. Ritchie, E. J. Salisbury and L. A. Harvey (secretary) who were members of the NRIC or its sub-committees. The British Ecological Society believed its membership 'included probably the great majority of those best qualified to advise on the right areas to be reserved', and the special committee accordingly sent circulars to all its members asking for details of potential reserves. This survey was at first quite independent of the NRIC, and Tansley's first letter to the NRIC met with a somewhat cool reply from Herbert Smith. But any misunderstanding was soon removed and a working relationship was achieved.[33]

The special committee of the British Ecological Society had two particular objectives in mind. First, it was anxious to select reserves on ecological criteria and secondly to protect vital field evidence for ecological research. It therefore drew up a list of vegetation types and areas which should be protected in the reserves (page 142), and a copy was sent to the NRIC in 1943.

It was soon decided to broaden the terms of reference of the special committee to include the whole question of nature conservation in Britain. Tansley prepared a memorandum which was presented to the Council of the British Ecological Society in April 1943, which set out the reasons for nature conservation and the role of ecologists in selecting and managing the reserves through the foundation of an Ecological Research Council. The memorandum was published in both journals of the Society, and a further 750 copies were specially printed and sold to the general public.[34]

The Reports of the NRIC

Once the NRIC had published its memorandum on *Nature conservation in Great Britain* in March 1943, all attention was devoted to identifying those sites and areas worthy of protection.

As early as June 1941, Herbert Smith had taken the initiative of inviting representatives from the various geological societies to attend the Conference on nature preservation, 'not only because they are directly interested in animals and plants, if in the fossil form, but also because they may be anxious that important geological features should be safeguarded'. At first there was no response to the invitation, but Smith was persistent and eventually the Geological Society nominated the President, H. L. Hawkins, and R. W. Pocock as its representatives. The Scott report on rural land use referred to the need to protect both biological and geological sites: it thought that geological features should be safeguarded in the same way as scheduled ancient monuments.[35]

At first, Smith represented the geologists' viewpoint on the NRIC and he was soon joined by W. G. Fearnsides, who was convener of the Peak District national sub-committee (page 138). Each regional sub-committee was asked to provide information on geological and physiographical features needing protection, but the response was uneven. Whilst some sub-committees suggested a large number of sites, others made no recommendations. The NRIC also realised that the measures required for protecting geological features were very different from those needed for conserving biological sites. To help overcome these dilemmas, the NRIC decided to appoint a gelogical sub-committee in April 1944. S. E. Hollingworth and G. H. Mitchell were nominated by the Director of the Geological Survey, and T. H. Whitehead and D. Williams were proposed by the Council of the Geological Society. So as to ensure the closest liaison with the NRIC, Herbert Smith served as chairman, and K. P. Oakley acted as secretary.[36]

The first task was to produce a balanced list of geological features for the whole of England and Wales, and further assistance was sought from the sub-committees. In addition, members of the Geologists' Association, Prehistoric Society and Mineralogical Society were invited to help, and eventually over fifty people gave assistance. For several months, Smith worked full-time in his capacity as chairman, collating the various reports and compiling the memorandum of the geological sub-committee.

A draft of the memorandum was completed in November 1944 and included a discussion of the concept of geological monuments and a list of both national and internationally important sites in England and Wales, together with those of the Isle of Man. Sites of purely local interest were rigorously excluded: there were plans to publish a second list of sites of local and educational value at a later date, but this report never appeared.[37]

The report of the geological sub-committee was published in September 1945 and 'had a wonderful press'. A second batch of 1,000 copies of the memorandum had to be printed one month later. A leader in *The Times* pointed out how many of the proposed geological monuments fell within areas of outstanding natural beauty and wildlife interest. The Avon Gorge, for instance, contained not only 'classic sections of Carboniferous Limestone', but also the rare Bristol rock cress *Arabis stricta*. Dungeness was not only a fine example of a sequence of shingle banks, but also the only British nesting station of the Kentish plover.[38]

Whilst the geological sub-committee was at work, the main committee of the NRIC was preparing a similar list of proposed national nature reserves. It was originally intended to publish this list before its geological counterpart, but progress was badly delayed by the poor quality of some of the regional sub-committee reports and by the sheer immensity of the task. The NRIC met twenty-one times between April 1944 and September 1945 before the final selection of proposed national nature reserves could be made. Again, most of the paperwork devolved on Herbert Smith. Eventually, drafts of the lists were sent to the Ministry of Town and Country Planning in August 1945, and the lists themselves were published in December 1945.[39]

In spite of the delay, the NRIC claimed 'there could have been no more opportune moment for the publication of a well-informed survey of our natural history resources than the present, when our minds, set free from the destructive occupations of war, are able once more to turn with re-awakened consciousness to the gracious appreciation of Nature'. Herbert Smith described the work of the Conference on nature preservation, and then the NRIC, as 'a big job', started just after London had experienced the worst of the blitz and completed as V1 and V2 rockets fell on the city. A great deal of the credit must be accorded to Smith himself, who co-ordinated work, maintained continuity and indeed 'discipline'.[40]

As early as 1943, Geoffrey Dent warned that the proposed reserves would be of little use unless wildlife was given greater protection throughout the countryside. He drew up a detailed memorandum on ways of improving legislation and law enforcement, and of regulating changes in the habitat, but the NRIC decided to postpone further discussions on these points until the lists of proposed geological monuments and nature reserves had been published. It also had plans to publish memoranda on plants and animals on the verge of extinction. But, in the event, these reports were never published. The work of the NRIC was overtaken by an unexpected turn of events.[41]

The Progress of Government Enquiries

During a Parliamentary debate of 30 November 1943, the Minister of Town and Country Planning, W. S. Morrison, confirmed that the government had accepted a responsibility for preserving the natural beauty of the countryside and for providing facilities for outdoor recreation. This was highly significant for the proponents of nature conservation because in accepting a responsibility for amenity the government had to some extent accepted an obligation for wildlife, since plants and animals were widely regarded as an essential ingredient of amenity. Morrison described how 'surveys were being made of areas suitable for national parks, nature reserves and recreational purposes'.[42]

Although Dower's terms of reference were widened after the publication of the Scott report, his enquiry continued to be purely for the guidance of the Ministry, and there was at first no intention of publishing his findings. However, Morrison referred to Dower and his investigations during a speech to the Annual Conference of the CPRE in December 1943 in order to underline the government's sincerity in trying to protect amenity and encourage outdoor recreation. This aroused so much interest in Dower's work that there were soon demands for the publication of Dower's report. This led to procedural problems since Dower had been acting simply as a research officer of the Ministry, and there were discussions as to whether his name should appear on the cover or, indeed, anywhere in a published report. A Cabinet committee debated whether the Minister should accept any responsibility for the report, and finally it was decided to publish the report as the findings of an officer in the Ministry 'acting as a consultant'.[43]

Meanwhile, the Scottish Council for National Parks pressed the Scottish Secretary, Thomas Johnston, for a survey of potential national parks in Scotland, and in November 1943 Johnston discussed with his heads of departments the value of inviting Dower to carry out a survey of Scotland. In the event, it was decided to appoint A. Geddes, a planning officer of the Department of Health, to undertake a survey under the supervision of a committee of four Scotsmen. The chairman of this committee was Sir J. Douglas Ramsay, formerly His Majesty's Commissioner to the Balmoral Estate and a member of the Scottish Council for National Parks. The other members were F. Fraser Darling, a naturalist and authority on life in the remoter Highlands and Islands, and D. G. Moir, the secretary of the Scottish Youth Hostels Association. Another member, P. Thomsen, died just before the report of the committee was completed.[44]

The Douglas Ramsay Supervisory Committee completed its work in

October 1944 and its report, together with that of John Dower, was published in mid-1945. It supported Dower's investigations in emphasising the need for a series of national parks, and gradually attention focussed on the question of how the parks should be administered. This had already been the subject of considerable debate within the voluntary bodies since the publication of the Addison Committee's report of 1931.

Some commentators believed the parks could be administered by simply strengthening the planning powers of the government, especially after the creation of the Ministry of Works and Planning in 1942. But the Standing Committee was quick to reject the idea: the Ministry had so many responsibilities that it could never devote sufficient attention and resources to national parks. Such tasks as the protection of wildlife, footpaths and bridleways required the attention of a 'specialised and whole-time body'.[45]

Other commentators accepted the need for a specialist body, but thought it was useless to press for an executive body during a time of financial stringency and international crises. The government was much more likely to accept an advisory national parks authority. But John Dower rejected such a compromise. He warned the Standing Committee in 1939 that the Ministry would simply use an advisory authority to 'ward off criticism and provide a cloak for government inactivity'. It might improve liaison between government departments, local authorities and statutory undertakings in the planning field, 'but it could not reliably protect, still less positively create, national parks'.[46]

Dower drafted a model National Parks Bill on behalf of the Standing Committee in 1939, which envisaged a National Parks Commission with nine members. It would designate national parks and appoint an assistant commissioner and an advisory committee to each. It would facilitate access to all parts of the parks and have powers to grant compensation to landowners and occupiers who were adversely affected. The Commission would buy, lease or enter into agreements with landowners for land for national nature reserves for 'the preservation of flora and fauna and rocks and soils of geological interest'. These would be protected with the aid of by-laws, and wardens would be appointed to administer them.

Under the draft Bill, the national parks commission was to be the planning authority for the park areas and control even the developments proposed by government departments, local authorities and statutory undertakings. It would draw up planning schemes in conjunction with local authorities for enhancing the scenery and wildlife of the parks and for extending recreational facilities and the output of agriculture.

This positive role for the commission was developed by Dower and the Douglas Ramsay Committee in their reports published in 1945. The commission would 'try to conserve and, progressively, to recreate and enrich the scenic beauty' of the parks through such measures as tree-planting and the removal of eye-sores. It would reclaim derelict land and order the removal of jerry-built houses and badly-placed advertisements. The commission would establish long-distance pathways and other facilities for holiday-making.[47]

By this time, however, the Forestry Commission had established National Forest Parks in Argyllshire (1936), the Forest of Dean (1939) and Snowdonia (1940). Whilst they were less ambitious than national parks (page 86), the Forestry Commission claimed they were more practical and it criticised the Dower report for trying to create a completely new and relatively expensive system.[48] For its part, the Standing Committee on National Parks welcomed the creation of National Forest Parks, but it opposed the notion that they were an adequate substitute for national parks. They were of necessity confined to the properties of the Forestry Commission, and the provision of outdoor recreation would always be subsidiary to commercial considerations.

There remained, nevertheless, the strong possibility of the Forestry Commission remaining the only statutory body responsible for parks and, in October 1943, the Commissioners decided to appoint a committee to consider the value of converting Glentrool into a new National Forest Park. Sir Roy Robinson wrote to the Scottish Secretary, T. Johnston, inviting him to nominate a representative to the committee, observing that the Forestry Commission had 'already established a sufficient number of National Forest Parks to be able to regard the making of new ones as a routine matter'.[49]

Johnston, however, took the strongest exception to the fact that as minister with planning responsibilities in Scotland he had not been consulted when the idea of a new National Forest Park in Glentrool was first mooted. In a letter to the Lord Privy Seal, C. Atlee, he pointed out that a National Forest Park would raise important planning questions, and the advisory committee would cut right across the Scottish Secretary's liaison with local authorities and the voluntary bodies on the national parks issue. To exacerbate the situation, the Forestry Commission announced the formation of the advisory committee, and the names of those persons already nominated to the committee, before the Secretary had responded to the invitation to appoint his own representative.

The Lord Privy Seal supported the complaint, and soon afterwards Johnston met the Minister of Town and Country Planning, W. S. Morrison, to discuss ways of presenting 'a common front against any proposals by the Forestry Commission to pursue an independent policy with regard to national parks'. They affirmed that the primary responsibilities for national parks lay with the two planning ministers. It was decided to apprise the Treasury of the situation 'so that they would know not to commit themselves to approving any expenditure on the establishment of a National Park in the Glentrool area' without first consulting the two Ministers.

The determination of Johnston and Morrison to retain a responsibility for national parks enhanced the significance of the Douglas Ramsay and Dower reports. In his report, Dower proposed the creation of a preparatory national parks commission as soon as possible, under the terms of Section 8 of the Ministry of Town and Country Planning Act of 1943. Morrison agreed and drafted a memorandum asking for the approval of the Reconstruction Committee of the War Cabinet for such a preparatory commission. Johnston also agreed to the need for further investigations, but he suggested appointing a further committee of enquiry rather than a preparatory commission. He proposed re-appointing the Douglas Ramsay Committee to examine those aspects not covered by their earlier report, namely those related to the administration and finances of a national parks system.[50]

There ensued a highly confidential exchange of views. The Minister was afraid the Scottish preference for another committee of enquiry might prejudice the views of the Reconstruction Committee against a preparatory commission, and the Minister suggested that the Secretary of State should simply justify his preference for a committee on the grounds that he had no legal powers to set up a Scottish preparatory national parks commission. The latter refused, claiming that the Secretary did have the necessary legal powers, but simply believed a new Douglas Ramsay committee would suffice.

Dower defended the decision to recommend a preparatory commission in the following manner:

> . . . to appoint a mere Committee . . . will look like shelving the issue to a further round of inconclusive consideration. On the other hand, if put forward with a frank explanation of the difficulties which prevent immediate legislative and executive action, a Preparatory Commission with clear status under the Act of 1943, will, I believe, be just enough to satisfy both general and specialist opinion, for some time to come. It would give substantial form to the Government's acceptance of National Parks, and would look like getting on with the job.
>
> The next main body of work on National Parks is to get down to brass tacks in the various 'first choice' areas with the Local Planning Authorities concerned. I do not expect much, if any, real opposition from them—rather, on the contrary, much interest

and keenness. But we must expect all sorts of different opinions about areas, methods, &c, and a plentiful crop of misunderstandings and 'bargaining' disparities. It will be a tough job to get the requisite schemes of action worked out with a sufficient measure of agreement and goodwill: and it will, I suggest, make a great difference to the success and speed of this work that a Commission with a bit of 'red carpet', rather than a mere Committee, should be engaged in the requisite contacts with the Local Authorities.

The opportunity of service on a Commission is more likely to attract the best available men and to stimulate them to work enthusiastically than membership of a Committee. Moreover a Preparatory Commission could go on without any break into the full Commission—it would grow naturally into its task, and would be ready to proceed at once without delay or hesitation when the time for action arrived.

The Minister made use of these points at the meetings of the Reconstruction Committee, held on 7 May 1945, shortly before the National Government was dissolved. In view of the widespread desire for national parks, he emphasised the value of creating a preparatory national parks commission to delimit potential areas in consultation with local authorities and for advising the Minister on legislation, financial and administrative requirements for a national parks system.

Lord Woolton was in the chair, and Sir John Anderson (Chancellor of the Exchequer) began by questioning the appropriateness of setting up a preparatory commission under the 1943 Act which, he claimed, was intended by parliament as a means of establishing such permanent bodies as a Land Commission which would have executive powers and some measure of independence from the Minister. For this reason, special provisions had been included for supervision by parliament. He thought that to set up an advisory and provisional commission for national parks would be contrary 'to the sound principles of administration, and might well be an embarrassing precedent'. The proposed body would deal with such large issues as land ownership and other matters arousing perhaps 'acute political controversy'. This would closely involve the Minister and other government departments, and 'it would therefore be better entrusted to a committee appointed by the Minister than to a Commission'.

R. S. Hudson, the Minister of Agriculture, also opposed the creation of a preparatory commission: whilst supporting the concept of national parks, he thought the time was inopportune. In his view, 'food production must have first priority for some years to come; new arrangements for developing forestry had only recently been announced; and hill sheep farming presented problems which must be solved in the near future. The Government must avoid the danger of committing themselves to a larger programme than the limited available resources, especially manpower, could support.' Plans for a preparatory commission should be dropped. The Minister should simply use his 'existing powers to prevent the spoliation of areas suitable for use as national parks'.

Morrison replied that he wanted to implement a national parks policy which was 'positive, and not merely preventative'. Nevertheless, the Reconstruction Committee invited him to reconsider plans for a preparatory commission, and suggested that the Minister and the Scottish Secretary should appoint instead fresh committees to consider the earlier reports and decide where the first national parks should be located.[51]

In order to retain the initiative for national parks, Morrison had no alternative but to accede to the suggestion of a committee, and soon afterwards a National Parks Committee was appointed under the chairmanship of Sir Arthur Hobhouse, the chairman of the Somerset County Council. The members of the Committee included John Dower, who continued to exert considerable influence until his death in October 1947. In a letter of direction, the Minister asked the Committee to use the Dower report as the basis of their work and to assume that a national parks commission and a series of parks would be established. A similar committee was appointed for Scotland in January 1946, again under the chairmanship of Sir J. Douglas Ramsay. The Scottish committee reported a month earlier than its southern counterpart, in June 1947. Both endorsed the recommendations made two years earlier, and contained detailed proposals as to the size, management and cost of the parks, and the relationship of the national parks commission with central and local government.[52]

The Huxley and Ritchie Committees

John Dower was so impressed by the urgent and special needs of wildlife preservation that he proposed, in his report, that the national parks commission should set up an advisory wildlife conservation council. W. S. Morrison accepted this idea, and incorporated it in his recommendations to the Reconstruction Committee for a preparatory national parks commission. In view of this, the Ministry decided that the Hobhouse Committee should appoint a nature reserves sub-committee, 'both on its own merits and so as to keep on good terms with the "Nature Reserves" and wild life interests'.

However, Dower rejected the idea of a nature reserves sub-committee and proposed instead a wildlife conservation special committee, which would have both wider terms of reference and greater status. At first, the Ministry rejected this, fearing that critics would 'ridicule our interest in such a side line as "the conservation of wildlife and protection of our native plant and animal populations at a time when we appear to be doing nothing about our major problems". This is fiddling while Rome burns'. Dower retorted that the Ministry needed 'a committee of first class scientists', who would adopt 'a broad ecological approach' to wildlife: the Ministry could hardly ask them to limit their investigations to 'a small and unimportant range of subjects, such as nature reserves in national parks'.

In the event, a Wild Life Conservation Special Committee was formed, and was given the task of considering the references to wild-life conservation in the Dower report and to recommend any amendments or additions which might be desirable. In selecting the members for this Special Committee, the obvious step was to appoint members from the NRIC, but the Ministry believed the NRIC had been too academic in its approach to conservation, its methods too slow, and the quality of its work uneven. A member of the Ministry had checked the lists submitted by one of the regional sub-committees, and found that several sites of outstanding value for wildlife had been omitted, and others of little merit had been included.

Accordingly, the Ministry decided on a fresh appraisal of nature conservation. An 'advocate of nature reserves' and member of the Hobhouse Committee, J. S. Huxley, was appointed chairman of the Wild Life Conservation Special Committee, and the other members were A. G. Tansley (vice-chairman), E. N. Buxton (also on the Hobhouse Committee), C. Diver, C. S. Elton, E. B. Ford, J. S. L. Gilmour, E. M. Nicholson, and R. S. R. Fitter as secretary. Tansley became chairman in May 1946 when Huxley was appointed to UNESCO. Tansley, Diver and Elton had served on the special committee on nature conservation, convened by the British Ecological Society in 1943, and Diver, who was a clerk in the House of Commons, was also on the NRIC. Having drafted most of the NRIC memoranda, he played an equally important part in drafting the report of the Huxley Committee. A. E. Trueman and J. A. Steers were appointed special advisers to the committee on geology and coastal physiography respectively. Steers had just completed a survey of the coastlines of England and Wales for the Ministry. At first, it was intended to include a marine ecologist on the committee, in view of 'the importance of fishing and seaweed manufacture', but this idea was dropped in order 'to avoid offence to the Ministry of Agriculture and Fisheries'.[53]

The proceedings of the Reconstruction Committee and steps to appoint the Hobhouse and Huxley Committees were necessarily confidential and, not surprisingly, some members of the NRIC were both surprised and annoyed to learn of the new Special Committee. The Ministry was quick to assure them that the Huxley Committee would make full use of both the general and detailed recommendations contained in their memorandum, but this did little to allay ill-feeling. As Herbert Smith explained, 'the Committee feel indisposed to have their work revised by another Committee, whom they regard as of inferior calibre'. But with the aid of Lord Macmillan, who was president of the SPNR, confidence was soon established.

For its part, the Huxley Committee made generous acknowledgement of the work of the NRIC. In its report, published in 1947, the committee recorded 'it is no exaggeration to say that, in the limited time available, we could never have done what was required of us, had it not been for the work of the Nature Reserves Investigation Committee through three active years'. The Huxley Committee accepted most of the recommendations for proposed nature reserves and conservation areas, and concentrated most of its attention on the more difficult and, in some ways, more controversial question of the administration, management and costs of reserves.[54]

The NRIC saw no point in continuing its survey work and the publication of memoranda, and accordingly it ceased to meet. For some years, Smith was reluctant formally to dissolve the NRIC but, soon after his death in 1953, the opportunity was taken to wind up the committee and transfer its small financial reserves to the SPNR.[55]

In Scotland, the Douglas Ramsay Committee also appointed a special committee to review the needs of wildlife, under the chairmanship of one of its members, James Ritchie, who was Professor of Natural History at the University of Edinburgh. But the situation was very different from that in England and Wales. The special committee was severely hampered by the fact that so little preparatory work had been undertaken by the voluntary bodies in Scotland.

The Zoological Society of Edinburgh was founded in 1909 and incorporated in 1913. According to its royal charter, its primary objective was to study and preserve wild animals but, for the first twenty-five years of its existence, the Society devoted most of its resources to the establishment of a national zoo. To redress the balance, the Society set up a Scottish Nature Reserves Committee in 1938, which included representatives from the National Trust for Scotland, Association for the Preservation of Rural Scotland, Office of Works, Forestry Commission and several societies. The Reserves Committee wanted to establish extensive nature reserves for the protection of native fauna, a series of island sanctuaries and inland plant reserves, and generally to stimulate public interest in nature preservation. A few meetings were organised, but the Committee soon became moribund, following the outbreak of war.[56]

Nothing further happened until 1943 when the Association for the Preservation of Rural Scotland set up a Scottish Council for National Parks which was concerned, among other questions, with the preservation of the flora and fauna of the proposed park areas. This stimulated the Zoological Society into reviving the Reserves Committee. James Ritchie was made chairman and representatives from various voluntary bodies, together with a number of assessors from the Scottish departments, were invited to attend meetings. Plans were laid for a new survey of rare species and important sites in Scotland: botanical, zoological and geological sub-committees were established under the chairmanship of W. Wright-Smith, J. Ritchie and Murray MacGregor respectively.

G. Taylor compiled a list of rare plants in Scotland, and the geological sub-committee made some headway, but otherwise very little was achieved. This was partly due to the absence of a person like Herbert Smith to enlist help, organise meetings, co-ordinate work, draft reports and write hundreds of letters. It was also due to the lack of urgency for the protection of wildlife in Scotland. Taylor stressed that there had been very little change in the flora of Scotland during the twentieth century. Although some areas had been affected by the collection of plants by horticulturalists, the problem was comparatively slight. He warned that 'the formation of Nature Reserves in Scotland would be a doubtful palliative'. Whereas in England the reserves were comparatively small and easily wardened, those of Scotland would be immense, and to make such areas as Ben Lawers a nature reserve, without proper supervision on the spot, would probably attract more tourists with a consequent increase of damage to the flora.[57]

Throughout the period 1943–5, correspondents in Scotland gave the impression that some progress was being made, and the NRIC decided to confine its attention to England and Wales. It was, therefore, annoyed and frustrated to discover at the end of the war that so little had been achieved. The NRIC felt that the absence of activity and information in Scotland seriously weakened the case for nature conservation throughout the British Isles. As C. Diver wrote, 'the arbitrary political boundary has no meaning in regard to the distribution of the flora and fauna of Great Britain which must be considered scientifically as a unit'.

The 'backwardness' of Scotland in this field of enquiry was demonstrated by the Ritchie Committee as soon as it was appointed in January 1946. It consisted of F. Fraser Darling and Douglas Ramsay of the main committee, together with J. R. Matthews, J. Berry and Murray MacGregor, with J. W. Campbell as secretary. This committee had to start virtually from scratch and although it published an interim report simultaneously with that of its parent committee in 1947, the more detailed report, containing lists of proposed national nature reserves, was not produced until 1949.[58]

The Value of National Nature Reserves

As the work of the various committees progressed, it was clear that little would be achieved until the public became convinced of the *positive* benefits of nature reserves and nature conservation. As Geoffrey Dent remarked in 1943, 'unless we can back our suggestions by popular appeal, we shall get very little' in the way of government aid.[59]

There was already a great deal of latent public support. As early as 1936, J. S. Huxley had remarked, 'Man does not live by bread alone nor by machines alone. Some men at least need the beauty of nature, the interest of nature, even the wilderness of nature, the contact with wild animals living their own lives in their own surroundings'. The demand for natural history books was sustained and increasing, and ornithology was flourishing as never before. The war, far from stultifying interest, acted as a spur. C. M. Yonge described how many evacuees from the towns had become fascinated by wildlife: for others, the study of wildlife was a form of escapism from the horrors of human conflict.[60]

One of the first writers to set out the positive value of nature reserves was F. Fraser Darling in 1939, when he stressed how they would bring immediate benefits for the public. They would 'be a place in which the public could take pride and have healthy enjoyment: research into problems of conservation could be conducted with a scope and continuity of policy impossible' elsewhere.[61]

Perhaps the most brilliant publicist was A. G. Tansley, who wrote articles in such journals as the *Spectator* in 1943, and published a book called *Our heritage of wild nature* in 1945. In this, he gave three reasons for establishing reserves: 'first there is their natural beauty and the deep sentiment which attaches to them as wild country in which one can escape from the strains of modern life; secondly there is their scientific value which has also essential economic implications; and thirdly their value as instruments of education in the widest sense'.[62]

There was already widespread concern over the protection of amenity, old buildings and archaeological sites, and it was only logical to extend this concern to cover wildlife. The British Ecological Society pointed out, in its memorandum of 1944, that wildlife was an integral part of the national heritage, as much part of the cultural history of Britain as any castle or stately home. 'Together with and determined by the climate, the physical features and varied soils, the natural vegetation of the country, with the animals which haunt it, forms the original scene in which our history has unfolded and has largely conditioned the development of our culture and civilisation.'[63]

The government already gave some protection to sites of archaeological importance threatened with destruction. Under the Ancient Monuments Act of 1882 and subsequent legislation, the Inspectorate of Ancient Monuments could acquire outstanding sites and keep others under surveillance. As early as 1909, the Commissioner for the Care of Natural Monuments in Prussia, C. Conwentz, recommended that sites of biological importance should be protected in the same manner. Almost forty years later, the Huxley report of 1947 made an identical recommendation: the State had recognised its responsibility for museums and ancient monuments, and 'there is but a narrow gap between these and (nature) reserves, which are both ancient monuments and living museums—living embodiments of the past history of the land'.[64]

Some reserves would be chosen because their plant and animal communities were unique. Protection would be given to species on the margins of their geographical range, and to those species which had developed in partial or complete isolation from the main centres of their population. A special effort was needed to include within a series of national nature reserves those few remaining areas of near-primitive vegetation and animal life. On these sites, the ecologist would be able to measure the extent of human impact on the remaining countryside. Other reserves should be chosen because they were representative of wider tracts of countryside. They might range over two or more rock or soil formations, where the relationship between wildlife and physical conditions might be studied more closely.

The reserves had an extremely important research role. According to W. H. Crump, writing as long ago as 1913, 'a Nature Reserve is no mere refuge for vanishing or persecuted species. It is an outdoor workshop for the study of plants and animals in relation to their natural habitat; a twentieth-century instrument of research as indispensible for biological progress as a laboratory or an experimental station.'[65]

It was highly significant that Wicken Fen and Blakeney Point were among the first nature reserves to be established by the National Trust, for they were key sites for survey and experimental work. Coastal sites were especially valuable since they were 'the best examples of wild Nature absolutely free from human interference'. F. W. Oliver had already made a detailed study of Blakeney Point, with its growing shingle bank and the numerous lateral shingle banks or hooks, running back from the main bank for as much as half a mile. Behind the bank was a salt marsh and sand dunes. Oliver demonstrated how the hooks were formed in a succession as one tip of the major bank was replaced by another. This succession helped to fix the ages of the salt marshes between each hook and so determine the relative ages of the vegetation communities within them. Thus, the youngest salt marsh at the tip of the shingle bank was carpeted with a thick growth of *Salicornia europaea*, growing through a layer of detached seaweed prostrate on the mud. The older salt marshes had a mixed association of *Aster tripolium*, *Limonium vulgare*, *Armeria maritima* and *Frankenia laevis*. In the oldest and highest marshes, *Puccinellia maritima* formed a close turf.[66]

It was essential that such important research sites should be preserved for long-term survey and experimental work. Tansley made this point in the early 1920s when he tried to persuade the National Trust to take over Sharpham Moor Plot in Somerset. The area of 1.5 acres provided unique opportunities of studying the plant communities characteristic of 'aboriginal peat bog'. Tansley warned that any monitoring work or field trials would be ruined by a change in land use or management by the local farmer. It was essential that such sites should be owned and managed entirely for nature preservation.[67]

In view of the difficulty of securing suitable sites for survey and research work, the British Ecological Society eagerly took up a proposal made by Sir Roy Robinson, chairman of the Forestry Commission, at the conference of the British Association at Cambridge in 1938. At this meeting, he invited ecologists to join the Forestry Commission in assessing the feasibility of ecological reserves, set up on the Commission's properties. The reserves would be enclosed at the Commission's expense, and there would be no afforestation within them. Ecologists would be given the chance of monitoring their changes in plant and animal life, and of undertaking experimental work.[68]

Clearly, both parties would benefit from the reserves. There would be comparatively little risk of the surveys and research work being interrupted or abruptly ended by a change in owner or policy. On the other hand, the Commission would gain from the favourable publicity for the reserves, and relations with ecologists would improve. This was especially important in view of the need to manage the forests on a scientific basis. Already, foresters had become aware of the value of several species of birds in pest control. In 1942, the Commission initiated an experiment with bird boxes in the Forest of Dean. Clearly, there were practical lessons in forest management to be learnt from the ecological reserves.

A committee was set up to examine the concept of ecological reserves, with W. Wright Smith as chairman, and C. S. Elton, H. Godwin, W. H. Guillebaud, E. J. Salisbury and A. S. Watt as members. Circulars were sent to the heads of botany departments and other interested organisations, inviting their co-operation in drawing up a list of functions and locations for the reserves. It was suggested that each reserve should be from ten to thirty acres, located on sites which were representative of their environs. The vegetation should preferably be at 'a sufficiently early phase of the plant succession to provide the maximum change in a reasonable period of time'. By the time war broke out, about twenty-five people in twenty departments were actively engaged in selecting sites for the reserves, and the Botany Department of the University of Bristol actually chose two sites on the north slope of Stock Hill in the Mendips. The war prevented any further progress being made, but the Forestry Commission promised to avoid damaging any of the potential reserves during the war.[69]

The Huxley Committee was keen to demonstrate the benefits of nature reserves for such ecological survey and experimental work, and one of its members, J. S. L. Gilmour, prepared a memorandum on the subject in February 1946, setting out their potential for research. First, the reserves could be used for planting species otherwise outside their normal range. He noted 'we know very little about the method of operation of the various factors (temperature, rainfall, etc) which limit the distribution of plants and the best way to find out is to grow species in their *natural habitats*, outside their normal range, and to record in detail their behaviour.'

Secondly, the reserves could be used for genetical experiments on wild populations of known genetical constitution. 'Experiments of this type with *Centaurim umbellatum* and *C. littorale* on Ainsdale Sand Dunes would be interesting. . . . Or again a "variety" of known genetic behaviour (e.g. a white flowered variety) could be introduced in various proportions into a colony of individuals with coloured flowers, and the composition of the succeeding populations recorded.' Thirdly, the reserves could be used in studies of 'developmental ecology'. The value of this kind of enquiry had already been demonstrated by the use of rabbit exclosures on the Breckland in studying the impact of grazing on the character and composition of vegetation.[70]

These requirements in the botanical field were complemented in zoology by a demand for sites where wildfowl could be studied through long-term surveys and experimental work. In 1946, the Severn Wildfowl Trust was set up to promote the study of wildfowl and 'in particular to establish and maintain a wildfowl research observatory on the estuary of the river Severn'. This was intended to provide facilities for (i) a close study of the winter flocks of wild geese and other birds, (ii) the ringing of wild ducks in the decoy pools and of wild geese on the marshes for the further study of migration, and (iii) the study of a comparative collection of live waterfowl.[71]

The selection and management of reserves was justified on both scientific and economic grounds. During the 1914–18 war, doubts were expressed as to whether the SPNR should acquire and preserve sites when land was so desperately needed for food production. Rothschild replied that the sites were so important for scientific research that this overrode any short-term need for extra food. In the future, the reserves would be an essential aid to scientific agriculture. The NRIC made a similar point during the 1940s. Advances in agriculture and forestry were greatly influenced by scientific research, which could only be gained from field work. It was important to compare the distribution of species in the agricultural habitat with that in semi-natural conditions.[72]

J. C. F. Fryer, the Director of the Plant Pathology Laboratory of the Ministry of Agriculture and member of the NRIC, summarised the potential role of nature reserves in a rapidly changing agricultural habitat. Previously any increase in wild species had been more or less matched by a proportional increase in their natural predators. But this balance had been upset: extensive areas of farmland were planted with a single crop which favoured some species to the extent that they became a pest, whereas their natural enemies might find conditions unsuitable and disappear. Ways had to be found of sustaining and re-introducing the mechanisms of biological control and, in this search, the nature reserves would play an increasingly important role. They were often the only areas where the interaction of wild species could be studied and compared with that occurring in the agricultural habitat.[73]

The Ritchie Committee was no less emphatic in declaring the economic benefits of nature conservation. It stated, 'detailed investigations, over prolonged periods, of the natural balance of plant and animal life in different types of environment, and comparison with the changes caused by man in other similar localities, are of fundamental importance if the nation is to obtain information essential for the best economic development of agriculture, forestry, freshwater fisheries, veterinary science, pest control, and for the propogation of beneficial birds, insects and other forms of life'. In this broader context, a marsh, sand dune and meadow grassland were of equal economic importance to any field of wheat or plantation of conifers.[74]

Nature reserves were also a means of protecting sites of geological and physiographical interest. Although many features were 'safely hidden below the surface of the earth, and called for no special measures for their protection', others had to be preserved from destruction. W. J. Arkell provided an example in 1948 of the threat to stone quarries by the tipping of rubbish. He wrote, 'the filling up of quarries in southern England has proceeded so rapidly in recent years that if nothing is done to stop it geologists will find in a few years that many formations are no longer to be seen, no more material will be able to be collected by palaeontologists, and there will be an acute shortage of exposures for the training of students and research workers'. He gave as an example the Lamb and Flag Quarry, Kingston Bagpuize, which contained one of the most complete and most highly fossiliferous exposures of the Corallian Beds in existence. About half the quarry had already been infilled, through the systematic tipping of garbage.[75]

Britain had many classic geological sites, partly because of the unique variety of rocks and landforms for a country of its size, and partly because the foundations of the science of geology had been laid in Britain. It was especially important to protect and provide access to the sites described in the memoirs of the Geological Survey. The Huxley Committee thought the public, as well as geologists and physiographers, should have access to these geological monuments. Most people were fascinated by such questions as the origin of the rocks and the impact of the Ice Ages. Informative booklets should be published, and name-plates and brief descriptions should be affixed to the geological monuments.[76]

The Huxley Committee also made reference to the need to protect archaeological features in the countryside. For a long time, the proponents of national parks and nature reserves had been aware of a coincidence of interest. In 1930, O. G. S. Crawford, E. C. Curwen and A. G. Tansley presented a memorandum to the Addison Committee which proposed the designation of the South Downs as a national park in order to protect the downland turf. This was the habitat of many wild plants and animals, and the protective mantle over the earthworks of earlier field systems and settlement sites. They noted that 'certain areas still remain in exactly the condition they were in when abandoned by prehistoric man. That this is so after two thousand or more years is due to the presence of a protecting mantle of downland turf. The destruction of this mantle would be equivalent to the destruction of a priceless and unique manuscript'.[77]

The Huxley Committee made a similar point: many potential nature reserves were of interest to archaeologists. It remarked that 'the continuous turf covering the Neolithic pits at Maiden Castle in Dorset, for instance, was probably established in the Bronze Age, and the charcoals found at different levels throw light on the vegetation of the neighbourhood at different times, so that both archaeological and botanical evidence, coupled with the evidence to be derived from the sub-fossil remains of snails and other animals, contribute to the elucidation of human, biological and climatic prehistory'. Co-operation between the two disciplines would not only facilitate research but strengthen the basis for protecting individual sites.[78]

In 1944, the Council for British Archaeology (CBA) was formed as a voluntary body to represent and promote archaeology throughout Britain. In October of that year, K. P. Oakley, on behalf of the NRIC geological sub-committee, submitted a list of proposed geological monuments of potential interest to archaeologists. These included:

   i the Bride Stones, above Staindale near Pickering;
   ii Victoria Cave, Settle;
   iii the site of discovery of the Piltdown skull, Sussex;
   iv a typical Stonesfield slate mine, used since Roman times;
   v Kent's Cavern, Torquay;
   vi Carn Meini in the Prescelly Hills, the suggested source of rock for the Bluestone Circle at Stonehenge.

The NRIC hoped that archaeologists and biologists would share the burden of protecting sites of common interest, designating them as an ancient monument and as a nature reserve or geological monument.[79]

From an early date, reference was made to the educational value of reserves. In 1914, the Cumberland Nature Reserves Association made plans for an open-air museum on its nature reserve at King's Moor near Carlisle, modelled on the Norwegian open-air folk museums. This would provide 'a valuable educational asset to the town'. The NRIC believed that the reserves would make ideal class-rooms for demonstrating the principles learned from textbooks. It noted that 'the serious student, whatever his bent, and whether he be professional or amateur, should be able to find a wealth of material of unfailing interest'.[80]

There was, however, a widespread reluctance on the part of teachers to take their students into the field. F. H. C. Butler observed in 1943 that 'few teachers—including even university graduates in the biological sciences—have the requisite first-hand knowledge and experience of field-work to teach natural history with competence and enthusiasm. It is far easier to teach and examine classes of school and university pupils in the laboratory than it is in the field.' Butler accordingly proposed the creation of a series of hostels for field studies, with accommodation for up to forty students, equipped with a common room, library, field laboratory and museum. A warden would be appointed to each centre for teaching students in the field and for assisting the teachers who would accompany the parties of students.[81]

The idea was well received, and a Council for the Promotion of Field Studies was formed in 1943: it soon became known as the Field Studies Council. Plans were laid for building five field centres after the war. Every one would be located in an area outstanding 'for the richness and variety of its ecological features, geological and geographical interest, and archaeological and historical importance'. The first president of the Council was W. H. Pearsall. He was a member of the NRIC, and the close affinity between the creation of the field centres and nature reserves was recognised right from the start. The first centre was opened at Flatford Mill, Suffolk, and in 1948 the SPNR gave the Council £75 toward the cost of equipping a further two centres, at Juniper Hall in Surrey and Dale Fort in Pembrokeshire. Each was near sites of biological interest worthy of being designated nature reserves.[82]

According to some observers, nature preservation had an even wider significance. 'The decline in interest in living things and the increasing preoccupation with mechanical achievements have had a profound and disturbing influence on national outlook.' The reserves were one way of redressing the balance. Both adults and children would be given the opportunity of studying wildlife; the NRIC regarded this as 'a liberal education in one of the most stimulating and formative fields of thought'.[83]

Chapter Six

The Selection of Nature Reserves

In view of the difficulties of acquiring and managing nature reserves, the sites had to be chosen with great care. In order to discover which species and communities were most in danger of extinction, the abundance and distribution of each had to be carefully recorded. Fortunately, a lot of information was already available.

From the medieval period onwards, a few people had toured the country in order to discover the character of the land and its people, and accounts of their journeys often provide a valuable insight into the wildlife of the past. There are, for example, several detailed descriptions of the cliff-line of Wales, Devon and Cornwall, where topographers marvelled at the sight of the large colonies of seabirds. John Ray visited an island near Caldy Island, Pembrokeshire, where he described the colonies of 'puits, gulls and sea-swallows'. The nests were 'so thick that a man can scarce walk but he must needs set his foot upon them'.[1]

One of the earliest lists of important sites for wildlife was compiled by Francis Willughby in the mid-seventeenth century, and published in his book *The Ornithology*. He included a list of the chief strongholds of seabirds, some of which have since become sanctuaries. They are identified in Table 3.[2]

It is not the task of this book to trace the development of natural history or, indeed, of ecology. The following section will simply draw attention to the way in which much of the information relevant to nature conservation was acquired and later published in the form of books, articles and maps.

Early interest in natural history was aroused by such writers as George Montagu and Gilbert White, who provided the framework and ideas for later studies. Montagu helped to systematise the description of birds, distinguishing the truly distinctive species, and Gilbert White demonstrated the value of making regular observations. In this context,

Of some remarkable Isles, Cliffs, and Rocks about England [sic], where Sea-fowl do yearly build and breed in great numbers.
The more noted and famous places of this kind about England are:

1   *The Basse Island in the great Bay called Edinburgh-Frith or Forth, not far from the shore*
2   *Farne Islands*
3   *Sea-cliffs about Scarborough*
4   *A noted island not far from Lancaster, called the Pile of Foudres*
5   *Isle of Man with a little adjacent Islet, called the Calf of Man*
6   *Prestholm, a small uninhabited island near Beaumaris in the Isle of Anglesey*
7   *Bardsey Island*
8   *Lundy Island*
9   *Cliffs by the sea-side near Tenby*
10   *Godreve, an island or rather a rock, not far from St Ives in Cornwall*
11   *Scilly Islands*
12   *Caldey Island*
13   *Isle of Erm near Guernsey*

Table 3

Chief strongholds of seabirds identified by Francis Willughby in the seventeenth century

James Fisher has drawn attention to the contribution made by clergymen who compiled and published records of their observations. He noted that 'no other, better system could have been devised for placing educated, simple, honourable, truthful and contemplative men in the places where they were most needed—dotted evenly all over the countryside, where they could record nature'.[3]

In addition to ornithologists, both botanists and entomologists were venturing into the field. In 1908, for example, several large landowners in Huntingdonshire gave permission for the Reverend Augustin Ley to 'botanise' in their woods for various types of bramble and wild rose. Many of the earliest botanists were women: as early as 1798, Charles Abbot drew attention, in his *Flora Bedfordiensis*, to the contribution of 'the female sex', especially the unmarried daughters of well-to-do families. As an example of their work, the Bedfordshire Record Office has preserved the sketches made of flowers by the Alston sisters in Odell Wood in the 1830s, and the lists of indigenous plants compiled by the Squire family of Basmead Manor about 1860. Perhaps the most remarkable female naturalist in the nineteenth century was Beatrix

Potter, the daughter of a prosperous London family. She spent her holidays in Scotland, the Lake District and Devon and kept a daily journal of her many detailed observations on natural history and geology.[4]

One of the most difficult tasks was to trace the movements of individual bird species throughout the year. The first 'sensible and balanced' views on migration were put forward by Sir Thomas Browne in the seventeenth century. He noted how the migrants of spring came mostly from the south, and those of autumn and winter from the north, entering on a north-east wind and departing on a south-westerly. These remarkable observations could not be accurately tested until the present century. The first birds were ringed in the 1890s when a land-owner carried out experiments by ringing the legs of young woodcock, whilst still on the nest. Large scale ringing was first undertaken in 1909 by H. F. Witherby and A. Landsborough Thomson in England and Scotland respectively. From the 1930s onwards, the data gained from the return of rings were supplemented by permanent observations from bird observatories: the first were established on the island of Skokholm in Pembrokeshire and the Isle of May in the Firth of the Forth.

Some naturalists published what they had seen, measured and dissected, and, from these local and county studies, the national distribution and abundance of species could be deduced. One of the finest examples was Edward Newman's book *British Butterflies*, published in 1869, which was based on the county lists of a large number of friends, supplemented by his own remarkable observations.[5]

Some recorders tried to map the complex patterns of distribution and abundance. In France, Charles Flahault experimented with ways of depicting vegetation at a variety of scales and in 1894 one of his students, Robert Smith, began an extremely comprehensive survey of Scotland. He died before much was accomplished, but his example gave encouragement to others. The Royal Geographical Society and the Geographical Society of Edinburgh played a major role in publishing the maps and memoirs. In 1905, the Royal Irish Academy published a coloured map of the Wicklow Mountains, clearly showing the altitudinal zonation of plant communities.[6]

In 1909, H. Conwentz suggested that special surveys should be made of those plants and animals facing extinction, so that a register could be compiled of species and sites which should be preserved at all costs. He stressed the need to store all the information in a central place so that it could be easily obtained.[7]

The need for a central data bank increased as more and more observers watched from cars, boats and aircraft. Beside the professional observers, there were many amateurs, including school children, who amassed records which needed to be collated, sifted, sorted and published. To some extent, the Natural History Museum served as a repository for records. The results of a survey of the Goyt Valley, Derbyshire, in 1931 were deposited in the Museum prior to the construction of the reservoir in the valley, but James Fisher, writing in 1942, thought this was a role for the local natural history societies, and he drew attention to advances being made in data collection and retrieval. He wrote:

> ... perhaps one day, not very far ahead, some zoologists may press a button in London and Oxford, or Cambridge or Aberystwyth or Edinburgh, a machine will hum, and a stack of cards giving all the records of crossbill irruptions in East Anglia, or the history of the pied flycatcher in Wales, or the migrations of the woodpigeon in Scotland, will fall into a tray.[8]

Detailed records, and especially maps, not only helped to identify the location and abundance of species, but they made it easier to relate the plants and animals to other features in the landscape. C. B. Crampton published a significant paper in 1911 which related the vegetation of Caithness to the geology, topography and soils of the county. A member of the Geological Survey, Crampton had been able to study the vegetation during the geological survey of Caithness in 1907–8. He recognised the considerable influence exerted by physiographical factors, and especially glaciation, on the development and distribution of vegetation types. He noted how the moorland peat was confined to the more stable parts of the landscape, and was absent from the coast, flood plains, and higher ground where erosion and deposition were more pronounced. Although H. C. Cowles and F. E. Clements had stressed the significance of plant succession in America, Crampton was the first to illustrate the dynamic plant–physiography relationship in Britain.[9]

A. G. Tansley has drawn attention to what he regarded as a scientific rennaissance in the late nineteenth century when atomic physics, biochemistry, genetics and ecology either developed or gained great impetus. He regarded the publication of the books *Plantesamfund: Grondtrak af den okologiske Plantegeografi* by E. Warming and *Pflanzengeographie auf physiologischer Grundlage* by A. F. W. Schimper as the foundations of ecology, offering a challenge to botanists to see whether they could discover a pattern of plant communities matching those described in these volumes.[10]

Tansley played a major role in co-ordinating research. The surveyors had used a wide variety of criteria and techniques, which made it difficult to compare the patterns of one area with another, and in a paper to the British Association conference in 1904, Tansley suggested the formation of a central committee for the systematic survey and mapping of the vegetation of the British Isles. By the end of the year, the British Vegetation Committee was formed which, at its first meeting, decided on a standard scale and laid down rules as to how maps should be coloured. The Committee gave the fullest support to efforts to establish a national collection of photographs of plants and vegetation types.[11]

Perhaps the finest coloured maps were those compiled by C. E. Moss and contained in the *Vegetation of the Peak District*, published in 1912. It was hoped that the entire country would eventually be covered by a series of maps and accompanying memoirs, parallel with those published by the Geological Survey. The Board of Agriculture gave its support, but the Treasury refused to sanction any financial assistance, and consequently the British Vegetation Committee had no alternative but to abandon such a grandiose scheme for lack of funds.

The Committee not only discussed the objectives and organisation of primary surveys but also the detailed studies that were being undertaken in such localities as Blakeney Point in Norfolk and the woodlands of the West Riding. These discussions formed the background of a series of major papers on the concept of plant communities and the character of various habitats, published in the *New Phytologist*. Field excursions were arranged and, in 1911, Tansley organised an International Phytogeographical Excursion attended by over a dozen foreign workers. Tansley edited, and largely wrote, a guide-book for the four-week tour, called *Types of British Vegetation*, which soon became an important landmark in the history of ecology, classifying for the first time some of the plant communities in Britain.[12]

At first, the British Vegetation Committee consisted of only eight members, and there were soon attempts on the part of Moss and others to invite a wider membership. This was at first opposed because it was felt that active field-workers could meet more easily as a small committee, exchange views, and directly influence decisions. On the other hand, the number of students taking up ecological work was increasing, and there was a growing need for an ecological journal. Thus, in 1913, the British Ecological Society was founded, with its own journal, and gradually the work of the British Vegetation Committee was absorbed into the larger society.

The new Society's journal, the *Journal of Ecology*, provided a valuable outlet for publishing the many case studies of the inter-war period which further developed the concepts of the plant community and the ecosystem. In his presidential lecture to the Society in 1939, Tansley described how, for example, the experiments undertaken by E. P. Farrow on the Breckland grass-heaths had contributed both to ecological knowledge and ecological techniques. He had shown how one plant community, the *Callunetum*, could be replaced by another, an *Agrostis-Festuca* grassland, as a result of an increase of rabbit grazing pressure. Studies of lakes, marshes, fens and bogs had indicated how an external force, such as mowing or grazing, could 'deflect' plant succession. H. Godwin had shown at Wicken Fen how the frequent cutting of *Cladium*, the fen pioneer, had led to the appearance of *Molinia*, and the transformation of *Cladietum* into *Cladio-Molinietum*, and eventually a pure *Molinietum*, which was otherwise absent from the ecosystem. If mowing stopped, bushes would colonise the *Cladietum-Molinietum* communities, and the 'normal' succession, would be resumed.[13]

These studies of the dynamism of plant communities, and the rapidity and direction of plant succession, were clearly relevant to an understanding of the distribution and abundance of species. The scope for 'manipulating' succession through various management practices had important implications for the conservation of wildlife on individual reserves.

The Rothschild List of 1915

From the late nineteenth century onwards, various sites were nominated as nature reserves. In 1913, the Cumberland Nature Reserves Association and Carlisle Corporation designated the remnants of King's Moor as a reserve. Bird boxes were placed in nearby woods and several ponds were enlarged as drinking places for birds and mammals. The Hampstead Scientific Society suggested turning parts of the Brent reservoir into a bird sanctuary: about sixty-seven species of waterfowl visited the reservoir and the area of the proposed sanctuary had little agricultural value.[14]

Whilst this kind of local initiative was very encouraging, Rothschild and a few other naturalists were worried at the way reserves were chosen on an *ad hoc* basis, with little reference to their regional or national importance. Every effort should be made to preserve the finest sites in the country, rather than dissipate resources on the less significant areas.

One of the objectives in founding the Society for the Promotion of Nature Reserves in 1912 was to identify these nationally important sites. Rothschild immediately organised a survey of all areas 'worthy of protection'. Once they had been identified, each could be kept under close surveillance, so that if and when they were threatened with destruction, steps could be taken to acquire them as nature reserves.

The survey had already made considerable progress by the outbreak of war in August 1914, when T. F. Husband of the Board of Agriculture, who was a member of the executive committee of the

SPNR, wrote a letter to Rothschild describing plans of the Development Commission to reclaim extensive areas of 'wasteland' for increased food production. There was, for example, a project to plough up 200 acres of sandy heathland at Brandon in Suffolk by way of an experiment. Circulars were being sent to each county council asking them to identify further areas suitable for acquisition and reclamation for agriculture.[15]

Rothschild interpreted Husband's letter as a 'straight tip' that very extensive works were contemplated and that the Society should complete its survey as quickly as possible, so as to provide the Development Commission with lists of areas which should be left in their 'primitive state'. Further naturalists were asked to help in the project: in order to ensure an equally comprehensive survey of each area, a standard questionnaire was sent to each surveyor, and an example of a completed form is given in Figure 2. Identical questionnaires were prepared for overseas use, written in French and German. Each completed questionnaire was filed by W. R. Ogilvie-Grant in a blue envelope, with other relevant notes and correspondence. Each area was marked on a one-inch, and sometimes on a six-inch, Ordnance Survey map.[16]

Rothschild and G. C. Druce nominated many areas: Druce visited Ireland on behalf of the SPNR in 1914 to inspect parts of Lord Lansdowne's property which had been suggested as a nature reserve. He took the opportunity to visit several areas which were later nominated as worthy of protection. W. R. Ogilvie-Grant, A. G. Tansley and other members of the Council of the SPNR nominated areas, local naturalists provided valuable help, but almost inevitably the final lists of areas reflected the extent of knowledge of a comparatively small number of surveyors rather than the actual distribution of important areas.[17]

N. C. Rothschild, G. C. Druce, F. R. Henley and W. R. Ogilvie-Grant began the task of analysing the recommendations in June 1914. Rothschild's solicitors provided the names and addresses of the owners of each area. The lists of areas worthy of protection were compiled very much 'with an eye to Europe as a whole', and accordingly special attention was given to those habitats which had no exact counterpart on the Continent of Europe, namely the mosses, saltings, shingle beaches and sand dunes of England and the mountain bogs of Scotland.[18]

A provisional set of lists for England, Wales, Scotland and Ireland was sent to the Board of Agriculture in June 1915, and a revised set a year later. The nominated areas were divided into three categories. Those in category A would be preserved in their entirety since 'they represented various ecological types'. Although they were distributed

Answers will be treated as strictly confidential, and will be
at the disposal of the Executive Committee only.

1 in O.S. map. 267
6 in Berk. 42. N.W.

Name of Place ___The Crocus Field___

District and County where area is situated. ___Nr. Inkpen Berkshire___

Name and address of Society or person giving information. ___G. C. Druce___
___9 Crick Rd. Oxford.___

A. Is the suggested area worthy of permanent preservation as :—

1. A piece of typical primeval country? ___Old pasture___

2. A breeding-place of one or more scarce creatures? ___No___

3. A locality for one or more scarce plants? ___Yes Crocus Vernus___

4. Showing some section or feature of special geological interest? _____

B. Is the place recommended primarily for birds, insects, or plants? ___Plants___

1. To whom does it belong? ___Owner J. Buckeridge 88 Ewell Road, Surbiton Hill, Surrey___
___Jason Buckridge. The Pottery___
___Inkpen. Hungerford. Berks. only farms it___
fld N-ck 30.8.16

2. Would the owner be willing to sell, or could the area be leased? _____

3. Could you get local financial aid should it be considered desirable to acquire the area? _____

4. Is the place or site locally popular as a pleasure resort? ___No, but well known___

This form should be filled up and returned to The SECRETARY:
Society for Promotion of Nature Reserves, c/o Natural History Museum,
Cromwell Road, London, S.W.

Figure 2
Completed questionnaire received by the SPNR (reproduced by kind permission of the SPNR)

unevenly over the country, the SPNR tried to ensure as even a spread of these potential reserves as possible. Those in category B would be preserved since they were 'the home of unique or local species'. The areas in category C were in no immediate danger of being destroyed: the New Forest, for example, was placed in this category since the 'various Acts of Parliament regulating its management preserved to some extent the natural features of the locality'.[19]

Figure 3 indicates the general location of the 251 areas nominated in England, Wales and Scotland, and identifies by name the fifty-two areas in category A. The areas in categories B and C were subdivided into thirteen 'ecological types', of which twenty-three were downland, twenty-two were heath and moorland, and twenty-one were wooded areas. Twelve areas were made up of two or more types. The lists described the 'virgin yew forest' of Kingley Bottom in Sussex as unique in Europe, and the area of Rannoch in Perthshire as remarkable for insects and plants. The holly bushes of Dungeness, the peregrine falcons of Ballard Down and Steepholm, the fine limestone pavement of Kilnsey Crag, and the archaeological interest of Pewsey Camp, Berkshire, were noted. Of the eleven areas in category A in Ireland, six were bogs of 'general and botanical interest'. The Burren of County Clare was nominated for its 'great botanical interest', Errisberg and Lough Nagraiguebeg in Galway for their Lusitanian flora, and Lough Neagh for its rare plants.[20]

In submitting the lists to the Board of Agriculture, the SPNR emphasised their provisional nature and noted that further areas might be added at a later date. In the event, only a further nine areas were added to the lists, and the Board appears to have made little use of the information during and after the war.[21]

The Lists of the Inter-war Period

Between the wars, there was a keen debate as to whether a large number of relatively small reserves should be established, or one or two national parks for wildlife preservation. The origins of this debate may be detected in the years leading up to the 1914–18 war. In 1909, Charles Stewart advocated a national park in the Scottish Highlands and Islands for the protection of indigenous fauna (page 73). On the other hand, the SPNR nominated 273 less extensive areas for preservation during its surveys of 1912–16.

In presenting evidence to the Addison Committee in 1929, the British Correlating Committee (page 19) tried to strike a compromise. It submitted a list of sixty-six areas 'where nature reserves are most required', and it also recommended a large wildlife park in Scotland.

1915

Figure 3
Distribution of areas 'worthy of protection', selected by the SPNR

Legend:
- named • Category A
- • Category B
- ▲ Category C

Orkney Islands — Tafts Ness
Shetland Islands — Burrafirth

Betty Hill
Culbin Sands
Loch Laide
Loch Ruthven
Creag an Dail Bheag
Lochs Kander and Nagar
Caenlochan — Glens Doll and Fee
Kilrannoch
Rannoch
Ben Lawers
Barry Links
Newham Lough
Glen Luce Sands
Port William Beach
Widdybank
Meathop Moss
Fleetwood
Ainsdale
Freshfield
Llyn Llywenan
Aberffraw
Llanddwyn Island
Clogwyn
Abbots Moss
Wybunbury Fen
Burnham Overy
Winterton
Broads
Red Lodge
Newmarket
Wicken Fen
Chippenham Fen
Hemley
Cothill
St Osyth
Shoeburyness
Kenfig
Sandwich
Steepholm
Braunton Burrows
Langstone Harbour
Kingley Bottom
Chichester Harbour
Littlesea
Dungeness
Ballard Down
Kynance Cove

0   50   100
MILES

131

A conference attended by delegates from twelve scientific and natural history societies in 1937 called upon the government to establish at least one national park specifically for the protection of plants and animals. Lord Onslow described how an extensive deer forest might be converted into a national park, where the public could see deer, goats, foxes, badgers, stoats, weasels and otters in their natural surroundings. He realised that the number of animals would have to be controlled, and he stressed the need to cull deer, otherwise they would soon outstrip their food supplies and cause damage to neighbouring estates. Lord Onslow also suggested the re-introduction of reindeer, wild pigs and beavers into the area, and thought a 'beaver-dam and a number of beavers on a river in the national park could be a great attraction for the public'. But he appreciated the dangers of introducing species: a great deal of damage to forestry and farming had resulted from the spread of aliens, such as the grey squirrel and muskrat.[22]

This concept of one or two large parks was severly criticised by other commentators. The parks would be necessarily confined to thinly-peopled parts of Britain, and therefore the more remote and rugged regions. They would include only a small fragment of the rich variety of scenery and wildlife which characterised Britain. Accordingly, Vaughan Cornish, a geographer, urged the Addison Committee in 1929 to recommend not one but at least six national parks, so as to include coastland, mountains, moorland, downs, river gorges, woodland and undrained fen. The series would thereby contain a wide range of habitats for wildlife, and the complete range of rock types, from the Pre-Cambrian to the Quaternary.

Cornish was the first to make a comprehensive review of potential areas: he concluded that any systematic study of the coastline 'soon reduced the choice of suitable areas for seaside parks' to the West Country and, in particular, Cornwall and Pembrokeshire. Likewise, the Lake District and Snowdonia were the two outstanding candidates as mountain national parks. Dartmoor would be an ideal moorland park, but the Pennine Chain, Northumbrian moors, Dovedale and tracts of the Welsh Borderland were worthy of consideration. In lowland England, Cornish rejected many areas as being predominantly under cultivation, but he nominated the 'nine-mile block' of the South Downs between the rivers Arun and Adur as a national park. The New Forest was ripe for designation as a national park because it was already intensively used by the public for outdoor recreation. In the east of England, where the youngest rocks occurred, most of the land was farmed, except for the 'amphibious region' of the Broads which had become a popular resort for pleasure-boating. A national park in that area would include parts of the River Ure and its tributaries, the Ant and Thurne.

In the same way as one park could not include every form of landscape, so one reserve could not safeguard all the rare and disappearing plants and animals. According to Anthony Collett, in his book *The Changing Face of England*:

> ...they do not lend themselves to mass treatment...no persuasion will induce all our scarcer birds and beasts to be happy together; their demands are too various, and they have been fostered by too great contrasts of scenery and climate. What scene would suit the needs of the golden eagle and the peregrine falcon, as well as of the bearded reedling and the bittern? We cannot transplant the Kentish plover from its pebble-beaches, or tempt the nesting snow-buntings down from the mountain-tops of Scotland to join the avocet.

Instead of a single extensive reserve, a large number of smaller areas had to be preserved in order to take account of 'the great variety of scenery, and its dependent life, in our island'.[23]

The British Correlating Committee came to a similar conclusion in 1929 and decided to submit to the Addison Committee a list of areas where reserves were urgently required. Unfortunately, it had only one month to compile the list, and the choice was accordingly incomplete and ill-balanced. The secretary of the British Correlating Committee simply asked the RSPB and thirteen other correspondents to suggest reserves: every suggestion was accepted.

Sir Arthur Hill and E. J. Salisbury provided information on the key areas for plants, and E. G. B. Meade-Waldo on the distribution of pine martens and wild cats in the Lake District and Snowdonia. The RSPB submitted a list of twelve areas of importance for bird life, which were likely to fall within the boundaries of future national parks. In response to requests, N. D. Riley asked members of the Royal Entomological Society for suggestions: accordingly, Claude Morley nominated six areas in Suffolk, and Heslop Harrison proposed the Blackhalls cliffs and tops, Waldridge Fell and Newham Bog in the north-east of England.[24]

Figure 4 indicates the wide variety of areas included in the eventual list. Two areas were recommended in Breckland, in the South Downs and in the Lake District. Since the list was to be published in the report of the Addison Committee, the precise location of each area and its biological interest were not given lest the details should help the unscrupulous collector. The interest of each site was simply classified under five general headings: mammals, birds, insects, plants and geology. For example, the Lake District was important in all five aspects: Tentsmuir for birds, Blean Woods for insects, Caenlochan,

1929

Coastal area

Figure 4
Distribution of areas where 'nature reserves are most required', selected by the
British Correlating Committee

Ben Lawers and Studland Heath for plants, and the Lyme Regis undercliff for its geological interest.

A Reserves Review, 1941–2

The Addison Committee was reluctant to propose any potential parks in case its recommendations tied the hands of a national parks authority, but in the event the government failed to implement any part of its report. John Dower undertook a fresh survey of potential national parks on behalf of the Standing Committee on National Parks in 1935, and his confidential list of areas is given in Table 4. He recommended that about a third of the country should eventually be included in the parks. In 1938, R. B. Burrowes published a booklet advocating the designation of four nature reserves which would include the major habitat types of Britain (page 141), but this aroused comparatively little interest. The mood began to change in 1941 when the government began to accept a greater role in land-use planning.

In April 1941, Herbert Smith, the secretary of the SPNR, suggested that a complete list of existing nature reserves should be compiled. The Executive Committee of the SPNR agreed, and within a month Smith had sent a letter and questionnaire to 'public authorities, national societies, unions of scientific societies, and other interested bodies and persons'. In view of the war situation, the response was very good, and the Nature Reserves Investigation Committee (NRIC) resuscitated the survey in 1942. Eventually, details on sixty-one areas were obtained, described by their owners as nature reserves.[25]

The National Trust gave the surveys its full support. The secretary, D. M. Matheson, commented in the *Manchester Guardian* that 'too often in the past we have been hampered by lack of knowledge of what is most important to be preserved as well as by lack of funds, and a nation-wide survey will be of great value'. He provided the NRIC with a list of thirty-two properties which he believed to have some wildlife interest. They ranged from extensive tracts of Devon and Cornwall to the Ruskin reserve of 4.5 acres at Cothill in Berkshire.[26]

The RSPB submitted the information that had recently been obtained by Geoffrey Dent and his sub-committee on existing bird sanctuaries and those species and areas in need of special protection. Figure 5 identifies the sanctuaries and those recommended for protection: the areas 'of special importance' are distinguished by name.[27]

A number of county councils and local natural history societies proposed a wide range of areas suitable as reserves. The 'county planning consultant' for Hertfordshire nominated the downs of

Scotland
North-West Highlands and Islands (one or two areas)
Central Highlands (Cairngorms and/or Ben Lawers)
Argyll Highlands and Islands (including perhaps National Forest Park)
Southern Uplands (St Mary's Loch)

Northern England
Cheviots and Roman Wall
Lake District
Northern Pennines (Cross Fell)
Mid Pennines (Bowland and Malham and/or Ingleborough, Whernside and Penygent)
South Pennines (High Peak and Dovedale)
Cleveland Hills

Wales
Snowdonia
Mid Wales (Cader Idris, Plynlimon and Radnor Forest)
Brecon Beacons and Black Mountains
Forest of Dean and Wye Valley
Pembrokeshire Coast

Southern England
Norfolk Broads
New Forest
Dartmoor
Exmoor
Coast of South-West Peninsula

Table 4
Areas proposed as national parks by John Dower on behalf of the
Standing Committee on National Parks in 1935

Royston Heath and Lilley Hoo, the wooded areas of Ashridge Park,
Broxbourne and Oxhey Woods, tracts of the river Gade and the Lea
Valley, and the reservoirs of Aldernham, Tringford and Wilstone
for their wildfowl. Individual naturalists often provided a great deal
of data on sites: J. R. Norman of the Zoological Museum at Tring
identified three areas in that part of Hertfordshire where the
fritillary *Fritillaria mealagris,* pasque flower *Pulsatilla vulgaris* and bogbean *Menyanthes trifoliata* grew. The site of the latter on the river Gade
was threatened by the construction of watercress beds.[28]

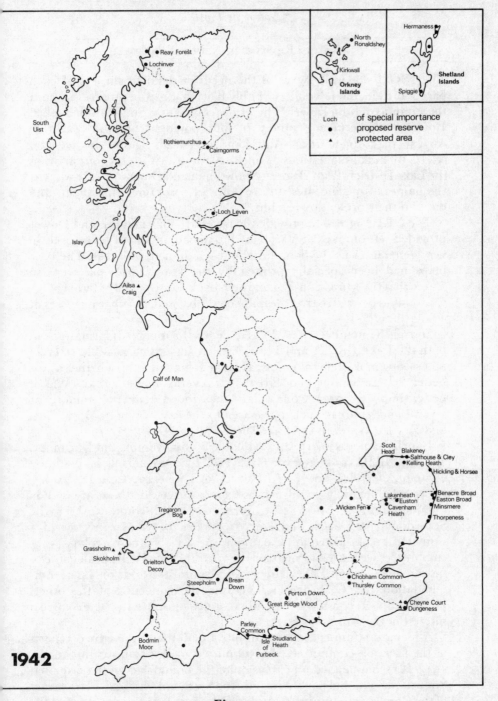

1942

Figure 5
Distribution of existing sanctuaries and those proposed as bird sanctuaries,
as indicated by the RSPB in 1942

The NRIC was well aware of the need for detailed surveys of each part of Britain, but it would probably have made little progress without the stimulus of John Dower. The Minister of Works and Planning asked Dower to undertake a survey of four potential national parks in August 1942 (page 101). And soon afterwards Dower invited the NRIC to 'make suggestions as to reservations' within the four areas of the Lake District, Peak District, Snowdonia and Dartmoor. He wanted the names of specific sites, the reasons for recommending them, and data on their present ownership.[29]

The NRIC agreed to provide the necessary information, and Dower provided sets of maps at a scale of 1:250,000 on which he marked in very general terms the boundaries of each of the park areas. The base maps had been specially printed by the War Office and were so scarce that the Ministry asked for them back. Only pencil or light colour wash was to be used so that the maps could be used for other purposes at a later date![30]

During September 1942, W. H. Pearsall supplied information on both the Lake District and Peak District, suggesting possible reserves and raising more general points. He asked, for example, whether it was better 'to reserve one good area...or several smaller areas'. Was it better simply to preserve one upland moss moor, such as Stainmore, or several smaller areas, such as the area to the east of Knotts Dock Tarn and Devoke Water in the Lake District?[31]

Information was less readily available for Snowdonia and Dartmoor, and the NRIC contacted Sir Cyril Fox, the Director of the National Museum of Wales, and L. A. Harvey of University College, Exeter, to see whether they could arrange for a survey of those areas. Fox nominated F. J. North as convener of a sub-committee for the Snowdonia park area, and Harvey agreed to act as convener of a similar sub-committee for Dartmoor. As an obvious corrolary, sub-committees were then formed for the two other parks: Pearsall chose to be convenor of the Lake District sub-committee and, on his recom-mendation, W. G. Fearnsides became the convenor of the other. Herbert Smith consulted a number of geologists as to the geological interest of the four areas.[32]

A memorandum containing an introduction and the edited reports of the four sub-committees was submitted to the Ministry in August 1943. It recommended an extension of the boundaries of the proposed Snowdonia national park to include the Sychnant Pass and a large tract of the Conway mountain. Pearsall and his sub-committee proposed the designation of such sites as Naddle Low Forest, Roudsea Wood and North Fen, Esthwaite Water, as nature reserves. But in general the

NRIC saw little point in creating reserves in the park areas since the national parks authority would have sufficient powers to prevent harmful changes taking place. The Committee recommended that deciduous woodland should be preserved and that experiments should be carried out to assess the impact of burning or swaling on wildlife. Commercial peat-working and further mineral exploitation should be forbidden unless the consent of the national parks authority had been obtained.[33]

The memorandum *Potential national parks* was treated as a 'strictly confidential' document, which was just as well. Although John Dower was very pleased with the detailed recommendations of the report, he was highly embarrassed by the introduction which assumed the four areas had actually been designated as national parks and that their boundaries had been decided. He emphatically denied this and asserted that the boundaries marked on the maps loaned to the NRIC were only 'rough indications'. Consequently, the erroneous introduction and all references to adjusting the boundaries of the parks were removed before the detailed recommendations were sent to the Regional Planning Officers of the Ministry for their information.[34]

Preparations for a National Survey

On the same day as the memorandum on potential national parks was delivered to the Ministry, John Dower asked for information on fifteen proposed 'amenity areas'. A few months later, he widened his request into an invitation to the NRIC to undertake a survey of all England and Wales, on behalf of the Ministry. The NRIC accepted the challenge, and sought the assistance of various learned societies.[35]

It was soon decided to set up sub-committees for each part of the country for it was impossible for a committee in London to undertake such a comprehensive survey of all England and Wales. Such societies as the Yorkshire Naturalists' Union and the South-east Union of Scientific Societies immediately offered help, and eventually over 200 people assisted in the collection and collation of data. Twenty-four regional sub-committees were established: some worked very hard and provided a great deal of information, but Herbert Smith frequently complained of the many laggards.[36]

In drawing up the lists of national nature reserves for the entire country, the first task was to decide how many areas should be nominated. So many sites were considered important by the regional sub-committees, but proved to be less significant when examined in their national context. The Ministry for its part was extremely reluctant to lay down any guidelines, and simply asked the NRIC to grade each site according to its need for protection. Eventually, John Dower conceded that twenty-five to thirty proposed reserves would be a reasonable number. The NRIC thought this was far too low. The special committee of the British Ecological Society faced a similar problem and its chairman, A. G. Tansley, finally set an arbitrary limit of fifty reserves.[37]

These discussions as to the optimum number of reserves were part of a larger debate as to the objectives of a series of national nature reserves. As long ago as 1913, N. C. Rothschild had distinguished two kinds of reserve, namely typical areas of plant and animal life, and smaller sites where one or more rare species were found. The British Correlating Committee made a similar division in 1929, distinguishing community reserves from species reserves. The concepts were defined more closely by J. C. F. Fryer in 1942: community reserves should contain a community of plants and animals, rich in species. Each should be sufficiently large to enable the communities 'to withstand natural catastrophes' and those practices which had established and maintained them, such as grazing or coppicing, should be allowed to continue. Species reserves were required to protect the breeding grounds of rare and local species which might otherwise be eliminated.[38]

The most obvious form of species reserve was a bird sanctuary, such as those identified or proposed by Geoffrey Dent and his sub-committee for the RSPB in 1940–1. Each was large enough to provide nesting space and some feeding ground for the endangered species, and a warden was usually employed during the breeding season in order to fend off collectors. The nature reserve acquired by the Cotteswold Naturalists' Field Club in 1932 at Badgeworth Marsh in Gloucestershire was a species reserve, specifically designed to preserve the snakes-tongue buttercup from extinction (page 56).

Geoffrey Dent proposed a more sophisticated classification of reserves in August 1942,[39] which consisted of:

a) ecological reserves, for the preservation of communities and species peculiar to a given type of country, or geological formation, mainly designated for scientific purposes;

b) species reserves, for rare animals or plants, which might other-wise disappear;

c) educational reserves, for schools and elementary biological study;

d) amenity reserves, to give the public the chance of seeing the beauty of wild flowers, trees, butterflies and birds;

e) economic reserves, for the breeding of species beneficial to farming.

These various concepts were considered by the NRIC in 1943, and its memorandum *Nature conservation in Great Britain* advocated four kinds of reserve, namely community or habitat reserve, species reserve, educational reserve and amenity reserve.[40]

John Dower thought this was 'needlessly elaborate' since one type graded into the other.[41] Some ecologists agreed with him, and C. Diver was especially critical of the concept of species reserves. In a letter of September 1942, he wrote, 'rare species have a wide emotional appeal, and there is no reason why we should voluntarily forgo the benefits of this fact, but the really important provision which we must make for the work of the naturalist, the scientist, and the educationalist of the future is the preservation of interesting communities on a scale which will include the widest possible range (in numbers of species) of our flora and fauna. Every real naturalist likes to see rare species, and to secure their continued existence if possible, but the fundamental work of science, whether pure or applied, is carried out on the commoner forms.'[42]

In drawing up his lists of proposed bird sanctuaries in 1940–1, Geoffrey Dent soon discovered the artificial distinction between community and species reserves. The species reserves would provide protection for a wide range of other animals and plants. A national series of bird sanctuaries would, for example, include:

> ... fen and marsh areas such as the Broads and Wicken and so on; heaths and moorlands of the south and west; breck and downland; mountain areas, including those in Scotland, Wales and the Lake District; cliffs and islands; beaches such as Blakeney, Scolt Head, and Dungeness; old deciduous woodlands; and old pine forests such as the Spey Valley. Thus the typical fauna and flora of each type of country would be preserved ... thus the pine marten and wild cat would find sanctuary in the Scottish areas, the otter and the swallow tail butterfly in the Broads and Wicken Fen, and the polecat would share the wilds of Brecon with the kite.[43]

It was generally decided to abandon the concept of species reserves and concentrate entirely on the habitat reserves. E. J. Salisbury concluded that the fauna would be automatically preserved if the vegetation cover was maintained: J. C. F. Fryer and H. M. Edelsten commented that if the plant communities were preserved, the insects were likely to flourish, thereby making a species reserve unnecessary.[44]

National Habitat Reserves

One of the first attempts to draw up a list of habitat reserves was made in 1938 by R. B. Burrowes, who advocated a series of four reserves, which would include the four major habitats of upland, fen, wood-land and heath. Each would cover at least 10,000 acres. There was a wide choice of sites for an upland reserve: the fen reserve might be located in the Broads or on a completely artificial site, formed by damming a river flowing through the fenland. A woodland reserve might include the remnants of old woodland in the New Forest, Sherwood or Charnwood Forest, or the Forest of Dean. A heathland reserve might be established in the Ashdown Forest, Cannock Chase or at Hindhead in Surrey. Burrowes believed the wildlife of these areas would soon increase. Rare wading-birds and marsh hawks would soon colonise the fenland reserve, and red deer and blackgame might be introduced to the heathland reserve.[45]

During November 1942, E. J. Salisbury submitted a list to the NRIC of existing and proposed nature reserves, classified by habitat type. Each included the finest example of its respective habitat. He noted, for example, how the reserves at Wicken Fen, Woodwalton Fen and Alderfen already protected valuable tracts of fen, bog and aquatic vegetation. In order to secure a full range of wetland reserves, he nominated as proposed nature reserves Esthwaite Fen in the Lake District, Hickling Broad and Heigham Sound, Horsey Mere and the Breckland Meres in Norfolk, the Tring reservoirs in Hertfordshire, Wisley ponds in Surrey, the fritillary meadows of Oxford, the water-meadows on the River Test in Hampshire, and Shapwick Moor in Somerset.[46]

E. J. Salisbury was a member of both the NRIC and the special committee of the British Ecological Society which compiled a list of proposed national habitat reserves in 1943. A total of sixty-seven habitat types was distinguished and the special committee tried to ensure that examples of each habitat were included in at least one of the proposed reserves. A special effort was made to preserve as many examples of oakwood as possible, owing to the habitat's intrinsic biological interest and because so many of the finest woods were being threatened with destruction.[47]

The special committee nominated forty-nine national habitat reserves, together with a range of scheduled areas (page 157). In two cases, the Committee proposed alternative sites for protection, either the downland behind Folkestone or the Wye Downs in Kent, and either the Aberffraw Dunes or Newborough Warren in Anglesey. A reserve was also proposed in the Essex marshes and on the sandy areas of east Norfolk or Suffolk, but the committee decided that further survey work was required before the reserve areas could be selected.

The special committee insisted that it was only a provisional list: as the secretary, L. A. Harvey, stressed, it was very much 'a personal list, though based on information from many different sources'. If another group of ecologists had compiled the list, they would have included further localities and omitted others.[48] About a quarter of the forty-nine proposed national habitat reserves had been described in papers published in the Society's *Journal of Ecology*. E. J. Salisbury had described Wormley Wood and other oak-hornbeam woods in Hertfordshire in 1918, and a paper on Studland Heath and its environs was included in the journal for 1935. The special committee was particularly anxious to preserve North Fen and other sites where changes in the ecosystem had been studied and recorded over long periods of time.

Nineteen of the proposed reserves were described as of 'outstanding importance', and their names are given in Figure 6. They included such areas as Ainsdale, Braunton Burrows, Kingley Vale and Tregaron Bog, which had been included in the earlier Rothschild list of 1915. But several other areas appeared on the list for the first time. They included the woods to the south of Loch Maree in Inverness, which contained the only example of self-regenerating pines in the Highlands, and the area of North Side in the South Downs, which was the finest example of succession to beechwood in lowland England. Reference was also made to eight sites which were already protected for their wildlife interest: they were Wicken Fen, Blakeney Point, Scolt Head and Dovedale owned by the National Trust, Woodwalton Fen by the SPNR, Brean Down by the RSPB, Longshaw and Eccleshall Woods by Sheffield Corporation and the National Trust, and Burnham Beeches by the City of London. The special committee recommended that the protected area of Burnham Beeches should be extended in order to save some of the surrounding woodlands from building development.

About half the proposed reserves were east of a line linking the mouths of the rivers Tees and Exe. According to the special committee, the bias toward lowland England reflected both the comparative lack of information on wildlife in Scotland and the profound differences in the character of the two parts of Britain. The soils and vegetation of lowland England were much more varied, and were 'constantly under threat of destruction', whereas the extensive tracts of relatively uniform vegetation in the north and west were less likely to disappear.

The NRIC List of Nature Reserves

By June 1944, the NRIC had received lists of proposed reserves from the RSPB, British Ecological Society and the Royal Entomological Society, together with submissions from its own regional sub-

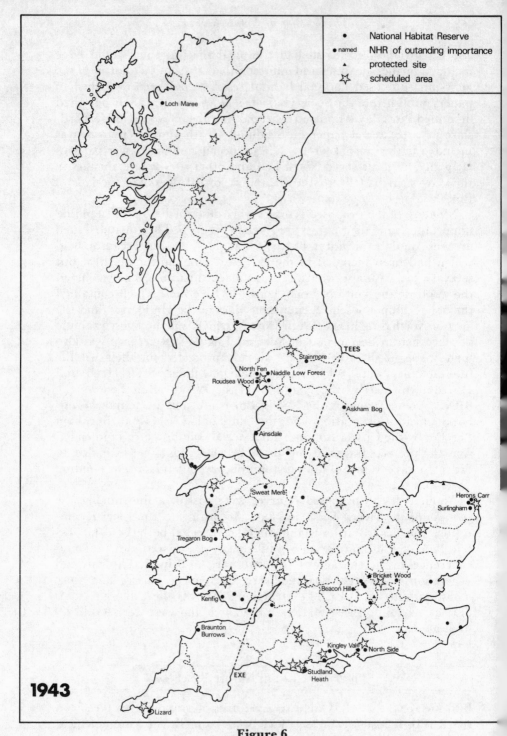

Figure 6

Distribution of national habitat reserves and scheduled areas, proposed by the
British Ecological Society

144

committees. Many sites appeared on more than one list.

The composition of the lists compiled by the RSPB and British Ecological Society has been noted on pages 135 and 142. The list of the Royal Entomological Society was submitted by H. M. Edelsten in 1943 and included over 100 areas outstanding for their insect life, classified by habitat type. As an example, the following fens and marshes were nominated: Wicken Fen and Chippenham Fen, Slapton Ley in Devon, Morden Decoy in Dorset, the Test marshes of Hampshire, Tring reservoirs of Hertfordshire, Woodwalton and Holme Fens in Huntingdonshire, Sandwich marshes in Kent, Norfolk Broads, Shapwick Moor in Somerset, Tuddenham Fen and Benacre Broad in Suffolk, Felbridge Ponds in Surrey, Lewes marshes in Sussex, and the Brading marshes in the Isle of Wight.[49]

The NRIC sub-committees varied in their zeal: most of the survey work devolved on one or two people. Thus, C. A. Cheetham, the secretary of the Yorkshire Naturalists' Union, was largely responsible for the compilation of the Yorkshire list. One of the most detailed and informative surveys was undertaken by the London Natural History Society, which invited its members and later other natural history clubs and societies to nominate reserves in the London area. A preliminary list was completed in 1943 and a final one was published in the *London Naturalist* in 1947.[50]

Each sub-committee tried to include the finest examples of every habitat type within its region. Thus, the Cambridgeshire sub-committee nominated Chippenham Fen, the oxslip-coppicewood of Hayley Wood on the heavy chalky boulder-clay, and even a tract of scrubland at Croydon Wilds. Much of this scrubland had developed since the mid-nineteenth century and was 'of scientific interest and considerable economic interest in relation to the regeneration of natural woodland'.[51]

The NRIC compared the various lists with those compiled by Rothschild in 1915 and the British Correlating Committee in 1929. In England, the regional sub-committees nominated 150 of those included in the Rothschild list, and indeed the lists for Kent, Surrey and Sussex were very similar. Of the remaining twenty-four areas on Rothschild's list, the regional sub-committees reported that twelve had been destroyed and the remainder were of no special interest. Of the twelve areas that had been ruined, five had been affected by building development, three by afforestation, three by cultivation, and one by the uncontrolled spread of bracken. The area and value of many more areas had diminished during the inter-war years.[52]

The extent of these changes may be illustrated by reference to events in Northamptonshire. The status of only one area on the 1915 list had remained unchanged, namely that of Whitewater Bog.

Swaddiwell Field had been damaged by the extension of the adjacent quarry. Helpston Heath was partially ploughed, Harlestone Heath was reduced to an area of secondary importance owing to building development. Oakley Purlieus had been clear-felled and Sutton Heath and Bog was totally destroyed by drainage and ploughing.[53]

This meant that many of the areas excluded from the 1915 list became relatively important. Monks Wood in Huntingdonshire, for example, was excluded from the list because there were other woodlands in the East Midlands richer in invertebrate life. In 1921, the owner started to fell trees in the wood as a speculative venture, and immediately incurred the wrath of entomologists. He accordingly offered to sell Monks Wood to the National Trust, which sought an appraisal of the woodland from the SPNR. N. C. Rothschild replied that 'I know Monks Wood well and it is certainly rich in insects. I do not, however, think that its acquisition by the National Trust is really desirable at the present time, bearing in mind the very large number of still more interesting areas, which are worthy of protection even more than this one.' Consequently, the National Trust refused to take up the offer. But the quality of many of the proposed reserves on the 1915 list declined so dramatically in the inter-war period that Monks Wood became one of the finest examples in the East Midlands. Although 'damaged by felling', it had suffered less than many other sites, and its status as a potential nature reserve rose accordingly.[54]

Now began the task of deciding which areas should be nominated by the NRIC as national nature reserves. The meetings held in June and July 1944 produced a short list of fifty-six sites, and each member of the committee was invited to vote for his choice of potential reserves at a meeting of 11 August. Table 5 gives the names of the 'top' twenty-two areas, as recorded in the ballot.[55]

As noted, the Ministry wanted the reserves to be graded, according to their individual importance. The NRIC found this very difficult because each site had been selected as the finest example of its type and it was, for example, impossible to compare the value of a peat-bog with that of a yew wood. Nevertheless, the NRIC drew up a tentative classification which divided the reserves into three categories, namely:

category A included those sites of outstanding merit which, in the committee's opinion, must be safeguarded;

category B included those of special importance, the destruction of which would be a serious loss to science; and

category C included those which should find a place in any complete national scheme.

It was hoped category A sites would be immediately safeguarded and that category B sites could be acquired and protected in due course.

Name of site	Number of votes received	Status in Conference memorandum, number 6
Upper Teesdale	6	Conservation area
Tregaron Bog	6	A
Cavenham Heath	6	A
Lakenheath Warren	6	B
Braunton Burrows	6	A
Ainsdale Dunes	5	A
Askham Bog	4	B
Newborough Dunes	4	B
Tring Reservoirs	4	C
North Fen	4	A
Bedford Purlieus	4	Omitted
Horsey—Hickling Broads & Winterton Dunes	4	A
Kingley Vale	4	A
Goonhilly Downs	4	Part of conservation
Hartland Point	4	area
Kenfig Dunes	3	B
Bricket Wood Scrubs	3	A
Monks Wood	3	A
Horsey Island	3	A
Wychwood	3	C
Basingstoke Canal	3	B
Matley Bog	3	A
Cranham Woods	3	A

Table 5

The number of votes cast for the 'top' 22 areas considered at a meeting of the NRIC, 11 August 1944, and the status accorded to these areas in the lists of Conference memorandum, number 6

The NRIC realised that the acquisition of category C might be beyond the resources of the government for some years to come, but nevertheless the planning authorities should absolutely prohibit any harmful development on those sites.[56]

As indicated in Table 5, twenty-two sites obtained three or more votes in the ballot, and Diver suggested that they should constitute the bulk of the category A reserves. They should, however, first be scrutinised to see whether all the major habitat types had been included and if a wide range of animal life was represented. Wherever possible, the NRIC tried to include sites which had been included in the list presented by the British Correlating Committee to the Addison Committee in 1929, since this might enhance their value in the eyes of the Ministry.[57]

The final list included twenty-six reserves in category A, fourteen in category B and seven in category C. The final task was to prepare the scientific case for preserving each site. In many instances, the regional sub-committees had provided insufficient data and more up-to-date information had to be obtained.[58]

The list of forty-seven proposed national nature reserves was published in December 1945. A further eight areas were already protected (Figure 7), and the combined area of the fifty-five reserves represented 0.2 per cent of the land surface of England and Wales, an area smaller than the Isle of Wight. Fifteen had been included in the lists of the special committee of the British Ecological Society, and indeed the wording of several of the entries in the lists was identical: thus, both described Tregaron Bog as 'the best actively growing raised bog in England and Wales, and the only perfect example remaining of a once common type of vegetation', which should be protected from 'peat cutting, trampling, grazing and burning'.[59]

The Huxley Committee's List of Nature Reserves

The Committee drew up a new list of seventy-three proposed national nature reserves, which included nearly all of those recommended by the NRIC. Indeed, the bulk of the Committee's data was drawn from the memorandum published by the NRIC in 1945, and the description of many of the proposed reserves was identical: only the English of the text was improved![60]

Soon after the Committee was appointed, its secretary, R. S. R. Fitter, visited Kingley Vale and Pagham harbour in Sussex. At the former, he found a great deal of barbed wire and many notices warning of unexploded missiles. In addition, the lower and less steep slopes had been ploughed up for cultivation. Fitter concluded that all the prospective reserves should be visited as quickly as possible in order to ascertain their present condition.[61]

Accordingly, forty-five of the proposed national nature reserves were visited in the succeeding twelve months. A party consisting of A. G. Tansley, A. S. Watt and R. S. R. Fitter, for example, spent a day on the Breckland and discovered that the dune system at Laken-

Figure 7

Distribution of national nature reserves and conservation areas, proposed by
NRIC in 1945

heath Warren had been destroyed by the construction of an airfield.
Accordingly, they recommended that only the land to the east of the
new road should be proposed as a reserve. The various parties also took
the opportunity to assess in greater depth the scientific merits of
individual areas. There was a debate as to whether the site of
Wychwood in Oxfordshire should be excluded since it was not thought
to be primary woodland: it was eventually 'retained' since the proposed
reserve also included 'excellent limestone grasslands'.[62]

In compiling the new list of seventy-three reserves (Figure 8 and
Table 6), the Huxley Committee rejected four of the sites proposed by
the NRIC, namely the reserve at Butley, Staverton Park and the

Northern Group

1 Farne Islands
2 Naddle Low Forest
3 North Fen
4 Roudsea Wood
5 Hawes Water
6 Colt Park
7 Askham Bog
8 Skipwith Common
9 Ainsdale Sand Dunes
10 Rostherne Mere
11 Alderley Edge
12 Wybunbury Moss
13 Dovedale Ashwood

Western Group

14 Newborough Dunes & Llanddwyn Island
15 Eglwyseg Mountain
16 Clarepool Moss
17 Sweat Mere
18 Tregaron Bog
19 Skomer, Skokholm & Grassholm
20 Worms Head
21 Kenfig Dunes
22 Avon Gorge
23 Cheddar Wood
24 Shapwick, Ashcott & Meare Heaths
25 Braunton Burrows
26 Isles of Scilly

Southern Group

27 Morden Bog & Old Decoy Pond
28 Heaths from Studland to Arne
29 Hurst Castle & Keyhaven
30 Matley & Denny area
31 Old Winchester Hill
32 Kingley Vale
33 Basingstoke Canal
34 Box Hill
35 High Halstow Marshes
36 Blean Woods
37 Deal Sand Hills
38 Wye and Crundale Downs
39 Ham Street Woods
40 Birdlip & Painswick area
41 Wychwood Forest
42 Aston Rowant Woods
43 Pulpit Hill & Lodge Wood
44 Tring Reservoirs
45 Burnham Beeches
46 Windsor Forest
47 Bricket Wood Scrubs
48 Water End Swallow Holes
49 Wormley Wood

Eastern and Central Group

50 Epping Forest
51 Hales Wood
52 Horsey Island
53 Shingle Street
54 Minsmere Level
55 Cavenham Heath
56 Lakenheath Warren
57 Barton Broad
58 Hickling Broad & Horsey Mere
59 Winterton Dunes
60 Blakeney Point
61 Scolt Head Island
62 Chippenham Fen & Poor's Fen
63 Wicken Fen
64 Fenland Wildfowl Reserve
65 Monks Wood & Bevill's Wood
66 Woodwalton Fen
67 Holme Fen
68 Castor Hanglands
69 Holywell & Pickworth Woods
70 Nottingham Sewage Farm
71 Creswell Crags
72 Leighfield Forest
73 Wren's Nest

Scottish Group

74 Hermaness, Unst
75 Noss
76 Bay of Nigg
77 Inverpolly Forest & Summer Isles
78 Oakwood at Ariundle
79 Treshnish Isles
80 Estuary of Ythan
81 Blackwood of Rannoch
82 Shingle Islands, Tay & Tummel
83 Gruinart Loch & Flats
84 St Cyrus
85 Tay Estuary, Mugdrum Island
86 Tentsmuir
87 St Serf's Island
88 Isle of May
89 Aberlady—Gullane
90 Bass Rock
91 Ailsa Craig
92 Reach of Solway
93 North Rona
94 St Kilda
95 Newton Estate, Haskeir, Pabbay & Shillay
96 Loch Druidibeg
97 Allt Volagir

Table 6

The national nature reserves nominated by the Huxley Committee in 1947 and the Ritchie Committee for Scotland in 1949 (Figure 8)

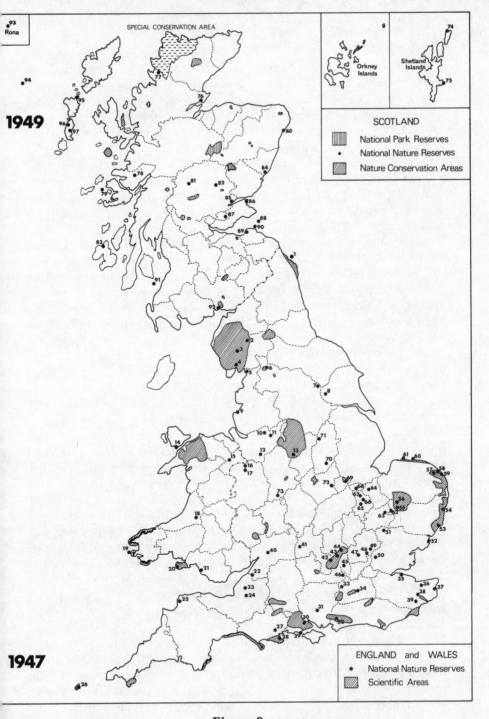

Figure 8
Distribution of national nature reserves and scientific areas, proposed by the
Huxley and Ritchie Committees (sites identified in Table 6)

Thicks, and Thorpeness, Whixall Moss and Fenn's Moss. It was decided to reject Butley, Staverton Park and the Thicks in Suffolk in the light of information received after the NRIC list had gone to press. E. J. Salisbury visited the area and claimed that the trees in Staverton Park and the Thicks were remnants of an old plantation rather than an ancient woodland. He accordingly recommended the removal of the site from any future list of proposed reserves.[63]

A party visited the Suffolk coast in 1946 in order to assess the value of the other proposed reserves. It consisted of A. G. Tansley, J. A. Steers, R. S. R. Fitter, and W. V. Lewis, a coastal geographer. It was decided to reject Thorpeness as a proposed reserve because it was too near unfenced roads and boating was allowed on the mere. The fen was already in sympathetic hands, and the RSPB rented North Warren. On the other hand, the party endorsed the recommendation of Minsmere as a national nature reserve. It was clearly outstanding for bird life, and Tansley stressed its potential value for ecological studies of brakish water conditions. The amount of flooding was 'just right' and every effort should be made to exclude the site from agricultural reclamation schemes.[64]

The Huxley Committee decided to reject Whixall Moss in Cheshire and Fenn's Moss in Shropshire, and replace them with Wybunbury and Clarepool Mosses respectively. This followed a visit to the sites by C. S. Elton and R. S. R. Fitter in July 1946. The NRIC had recommended these reserves on account of the presence of *Coenonympha tullia* and other 'northern' insects, but Elton and Fitter found only one specimen. Both sites had been badly affected by draining, and Fenn's Moss had been swept by fires started by sparks from a railway which ran through the site. It was 'badly covered with bracken and scattered bushes'.

In contrast, Elton and Fitter 'unhesitatingly' recommended the preservation of Wybunbury and Clarepool Mosses. The former was the 'last perfect peat moss in Cheshire', with *Erica tetralix, Empetrum, Drosera rotundifolia, Oxycoccus, Molinia, Melampyrum, Orchis maculata, Narthecium, Potentilla erecta, Andromeda,* etc. Clarepool Moss was situated on 'deep peat' and included a tract of pure Sphagnum quaking bog, with *Drosera* and *Oxycoccus,* turning to *Empetrum, Erica tetralix* and *Calluna* at the edges.[65]

The Huxley Committee developed the view of the NRIC that reserves should be chosen primarily for their scientific value. The series should include 'both the unique and the typical, the common and the rare, in such proportions as will best provide a foundation for a sound ecological study of wildlife conditions in this country'. In line with this objective, the Committee tried to ensure that each part of the country and major habitat were represented in the series of proposed reserves.

Accordingly, a small number of additional reserves was proposed to fill in the geographical 'gaps' in the NRIC list. These reserves included the Holywell and Pickworth Woods in Lincolnshire and Rutland, the Farne Islands, several of the Scilly Isles, and Skokholm, Skomer and Grassholm.[66]

The Committee planned to include a map in its report, showing 'the different types of habitat in broad outline' and a table showing how each type was represented in the series of reserves. In the event, the map and table were omitted, probably because of the difficulties in compiling them.[67]

Nevertheless, the Committee's approach may be illustrated by reference to a memorandum submitted by A. G. Tansley and A. S. Watt, following their visit to the Chilterns in June 1946. They distinguished five climax types, namely:

a) escarpment beechwood with sanicle field layer;
b) escarpment beechwood with mercury;
c) plateau beechwood on the richest soils;
d) plateau beechwood on intermediate soils;
e) plateau beechwood on podsolised soils.

There were, in addition, four seral types, namely:

f) early phases of colonisation by woody plants;
g) juniper sere on escarpment;
h) hawthorn sere on escarpment;
i) heath and grassland sere on plateau.

No one area included all nine types, and type (i) did not occur adjacent to any other type. Tansley and Watt concluded that it was not feasible to designate a national nature reserve simply to preserve this one kind of community, and so it was excluded from further consideration.

On the other hand, they recommended the designation of three national nature reserves to safeguard the remaining eight types. The Aston Rowant woods included tracts of (c) which were probably the finest examples of high beechwood in the Chilterns, together with types (a), (b), (d) and (f). Pulpit Hill was recommended for its particularly good examples of type (g): type (h) was present, and type (a) was very well represented. The third area, Lodge Wood, included the best examples of type (e) where the podsolised soils encouraged an entirely different flora from that of the other two proposed reserves.[68]

The Huxley Committee stressed the value of the reserves in ecological survey and experimental work, and accordingly it nominated three areas specifically as experimental reserves. One of these was Old Winchester Hill in Hampshire, which was particularly suitable for experiments on chalkland communities. The site was recommended by

J. Hope-Simpson, who noted that it covered only 450 acres and
included a plateau and slopes facing the north, west and south. It contained a wide variety of communities, including a well developed yew
wood, juniper scrub, hawthorn scrub, and heath on clay-with-flints,
chalkland heath, and tracts of chalk grassland. The proposed reserve
would be ideal for studying the relationship between calcicole and
calcifuge species. The acidic plateau, surrounded by calcareous
habitats, would form an excellent research site since the micro-
climatic factors were similar and it was much easier to compare the
soils and vegetation of two adjacent, rather than widely separated,
areas.[69]

The committee included two proposed experimental bird reserves
in its list, chosen with the following objectives in mind:

i) to attract back as many of the former marshland breeding birds
as possible;

ii) to establish a winter reserve for wildfowl, especially grey
geese;

iii) to set up a station for the study of bird migration, especially
in relation to waders and other aquatic birds;

iv) to further general ornithological research as far as possible within
the special aims of the reserve.

In the event, the Committee chose the High Halstow Marshes in Kent
as a proposed coastal wildfowl reserve, and the Whittlesey Washes in
Cambridgeshire were their first choice for an inland site. The Bedford
Levels in Cambridgeshire were made the second choice, but the Cowbit
Marshes were rejected as a reserve since the area was 'too narrow and
overlooked by public roads'.[70]

At the same time, the Committee decided to include a sewage farm
in its list of proposed reserves as an example of an 'important type of
artificial habitat'. Nottingham sewage works were nominated, but the
Committee stressed that there was no need to interfere in the operation
of the plant until plans were prepared for modernising the works. This
was expected to occur in the 1950s and, at that time, the Committe
recommended that several meadows should be taken out of the farm
and retained in a flooded condition.

The Huxley Committee refused to place its choice of reserves in any
order of priority, claiming that each was roughly equal in value and
had to be preserved in order to secure a balanced representation of
the major habitats of the country. At its first meeting in September
1945, the Committee decided that it was 'all or nothing': each one of the
seventy-three proposed reserves had to be protected, otherwise the
overall value of the entire series would be lost.[71]

The proposed national nature reserves occupied an area of 70,000 acres, and ranged from twenty acres to over 3,500 acres in size. About 3,000 to 4,000 acres of the aggregate area belonged to various departments of State, and a further 1,500 acres were held by organisations from whom acquisition would be neither practicable nor possible. Thirteen of the proposed reserves, covering about 11,000 acres, were already owned by a body concerned with nature conservation. The National Trust, for example, managed the Farne Islands, and the recently formed Yorkshire Naturalists' Trust had acquired Askham Bog (page 226). There was no intention of taking over these areas, but the Committee believed they should be given the status of national nature reserves in order to demonstrate their outstanding biological value to the relevant planning authorities.

Of the remaining 47,000 acres of proposed reserves, about 12,000 acres were wooded and of little commercial value, and the remainder could be regarded as waste land. The cost of acquiring geological monuments would be 'negligible'. The Committee, therefore, estimated that the total cost of buying the land occupied by the reserves would amount to £500,000. A further £10,000 would be needed each year for maintaining the areas: there would be a small return from the sale of reeds and other produce, and from the payments made by visiting research workers for accommodation provided on the sites.

Scientific Areas and National Parks

The NRIC and the Huxley Committee believed there was no substitute for owning a key site in order to protect its wildlife. But clearly some areas were too extensive to form nature reserves, and it was hoped they would fall within the boundaries of national parks and thereby obtain some protection. The two Committees therefore took the greatest interest in the choice of national parks made by John Dower and the Hobhouse Committee.

Dower believed the parks should be established in the wilder parts of the countryside, as indicated on the maps recently published by the Land Utilization Survey (Figure 9). He distinguished twenty-two areas which might be considered as suitable for national parks, covering 8,000 square miles, and he divided these into divisions A and B. Dower insisted that the ten proposed parks in division A should be established within five years, otherwise there might be a danger of visitors concentrating in just one or two areas, causing damage to the amenity, dislocation of local transport, and inconvenience to settlement within the park areas. This would soon discredit the parks concept.[72]

This selection provided a 'sound foundation' for the more detailed proposals of the Hobhouse Committee in 1947, which urged the

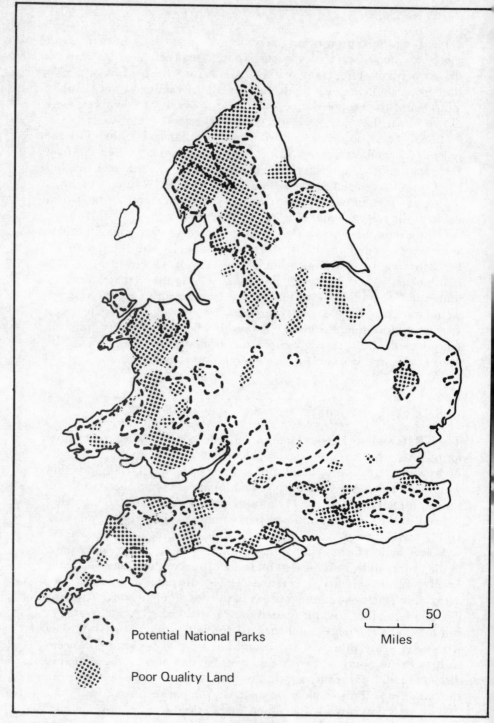

Figure 9
Distribution of poor quality land and areas suitable for national parks

government to designate twelve parks, covering 5,682 square miles, within three years (Figure 10). These included nine of those in Dower's division A, although some of their names and boundaries were changed.[73] The Hobhouse Committee decided to omit the national park proposed by Dower for the South-West Peninsula, which extended from Ilfracombe on the North Devon coast to Poole Harbour in Dorset. It would be very difficult to administer such a long and broken coastline of 396 miles.

In order to increase the variety of scenery represented in the series of parks, the Hobhouse Committee decided to upgrade two of the parks which Dower had consigned to his division B, namely the North Yorkshire Moors and the Broads. The latter was already a popular holiday area, and an overall planning authority was badly needed to draw up a scheme for the future recreational use of the area. Finally, the committee included in its proposals one park which Dower had rejected, the South Downs, in order to provide London with a nearby park.

Only a limited number of parks could be established, and many outstanding areas would have to be excluded. Dower assumed that the planning authorities would simply do their utmost to protect such areas from harmful development, but the Hobhouse Committee believed the areas should be given a special status so as to emphasise their value. It accordingly nominated fifty-two areas as conservation areas. Most were 'rejected national parks'. The Malverns and Cotswolds were too small and intensively exploited to make suitable national parks; the Breckland was too important for forestry, and the greater part of the Marlborough and Berkshire Downs was under cultivation. The list of conservation areas included fourteen tracts of coastline, among them the area of Devon, Dorset and Cornwall, designated by Dower as a proposed national park but rejected by the Hobhouse Committee.

Quite clearly, the proposed parks and conservation areas included many key sites and areas for wildlife. Nevertheless, some important tracts of land had been excluded, and even in the parks the preservation of wildlife was not the paramount interest. Consequently, the NRIC believed there was a need to schedule some areas explicitly for the protection of their wildlife, where planning authorities would be obliged to take account of the scientific interest whenever examining plans for a change in land use. There would be no attempt to interfere with existing agriculture or forestry, and new forms of husbandry would be allowed to maintain the profitability of farming and forestry. The NRIC simply hoped the scientific interest would be regarded as of equal importance, and the Huxley Committee endorsed this view.[74]

The special committee of the British Ecological Society drew up the

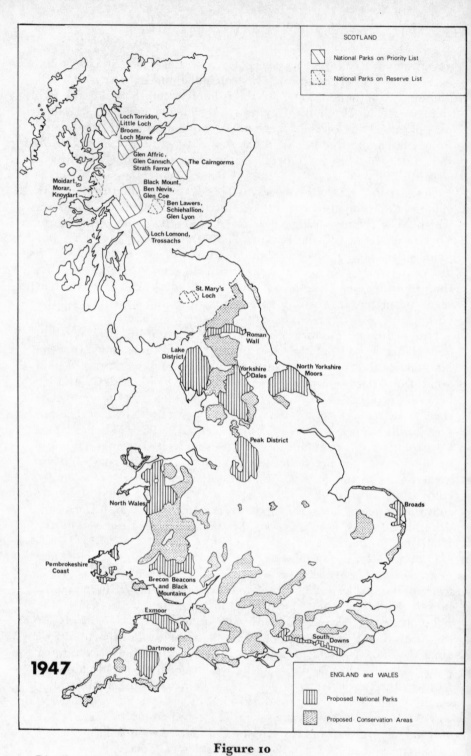

Figure 10
Distribution of national parks and conservation areas, proposed by the
Hobhouse and Douglas Ramsay Committees

first list of proposed scheduled areas to complement its list of national habitat reserves. The list included thirty-three areas where all developments inimical to wildlife should be banned or severely restricted (Figure 6). It included one area in Northern Ireland, around Lough Neagh, where there were plans to build a lake-side road. Two scheduled areas were proposed for the South Downs, and several national habitat reserves fell within the boundaries of a scheduled area: the reserve of Matley Bog, for example, was included in the New Forest scheduled area. The special committee's list gave little information as to the size and boundaries of the proposed areas, and it stressed the need for further survey work once the war had ended.[75]

John Dower claimed that the term 'scheduled area' was inexpressive and open to misunderstanding, and, at his suggestion, the NRIC used the term 'conservation area' in its memorandum published in 1945, which nominated forty-seven national nature reserves and twenty-five conservation areas (Figure 7). The latter included twelve of those proposed by the special committee of the British Ecological Society. Indeed, several were described in identical terms in the NRIC list. The conservation areas covered an aggregate area of 1,530 square miles, or about 2.6 per cent of England and Wales, an area slightly larger than Cumberland or Kent.[76]

While preparing the list, Diver suggested that the conservation areas should be graded in the same way as nature reserves. This was agreed, and nineteen of the areas were placed in category A, four in category B and two in category C. It was decided to place the Lake District, Peak District and Snowdonia in a seperate list since they were almost certain to become national parks and no special measures would be needed for the protection of wildlife once this happened.[77]

The Huxley Committee accepted all the conservation areas nominated by the NRIC, but changed their name to scientific areas in order to avoid confusion with the fifty-two conservation areas proposed on amenity grounds by the Hobhouse Committee. The Huxley Committee identified the Lake District, Peak District, Snowdonia and the Norfolk Broads as scientific areas, and five other areas on geological and physiographical grounds (page 163). Finally it recommended a further two scientific areas in order to fill in 'blanks' on the NRIC list (Figure 8 and Table 6).[78]

The first was an area between Clipsham and Holywell in the East Midlands, recommended by T. G. Tutin. This included a representative sample of wood and grass land on Jurassic limestone, intermediate between the Lincolnshire and Cotswold types. The pendunculate oak–hazel woods contained a rich field layer, and the grasslands were notable for containing a number of species with a continental type of distribution which reached their western limits in the East Midlands. The area included the Holywell and Pickworth Woods, nominated as a national nature reserve.[79]

The second scientific area was the Scilly Isles, recommended by J. E. Lousley, on account of their distinctive flora. Lousley estimated that forty-two per cent of the Mediterranean species listed in J. R. Matthews' paper in the *Journal of Ecology* in 1937 occurred in the Scilly Isles, which also contained forty-three per cent of all Oceanic southern species and thirty-four per cent of Oceanic western species. This was a very high proportion for a group of islands covering less than seven square miles of land.[80]

The Huxley Committee insisted that the scientific areas were an integral part of the system of national nature reserves: they were not an optional extra.[81] On the other hand, the conservation/scientific areas were the least well-defined and most contentious categories of land. As early as May 1945, W. L. Taylor of the Forestry Commission warned the NRIC of difficulties ahead. Either the scheduling of such areas would be so weak as to be ineffective in protecting wildlife, or it would inhibit land reclamation and afforestation, and thereby promote a tremendous clash between naturalists and other land-users. Taylor noticed that the NRIC had proposed the scheduling of Ingleborough, Breckland, St Leonards Forest and the Cleveland Hills, and he warned 'no Minister or other responsible person in charge of forestry could contemplate' the abandonment of afforestation in all these areas. At the larger scale, the NRIC had scheduled all the principal sand dune formations in the country: if the Forestry Commission was to expand its planting programme, it would have to afforest some of these dune systems in order to achieve its targets.[82]

Geological Sites

Many of the proposed nature reserves were of interest to the geologist and physiographer. The Rothschild list of 1915, for example, included eighteen areas of sand dunes and nine shingle beaches. It proposed the protection of such areas as the limestone of Hutton Roof in Westmorland, Kilnsey Crag in Yorkshire, and Whitecliff Bay in the Isle of Wight.

The British Correlating Committee also made reference to the geological interest of some of its proposed sixty-six areas worthy of protection. Eight were of special interest for geologists, including Snowdonia, the Lake District, Charnwood and Savernake Forests. In addition, the Geological Society of London submitted a memorandum which recognised five types of land which should be protected.[83] These were:

i) isolated outcrops—the Cheeswring in Liskeard, Cornwall, and Druid Stone in Blidworth, Nottinghamshire;

ii) glacial erratics—the boulder at High Onn, Staffordshire;

iii) natural sections—Pentire Point, Cornwall;

iv) sites of disused quarries—Arco Wood Quarry in Settle, Yorkshire, threatened with infilling;

v) extensive areas—Ingleborough, Malham, Wensleydale and Fylingdales in Yorkshire.

The evidence submitted to the Addison Committee contained only a few examples of each type of site: a full list of glacial erratics had been compiled by a committee of the British Association between 1896 and 1913, and the Geological Survey itself had set up a committee to compile a further list of sites worthy of protection.

The NRIC set up a geological sub-committee in April 1944 'to guide the regional sub-committees and supplement their lists of proposed reserves where necessary'. The first task was to draw up a classification of sites to be protected, for the regional sub-committees had already recommended geological monuments ranging in size from a small erratic boulder to the Lizard peninsula, and had included both natural sections and quarries still in active use. At its first meeting, the geological sub-committee decided to separate this wide range of features into four categories,[84] namely:

Geological monuments. The features, together with a small area of surrounding land, would be purchased and thereafter maintained at minimal expense. In drawing up the short-list of geological monuments, the committee took account of their 'public educational' appeal. Nearly all were 'likely to arouse interest on account of their arresting appearance or fame', and the committee suggested that a metal notice plate should be fixed to each, explaining the character and origins of the monument.

Controlled sections. Every attempt should be made to keep both natural sections and disused quarries open for scientific study and teaching purposes. For this reason, restrictions should be placed on building and other forms of development which prevented access to the sites. Most rock faces were so massive and extensive that there was no risk of their being entirely destroyed, but there were exceptions. There was a risk of some pits being filled with rubbish once they fell into disuse: this had to be prevented. In some cases, an entire rock might be removed by quarrying: every effort had to be made to preserve a typical column through the entire strata.

Registered sections. Some exposures of rock were so important that quarry owners should be asked to give notice of further excavation so that geologists could study the cliff faces as work proceeded. The special committee stressed, however, the need to preserve the goodwill of the owners: geologists should interfere in the management of quarries only when it was absolutely necessary.

Geological conservation areas. These were extensive areas of considerable topographical and geological interest. The scheduling of the areas would encourage local planning authorities to protect them from any threat.

In September 1945, the geological sub-committee published its memorandum which recommended the designation of forty-eight geological monuments, 198 controlled sections, seventy-three registered sections, and seventy geological conservation areas, and their distribution is indicated in Figure 11 and Table 7.

Geologists had to be pragmatic when choosing sites for preservation. Clement Reid made this point in 1913 when he was asked by the SPNR to nominate a submerged forest for protection as a nature reserve. He wrote:

> I do not quite see what means of protection could be taken, for when the submerged forest is hidden it is quite safe, and when it is exposed it is all the time being destroyed by the waves or weather. The great point for the study of these forests is that fresh surfaces should continually be exposed, as the coast is cut back. If a submerged forest were protected artificially it would soon get hopelessly obscured and muddy, through the action of weather, boring molluscs and annelids.[85]

The geological sub-committee of the NRIC tried to be equally realistic in selecting sites. It did not include a representative locality of every rock type or zone, for this would have produced an unwieldy list. It avoided nominating sites on the widespread zones of chalk since there was no risk of these becoming inaccessible to geologists. Clay pits were rejected as geological monuments because of the tremendous difficulties of protecting them from erosion and flooding. Thus, the published list of proposed sites was biassed toward inland artificial sections, situated on such resistant rocks as Carboniferous Limestone.

The Huxley Committee agreed with this approach and endorsed the nomination of forty-one of the proposed geological monuments. It also recommended Blackhalls Rocks in Durham, which the NRIC sub-committee had proposed as a small geological conservation area. The average size of the forty-two monuments was less than one acre. The Huxley Committee doubted whether many sites would have to be purchased; where this was necessary, the organisation responsible for national nature reserves should also acquire and look after the geological monuments. The Geological Survey had offered to make periodic inspections and supply material for display notices.[86]

The seven 'rejected' monuments, together with the 198 controlled sections and seventy-three registered sections nominated by the NRIC sub-committee, were recommended by the Huxley Committee as sites of special scientific interest, as defined elsewhere in its report. The Huxley Committee noted that most of the proposed geological conservation areas fell within proposed national parks, conservation and scientific areas, and it accordingly decided not to award them any special geological status: the preservation of their geological interest was already virtually assured. Of the remaining areas, the Huxley Committee decided to nominate the Woolhope area of Gloucestershire and Herefordshire as a scientific area on geological grounds; the Northumberland coast, Malvern Hills and Charnwood Forest were proposed on account of their geological and biological interest. Finally, the Committee added a scientific area which had not been proposed by the NRIC sub-committee, namely the north Norfolk coast which was of outstanding importance to the coastal physiographer.

Sites of Special Scientific Interest

The regional sub-committee and the special geological committee of the NRIC recommended hundreds of sites which could not be included in the final lists of proposed national nature reserves and geological monuments. Many were threatened with destruction. During a visit to the Suffolk coast in 1946, several members of the Huxley Committee discovered plans to excavate more shingle from Benacre Ness and to transform a naval camp at Covehithe Cliffs into a holiday resort.[87]

In order to draw attention to the scientific value of these sites, the Huxley Committee recommended that they should be scheduled as sites of special scientific interest, and that lists of such sites should be sent to the Ministry of Town and Country Planning, the appropriate local planning authorities and landowners, and made available for public inspection. Clearly, the scheduling should begin immediately, and the Committee recommended that the NRIC regional sub-committees should be given an official status under the Ministry of Town and Country Planning, and assess the scientific value of each site for scheduling. The sub-committees would begin work in the national parks, conservation and scientific areas, and add any further important sites to those already known.

In the course of time, booklets would be published describing the scientific value of the sites of special scientific interest in each region. The extra publicity would help to ensure that the scientific merits of

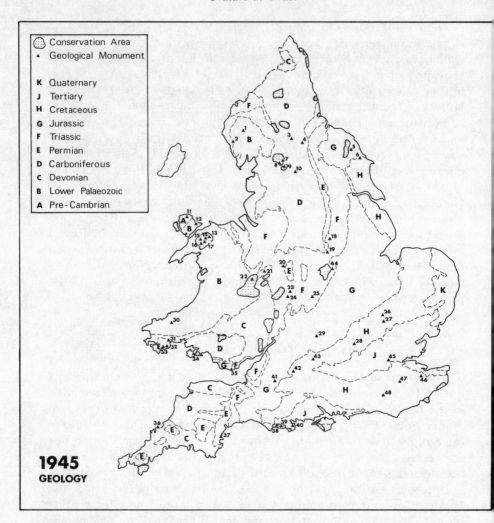

Figure 11

Distribution of geological monuments and geological conservation areas, proposed by NRIC in 1945 (monuments identified in Table 7)

each site were fully taken into account whenever a change in land use or management was proposed.

The Scottish Reserves

The supervisory committee appointed under Sir J. Douglas Ramsay in 1944 recommended two categories of national parks, as indicated in

1	*Crag in field, E. of Gosforth, Cumberland*
2	*Bowder Stone, Borrowdale, Cumberland*
3	*Carlow Stone, Semmer Water, North Riding*
4	*Brimham Rocks, near Pateley Bridge, West Riding*
5	*Bride Stones, near Pickering, North Riding*
6	*Wold Newton, N.W. of Bridlington, East Riding*
7	*Austwick Beck Head, N.W. of Settle, West Riding*
8	*Norber Brow, Austwick, West Riding*
9	*Victoria Cave, Settle, West Riding*
10	*Draughton Quarry, near Skipton, West Riding*
11	*Llaneilian, E. of Amlwch, Anglesey*
12	*Trwyn-dwlban, Red Wharf Bay, Anglesey*
13	*Glaciated pavement near Ogwen Cottage, Nant Ffrancon, Caernarvonshire*
14	*Group of moraines, Llyn Idwal, Caernarvonshire*
15	*Glaciated pavement, S.W. of Llyn Peris, Caernarvonshire*
16	*Erratic boulder, Maen Bras, Caernarvonshire*
17	*Erratic boulder, near head of Llanberis Pass, Caernarvonshire*
18	*Druid Stone, Blidworth, Nottinghamshire*
19	*Hemlock Stone, Bramcote, Nottinghamshire*
20	*High Onn, S.W. of Stafford*
21	*Lea Rock, Overley Hill, Shropshire*
22	*Devil's Chair & Cranberry Rock, S. W. of Haberley, Shropshire*
23	*Romsley Hill, S. of Halesowen, Worcestershire*
24	*Great Dodford, N.W. of Bromsgrove, Worcestershire*
25	*King's Hill, Finham, Warwickshire*
26	*Erratic boulder, Royston, Hertfordshire*
27	*Barkway chalk pit, near Royston, Hertfordshire*
28	*The Lee, N. of Great Missenden, Buckinghamshire*
29	*Stonesfield Slate Mine, S.W. of Charlbury, Oxfordshire*
30	*Carn Meini, near Mynachlog-ddu, Pembrokeshire*
31	*Saundersfoot, Pembrokeshire*
32	*Lydstep Haven, S.W. of Tenby, Pembrokeshire*
33	*Skrinkle Haven, S.W. of Tenby, Pembrokeshire*
34	*Minchin Hole, Oxwich Bay, Gower*
35	*Little Island, Barry, Glamorgan*
36	*Pentire Head, Cornwall*
37	*Kent's Hole, Torquay, Devon*
38	*Fossil, forest, Lulworth, Dorset*
39	*Durdle Door, Dorset*
40	*Agglestone, Dorset*
41	*Vallisvale Quarries, N.W. of Frome, Somerset*
42	*Quarry E. of Canal Bridge, Bradford-on-Avon, Wiltshire*
43	*Fyfield Down, Wiltshire*
44	*Mountsorrel Granite Quarry, Leicestershire*
45	*Charlton Sand Pit, London*
46	*Lenham Chalk Pit, S.E. of Maidstone, Kent*
47	*High Rocks, Tunbridge Wells, Kent*
48	*Fletching, N. of Lewes, Sussex*

Table 7

The geological monuments nominated by the NRIC in 1945

Figure 10. These had an aggregate area of 2,600 square miles, out of a total of 21,200 square miles of rough grazing, deer forest and woodlands in Scotland. In addition, the committee suggested that parts of the national parks should be set aside as nature reserves, and that three additional, small areas outside the park boundaries should be made reserves, namely the lower reaches of the Garry, Moriston, and the Black Wood of Rannoch.[88]

The second Douglas Ramsay Committee of 1946–7 supported these recommendations and urged the government to create five national parks within ten years. It also set up a Wild Life Conservation Special Committee to carry out a survey of potential national nature reserves in Scotland. Whereas the Huxley Committee, south of the Border, could draw on a large body of information amassed by the NRIC, this Committee under the chairmanship of James Ritchie had to start from scratch. Consequently, its lists of proposed nature reserves were not completed and published until 1949.[89]

Scientific bodies and individuals were asked to assist in the survey of potential reserves. Regional sub-committees were appointed, based on the universities, but their work varied in quality and a member of the Ritchie Committee confided in 1948 that they proved very disappointing and provided little aid to the Committee.

It was decided to recommend three kinds of nature reserve, which covered an aggregate area of 250,094 acres (Figure 8). The first was to be situated in the national park areas, as recommended by the Douglas Ramsay Committee, and would be called national park reserves. One would be located in the Northern Highlands and three in the Southern Highlands. They would act as nurseries for wildlife that would multiply and enhance the amenity of the remainder of the national park areas. Public access to the reserves would be very strictly controlled during the breeding season.

Outside the national parks, a series of national nature reserves would be established for 'safeguarding and perpetuating the natural assemblages of plants and animals which they now contain, plant and animal assemblages which might settle there under more favourable conditions, and special features of geological interest. Such reserves would offer invaluable opportunities for scientific study.' The Committee nominated twenty-four of these reserves, of which eight were in the Central Plain, six in the Northern Hebrides, four in the Southern Highlands, five in the Outer Hebrides, and one in the Southern Uplands (Figure 8 and Table 6).

The Committee recommended that the third category of reserves, the local nature reserves, should be situated near towns and large villages so that they could be fully utilised for educational and recreational purposes.

To these classes of reserve, a fourth category was added, namely the nature conservation areas where the countryside would be preserved as far as possible from harmful developments. There would be no interference with landownership or sporting rights, although the government would make available grants for the protection of wildlife and amenity. In many respects, the twenty-two areas proposed by the Committee would fulfill the same function as the scientific areas recommended by the Huxley Committee.

For many years, there had been proposals for a really extensive reserve in the Highlands, which would include a wide variety of habitat and a representative selection of Scottish flora and fauna. Writing in 1938, F. Fraser Darling claimed the West Highlands would be ideal 'for within a limited area there are sea cliffs, sand-dunes, saltings, glens with deciduous woods, birch, scrub, coniferous woods, deer grounds, and high tops. There are also plenty of freshwater lochs and rivers.'[90] The Ritchie Committee agreed upon the need for such an area, and 468,180 acres of north-west Sutherland was designated a special conservation area: the cliff formations and flora were unique, and the hinterland was the stronghold of the pine marten. The parishes of Assynt, Eddrachyllis, Durness and Tongue, which made up the area, contained only four persons per square mile, and the Committee believed the designation would help the landowners and occupiers to maintain and enhance the distinctive character of one of the wildest and least accessible parts of Britain.

Local Nature Reserves

In its evidence to the British Correlating Committee in 1929, the RSPB suggested that local authorities should have powers to establish bird sanctuaries on the outskirts of towns and cities in order to sustain the bird population and stimulate public interest in wildlife preservation. The Ritchie Committee, in its report of 1947, was especially concerned with the educational value of such local nature reserves. While nature study was included in the curricula of most schools, the Committee found it was poorly and unimaginatively taught by teachers who had little enthusiasm for the subject. This was largely because nature study was taught in the classroom: instead, it should be undertaken out-of-doors on land set aside for the purpose. The reserves would not have to be large or contain 'rare or extensive flora or fauna'. Indeed, many disused clay pits, abandoned quarries, old colliery sites and waste heaps would be ideal: they would have little commercial value and could soon be converted to this new use.[91]

The Ministry of Education was generally sympathetic toward such proposals but was naturally concerned as to the cost of providing reserves when it faced a heavy school building programme. Individual schools already made heavy demands on land, and the addition of nature reserves was out of the question. Representatives of the Ministry suggested in the 1940s that efforts should be concentrated on providing a nature reserve in the vicinity of each teacher training college, so that every teacher received some instruction on teaching nature study in the field as part of his formal training.[92]

Both the Ritchie and Huxley Committees called upon the government to introduce legislation to widen the involvement of local authorities in the provision of nature reserves. It was expected that the Treasury would provide assistance, in the form of grants toward the acquisition and management of such sites. Local field clubs and natural history societies would also lend assistance, especially in surveying changes in wildlife and in undertaking some of the management work.

Perhaps not surprisingly, the regional sub-committees of the NRIC were among the most enthusiastic advocates of educational and local nature reserves. The Lincolnshire committee, for example, drew up a list of those reserves which would be valuable for teaching purposes. Figure 12 indicates the distribution of these reserves and their proximity to the schools of local towns. The site of Twigmoor, Gull Ponds and Woodland, for instance, was within three miles of the schools in Brigg and five miles of those in Scunthorpe.[93]

Although the Lincolnshire sub-committee soon became defunct, the Lincolnshire Naturalists' Union continued to press for local nature reserves, and most especially the designation of Gibraltar Point, a site already owned by the Lindsey County Council. The reserve, equipped with a field study centre and bird observatory, would be intensively used by senior school children and colleges of adult education. Geographers would be able to trace the development of the marsh and dune systems through all their phases. Ecologists would discover the wildlife characteristic of each phase of development. Gibraltar Point was the only nesting site of several bird species and well placed on important migration routes.[94]

By 1950, an aggregate of over 500 areas had been recommended by the SPNR, the British Correlating Committee, the special committee of the British Ecological Society, the NRIC, and the Huxley and Ritchie Committees. Some were designed to protect a community, and others to safeguard a species. Most were selected on scientific criteria, but reference was made to their educational potential. Many were graded, and a hierarchy evolved, which distinguished national nature reserves from those of primarily local importance.

Initially, the voluntary bodies had expected to acquire and manage

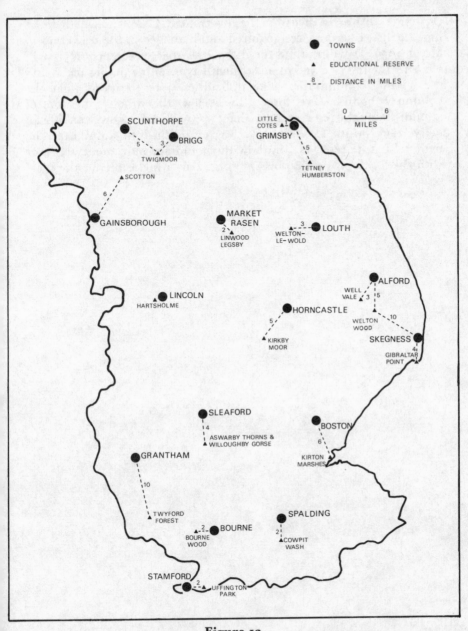

Figure 12
Distribution of reserves suitable for educational purposes, proposed by
Lincolnshire sub-committee of NRIC

these sites, with assistance from the government. Chapter 7 will describe how the first reserves were acquired and managed in the period up to about 1950. It will outline the difficulties that were encountered in securing the reserves and in subsequently controlling public access and the wildlife communities. The difficulties were so severe that the voluntary bodies were forced to review the whole question of administering the reserves, and Chapter 8 will indicate how an official body, the Nature Conservancy, was established to administer the national nature reserves, and how the voluntary movement, together with the local authorities, became primarily responsible for the local reserves.

Chapter Seven

The Acquisition and Management of Nature Reserves

Charles Waterton may be given the credit for establishing the first nature reserve, in the years after 1813 when he provided refuge for all kinds of wildlife, except rats and foxes, on his estate at Walton Hall, near Wakefield. The duties of the gamekeeper were transformed: instead of being paid to destroy hawks, magpies, carrion crows, owls, stoats and weasels, he had to protect and cherish them. A wall was built eight feet high around the grounds, and was raised to sixteen feet by the Hull to Barnsley canal so as to stop bargemen shooting the birds as they passed the grounds. The wall, three miles long, was built in stages, and took ten years to complete at a cost of £10,000.[1]

These protective measures were augmented by schemes to enhance the estate with additional forms of wildlife. Waterton provided the barn owl with new breeding sites. He wrote:

> . . . on the ruin of the old gateway . . . I made a place with stone and mortar, about four feet square, and fixed a thick oak stick firmly into it. Huge masses of ivy now quite cover it. In about a month or so after it was furnished, a pair of barn owls came and took up their abode . . . when I found that this first settlement on the gateway had succeeded so well, I set about forming other establishments . . . it will help to supply the places of those which, in this neighbourhood, are still unfortunately doomed to death by the hand of cruelty and superstition.

Having succeeded with barn owls, Waterton was encouraged to provide breeding sites for starlings, and made twenty-four holes in the old ruin which were soon occupied. He later constructed circular towers, similar in design to dovecotes for the birds. In a sunny, sheltered corner beside a grotto, a loose heap of rough stones was made for the weasels to inhabit.

Trees and bushes were planted and protected for shelter, food and as breeding places for the birds. Waterton discovered that holly, for example, was best planted in the last week of May so that it survived the drier summer months and reached almost one foot in height by September. He was keen to demonstrate how little damage was caused by birds and mammals (with the exception of the rat) to gardens and game preserves. He wrote with pride:

> . . . every bird, be his qualities bad or good, is now welcome here; and still nothing seems to go wrong, either in the orchard, or in the garden. . . . The dovecot is most productive, notwithstanding that a colony of starlings exists within a stone's throw of it. The pheasants are crying in every wood around; nor do the hoarse croakings of the carrion crows, or the frequent chatterings of the magpies, cause me any apprehension that there will be a deficiency in the usual supply of game.

The sanctuary at Walton Hall became only one of many estates where an owner either tolerated or took steps to encourage wild plants and animals. The owner of Castle Eden Dene on the coast between Sunderland and Hartlepool in Durham preserved the rare and distinctive plants which grew in the deeply incised valley, leading into the North Sea. *Daphne laureola, Cephalanthera longifolia, Ophrys apifera* and *O. muscifera insectifera*, and *Cypripedium calceolus* were present. At one time, the plants had been present in other denes on that part of the coast, but gradually the valleys had been overrun by holiday-makers or used for dumping refuse from nearby collieries.[2]

The value of these private reserves was enhanced between the wars as wildnerness areas were developed. E. C. Arnold described in his book *Bird Reserves*, published in 1940, how he bought a disused brickpit, a wood, and marshland in Sussex, and part of Salthouse Broad in Suffolk, for his own 'edification' and for posterity. He wrote: 'to my mind bird protection is nowadays far more a matter of preserving bird haunts than of making laws to protect birds, which may easily, like the Kentish plover, be exterminated by progress . . . the only wild land ultimately saved will be that which we save ourselves'. As a guide to others, he described how he acquired the reserves, wrestled with the problem of vandalism and the damage caused by stray cattle and sheep, and how he endeavoured to establish trees and shrubs in order to variegate the habitat and make it more attractive to birds.[3]

This chapter will trace the early experience of the voluntary bodies in acquiring reserves, often with the aid of public appeals. It will then outline the problems faced by these bodies in regulating public access and in implementing management programmes to preserve and enhance the wildlife communities on the reserves.

The Acquisition of Reserves

The early reserves tended to be established on wet-land sites or along the coast. This reflected their richness of wildlife and vulnerability to disturbance and destruction. Such entomologists as N. C. Rothschild, for example, took a leading role in establishing reserves at Wicken Fen and Woodwalton Fen in East Anglia, and at Meathop Moss in Westmorland. These were key sites for Lepidoptera and other insect groups, and were threatened by collectors and attempts to drain the land for peat-workings or cultivation. The RSPB was anxious to safeguard the famous bird colonies and resting grounds for migrants on the coast. Accordingly, a reserve was designated in Romney Marshes in 1928, and R. M. Lockley and W. H. Sheldon acquired the lease for Skokholm in Pembrokeshire in order to provide 'a flower-covered sanctuary' for the outstanding colonies of seabirds.

The SPNR and NRIC compiled an inventory of existing nature reserves in 1940–2 which clearly illustrated the role of the National Trust in protecting key areas of biological interest. Although many properties were acquired primarily for their amenity, thirty-two fulfilled the role of sanctuaries and provided early experience in tackling the problems of managing both upland and lowland areas for amenity, wildlife and outdoor recreation.[4]

Most of the reserves were obtained through the initiative of individuals, rather than as part of any comprehensive programme of acquisition on the part of the Trust. Wicken Fen was obtained in pieces: N. C. Rothschild gave a small strip of land in 1899, and in 1912 G. H. Verrall, another entomologist, gave 239 acres. Rothschild told a local naturalist, A. H. Evans, to keep a close watch for any further 'desirable acquisitions' which might come onto the market, and he subsequently bought and donated more land to the SPNR which, in turn, the Society presented to the National Trust.[5]

Even when sites were acquired by public subscription, most of the work devolved on individuals. J. R. B. Masefield was almost entirely responsible for obtaining 207 acres of woodland, valley, marsh and reedbeds at Hawksmoor in Staffordshire. The area already contained most of the ninety-five breeding birds in the county, and he hoped the reserve would protect and attract further species. He launched a successful appeal for funds to acquire the land, and collected most of the contributions himself.[6]

As indicated on page 60, the SPNR was formed in 1912 to stimulate the National Trust into acquiring more properties of interest to the naturalist. The National Trust enjoyed special privileges granted by parliament and had greater experience and resources to tackle the various land agency and management problems incurred by any landowner. But there were soon signs of disenchantment. There is no evidence that the Trust used the list of 273 areas proposed by the SPNR as the basis of its acquisition programme: the few new reserves continued to be selected and acquired on a piecemeal basis. Secondly, there was criticism of the standards of management of the Trust properties. As early as 1924, the Council of the RSPB discussed the poor state of some of the sites, but rather reluctantly concluded that this was a matter where it 'could not with propriety intervene'.[7]

This disenchantment had far reaching effects on the SPNR and the nature preservation movement in general. At first, the founders of the SPNR did not intend the Society to own or manage land, but the Society's honorary solicitor advised that its royal charter should grant such powers. Rothschild and the other founder-members were soon grateful for his insistence on this 'technical point' because they were not only concerned at the poor state of some of the Trust's properties, but the National Trust began to refuse custody of some potential reserves.[8]

By his will of 1916, N. C. Rothschild intended to leave his property at Woodwalton Fen to the National Trust, and in 1920 he bought another 'area worthy of protection', Ray Island in Essex. The National Trust was very reluctant to accept either area because they were exclusively of interest to the naturalist, and accordingly Rothschild was obliged to give the two reserves to the SPNR, which later sold Ray Island and used the revenue to finance the management of Woodwalton Fen.[9]

During the inter-war period, the SPNR obtained further sites which the National Trust had rejected owing to their small size and limited interest to non-naturalists. In 1915, for example, botanists discovered a sedge, which they identified as *Carex evoluta*, on a small plot of land in Sharpham Moor, Somerset. This was the first record of the plant in Britain, and A. G. Tansley and several other botanists were so keen to preserve it from destruction that they launched a small appeal for the purchase of the 1.5 acres of moor. The necessary funds were raised by thirty-three donors and, having failed to persuade the National Trust to accept custody, the plot of land was offered to the SPNR, which accepted on the condition that it was not responsible for meeting the cost of any outgoings.[10]

The RSPB was at first equally reluctant to become a landowner, and depended on the simple appointment of watchers. But clearly this was inadequate where damage was likely to be caused by the landowner or occupier, and accordingly the Society was obliged to buy the shooting lease of Brean Down in Somerset in 1912. This was a key ornithological site on the south-west coast, where the raven and peregrine falcon bred, together with sheld-ducks, sand pipers and rock pipits. The county council issued a protective order on the birds and their eggs. In addition to acquiring the shooting rights, the RSPB bought the area of the Old Fort in 1936 in order to prevent the land falling into the hands of an owner who might be hostile to bird protection.[11]

The RSPB was also forced to intervene at Dungeness which had a ternery and was a breeding site of the very rare Kentish plover. In 1896, the Kent County Council obtained an order to designate the area as a sanctuary and the RSPB appointed a watcher. During the 1920s, there was an increasing danger of the more accessible parts being developed for housing, and matters came to a head in 1925 when 1,100 acres of the eastern side of the promontary were offered for sale for £5,500. The Society hurriedly convened a conference of interested parties to discuss ways of raising sufficient funds to purchase the area and then hand it over to the National Trust. It failed to secure sufficient support, and after four months the Society was only able to offer £2,000. This was rejected by the vendor, and the land was later purchased by a building syndicate.[12]

The voluntary movement was at first extremely sceptical of the value of public appeals for funds to acquire and maintain sites. The publicity given to an area by an appeal might encourage the vendor to increase the purchase price and attract attention to the presence of rare plants and animals. The RSPB thought a public appeal for the purchase of Dungeness as a bird sanctuary would be a complete waste of 'money, time and energy'. The Society noted that 'its birds and desolation would not appeal to the British public in the least, but only to a limited number of people who care about fauna and wild places'.[13]

This disdain for appeals was encouraged by the belief that most landowners would give their land or make very generous arrangements for the sale of areas of high amenity or natural history value. But the SPNR and other bodies soon encountered owners who refused, irrespective of the sums and terms offered. In 1914, the Duke of Richmond refused to give or sell 'the remarkable wood of ancient yews at Kingley Bottom' in Sussex.[14] N. C. Rothschild was extremely anxious to secure Meathop Moss in Westmorland on behalf of the SPNR since it was one 'of the most interesting places' in England, where *Erica tetralix* grew in profusion, and *Myrica gale* and *Thelyptris palustris* were present. There was a very rich insect fauna, including the large heath butterfly *Coenonympha tullia*. The Society's honorary solicitor entered into negotiations with the owner in 1916, who died soon afterwards and the entire estate was sold to another person. The Society then began negotiations with the new owner, who refused to sell just the Moss. Eventually, Rothschild had to agree to a lease of twenty-one years at an annual rent of £25 per annum.[15]

The SPNR was generally reluctant to accept land on the basis of a lease or tenancy, especially after its experience with a nature reserve called Swaddiwell Field in the Soke of Peterborough. This was the site of a medieval building-stone quarry, and the grasslands contained several rare plants and animals. Soon after the war, at the behest of Rothschild, the National Trust took an annual tenancy of eight acres of the field: the SPNR paid the rent. In 1923, the owner of the field proposed to sell the land, and Rothschild made plans to buy the reserve in order to ensure its protection. However, he died before the purchase could be made and, since he had made no reference to the site in his will, his executors were unable to stop a local farmer from buying the land. The latter immediately demanded the right to excavate stone: the National Trust, on behalf of the SPNR, refused to grant permission, and the new owner consequently gave the Trust notice to quit within six months.[16]

The voluntary bodies became even more cautious in acquiring land after the experience of the RSPB at Dungeness in the 1930s. Following the debacle of 1925, the Society obtained an area of 253 acres of shingle and grass, called Walkers Outland, in 1931. A year later, R. B. Burrowes acquired a further 271 acres, called the Great Stones, where the Kentish plover nested. This left him in straitened circumstances, and an appeal was launched which contributed £2,350 toward the purchase price of £9,000, and the site was then transferred to the custody of the RSPB. As a condition of sale, the vendor agreed to leave a right of way, which ran along the shore and through the new reserve, as a rough track. However, the vendor soon used the money from the sale of the reserve area to buy further land to the south of the reserve and he straightway broke the covenant and converted the track into a road. This completely ruined the purpose of the reserve. After a protracted legal dispute, the vendor was forced to re-purchase the moribund reserve in 1935 for the original sale price.[17]

There was a widespread reluctance to acquire any land in the vicinity of built-up areas. The prices were considered too high, and the problems of subsequent management too formidable. Local residents would, for example, pick all the wild flowers and take the birds' nests. But a correspondent to the SPNR in 1925 criticised this defeatist attitude: nature reserves were most urgently wanted on the edge of urban areas, in order to preserve the last fragments of vegetation. They would also play an important part in convincing the inhabitants of towns of the benefits of nature preservation, and would help to win both their moral and financial support for further reserves in the same area and further afield.[18]

In view of these practical difficulties of acquiring land, especially in the vicinity of towns, there was an increasing need to secure the goodwill of landowners and the public at large. In this context, Section 34 of the Town and Country Planning Act of 1932 (page 78) was highly significant for it conferred powers on local authorities to enter into voluntary agreements with landowners whereby covenants were specifically drawn up to protect property from building development. Whilst this reduced the value of the land to the owner, it also reduced his liability for death duties. The National Trust obtained almost identical powers to the local authorities under the National Trust Act of 1937: the National Trust for Scotland negotiated its first agreement in 1938 with Sir John Stirling Maxwell for a large part of his Pollok Estate on the outskirts of Glasgow. In 1942, an agreement with restrictive covenants was secured for parts of Fleet Bay in Kirkcudbrightshire whereby all building development was banned, except that required for agricultural purposes. A further agreement for a tract of outstanding coastline was negotiated in 1944, which safeguarded the greater part of the famous West Links of North Berwick.[19]

But these agreements were exceptional, and the voluntary bodies usually had no alternative but to acquire the land which they wished to preserve. In the absence of rich benefactors, they had no option but to launch public appeals for funds, in spite of their distaste for such a method. By the 1930s, the SPNR and RSPB had also witnessed the success of a number of appeals launched by local amenity bodies. The Lynton, Lynmouth and District Association for the Preservation of Local Natural Beauties launched an appeal in 1932 for £8,500 for the purchase of the Valley of the Rocks and Watersmeet on Exmoor. The two owners of the land had agreed to sell the property for that amount, and the Association 'divided' the area of 340 acres into 1,600 numbered plots, which could be purchased by the public for £5 each. Once purchased, all the land would be 'kept in its natural wooded state as a charming, tranquil, health–providing river and wooded walk and retreat—for the *free* use and enjoyment of the nation'. It proved very difficult to raise the necessary funds before the options given by the owners expired, but eventually the target was reached and the Valley was transferred to the National Trust in 1934.[20]

The task of raising funds became increasingly difficult as the world financial climate worsened. Very often, reserves had to be bought in instalments and several schemes would have failed but for the last-minute intervention of a large donor. This was how Selsdon Wood was obtained for £11,000 between 1925 and 1936. The Surrey Committee of the Commons and Footpaths Preservation Committee launched an appeal and later published three well-illustrated brochures on the property. Special articles were written for *The Times* and *Daily News*, and the public were admitted and school visits were arranged to those parts which had been purchased. The appeal was well organised, but nevertheless the venture nearly ended in failure 'owing to the adverse monetary conditions' of the early 1930s. Eventually, the appeal and reserve were rescued by the donations of a small number of benefactors, including the London Parochial Charities.[21]

At first, little help was expected, or indeed received, from local authorities. The voluntary movement tended to regard the authorities with an air of hostility. Ray Lankester accused them in 1914 of trying to turn every open space into 'a London Park', football pitches or golf courses. He recalled how a small marsh above the Leg of Mutton pond on Hampstead Heath had been drained and reclaimed by the local authority, although there was plenty of dry ground for walking on the Heath. As a result, the Sundew *Drosera rotundilfolia* and Bogbean *Menyanthes trifoliata*, which depended on damp conditions, became locally extinct.[22]

Relations between the voluntary bodies and the local councils tended to grow worse owing to the requirements placed on the highway authorities to cut the grass on roadside banks and verges. Throughout the 1920s, the indiscriminate mowing of the verges was widely condemned and, in March 1934, the CPRE approached the County Councils Association and asked if the verges could be left uncut until July or the early autumn each year, and that only the sward and herbs near the road should be cut. In this way, the rich flora of many roads and lanes would be preserved, but the Association dismissed the recommendations as impracticable.[23]

There were many references to the apathy and even hostility of councils toward nature preservation and, in this context, the preservation of Belfairs Great Wood in Essex became a *cause célèbre*. The woodland was zoned under a town planning scheme for residential development, and a group of local people founded an organisation in 1931, called the South Essex Natural History Society, with the object of opposing the destruction of the wood. A sub-committee was set up, named the Southend-on-Sea Nature Reserve Committee, to persuade the local councils to buy the wood and protect it as a nature reserve. At first, the Southend Borough Council and two adjacent rural district councils were sympathetic and agreed to buy part of the woods. It was widely assumed that the Borough Council would contribute the greater part of the purchase money since it had a much higher rateable income. However, the Borough refused to make a higher contribution since the woods happened to be just outside the Borough boundary, and accordingly the two other councils withdrew their offers of support.

The Southend-on-Sea Nature Reserve Committee tried to force the hand of the Borough Council by launching an appeal for £1,000 toward the cost of purchase, and by organising a petition which called upon the authorities to save the wood. Over 2,000 local residents and ratepayers signed the petition, which made the petition the largest in the history of the Borough. Finally, in 1938, the Council relented and agreed to purchase 40.5 acres of woodland as a nature reserve on the condition that the Reserve Committee succeeded in raising £1,000. The SPNR gave £100 and eventually the target was reached.[24]

Naturalists were quick to point out that the remaining 112 acres of woodland remained unprotected, although they were 'in many respects the most interesting and valuable portion'. Soon after the war, the Borough Council decided to buy a further fifty-two acres. The Essex County Council contributed £1,000 and the SPNR and South Essex Natural History Society gave £100 each. The enlarged area greatly improved the value of the entire reserve.[25]

Gradually, the local authorities recognised the growing public interest in wildlife and nature reserves, and gave limited support. In 1927, an appeal was made for the purchase of 118 acres of Lesness Abbey Woods in Kent. The woodland had been closely studied by St John Marriott, and the discovery of deposits of Blackheath shell-beds on the site aroused considerable interest. Seventy-five acres were sold for development, but local naturalists obtained an option on the remainder. The Woolwich Borough Council agreed to contribute to the purchase fund and established a sub-committee of its town planning committee to organise an appeal and enlist the aid of the Kent County Council and local urban district councils. Eventually, all the authorities contributed, and the Borough Council raised the equivalent of a one penny rate. The London County Council, which gave the bulk of the purchase money, formally took over the reserve in 1931.[26]

The inventory of reserves drawn up by the SPNR and NRIC in 1940–2, although very incomplete, identified five sites actually owned by local authorities, namely The Camp at Little Kimble in Buckinghamshire, Belfairs Great Wood in Essex, Tile Hill in Coventry, the bird sanctuary at Echo Pit near Guildford, and the arboretum at Dinsmore Hill in Herefordshire.[27] The inventory also identified two very small reserves owned by public schools. An area of 2.5 acres of water-meadows on the River Itchen was turned into a sanctuary by Winchester College in 1936. Irrigation ceased, cattle were excluded, and bushes and trees were planted as cover for birds and insects. Eton College owned a sanctuary of similar size within part of an old osier bed on the River Thames, rich in warblers, especially the sedge and reed warbler. The area of marsh, willow and hawthorn was enclosed by a chestnut fence, a pond was excavated, shrubs were planted, and nesting-boxes installed.[28]

Various statutory bodies were also persuaded to manage part of their property as reserves. The London Natural History Society drew attention to the potential value of the Walthamstow reservoirs of the

Metropolitan Water Board as bird sanctuaries. At first, the Board refused to stop private shooting parties visiting the reservoirs on Saturday afternoons in the open season in case too many birds fouled the water. The RSPB circulated every member of the Board in 1923 and joined the Selborne Society in a deputation. Soon afterward, it was announced that all shooting was to end and the reservoirs became a bird sanctuary.[29]

Most commentators distinguished a special kind of reserve, the town sanctuary, created and administered by the Crown or urban authorities. In his book *Birds in London*, published in 1898, W. H. Hudson called upon urban authorities to convert part of their parks to bird sanctuaries, islands of refuge in the otherwise hostile environment of the city. Not surprisingly, the Office of Works and the larger city councils were the first to become interested in the concept. The former was responsible for managing the Royal Parks and, in 1922, Howard Russell persuaded the secretary to the Office, Sir Lionel Earle, to raise the question of bird sanctuaries in London with the newly appointed First Commissioner, Lord Crawford. Russell had read Hudson's book, and 'was afraid that unless some protection and encouragement were created for the birds they would gradually disappear'. Lord Crawford was sympathetic to the idea and appointed an advisory committee of experts to recommend where sanctuaries should be established.[30]

Whilst no part of the Royal Parks could be abandoned to grow wild, the advisory committee recommended that every opportunity should be taken to exploit the areas which were already enclosed. These should be left 'untidy' and no one should be allowed within them, except bird experts and observers. Two small sanctuaries were soon established in Hyde Park and another in Kensington Gardens, on the small Round Pond where the gadwall nested and the heron and kingfishers were seen. The cost of turning these areas into sanctuaries was small: barricades were erected against cats, and some extra covert was planted.

Perhaps the London park with the greatest potential was Richmond Park, where two very large sanctuaries of forty acres each were set aside. The clearance of dense undergrowth soon encouraged warblers and other species, and tracts of rhododendron were replaced by thorns, brambles and other native undergrowth. The Office of Works took steps to encourage water-birds: there was already a series of artificial islets, covered with vegetation, moored on the Pen Ponds, which provided nesting grounds for coot, moorhen and tufted duck.

In addition to these formal nature reserves, whether located in remote areas or towns, there were extensive tracts of land which were regarded by many as 'undeclared nature reserves'. These included the embankments and cuttings of railway lines, and in 1932 the RSPB appealed to the various railway companies to delay the cutting or burning of grass until the breeding season was over. These refuges were particularly valuable where changes in agriculture or forestry, and building or industrial development, had displaced wildlife on neighbouring land.[31]

Likewise, interest was shown in derelict land where wildlife could flourish comparatively undisturbed. In 1932 the *Lancashire Daily Post* drew attention to the value of disused brickworks and other derelict sites. In one example, abandoned during the First World War, the 'holes became pools, rushes appeared among abandoned tracks and rusting rails; grass tried to hide the desolation; and gradually there came to nest, amid the waste, Lapwings, Redshanks, Snipe, Waterhens, Wild Duck, Meadow Pipits, Reed Buntings, Wagtails Pied and Yellow, and Skylarks'.[32]

The Addison Committee drew attention in 1931 to the potential value of commonlands for amenity, wildlife and outdoor recreation, and indeed the Norfolk Naturalists' Trust (page 226) had bought three cottages in the village of Lakenheath with the express intention of securing three of the thirty common rights on Lakenheath Warren, and thereby preventing any changes in the management of the common land which might harm the wildlife of the area.[33]

The Commons, Open Spaces and Footpaths Preservation Society estimated that there were up to 1,750,000 acres of common land in England and Wales, although their function and value varied enormously. About four-fifths were rural commons in remote parts of upland Britain, which could not be enclosed without the sanction of the Ministry of Agriculture. This was very rarely given. Many commons in lowland England were subject to special Acts of Parliament and, as in the case of Epping Forest and Burnham Beeches, they were administered by Boards of Conservators. The National Trust owned some commons, including Hindhead Common in Surrey and Minchinhampton Common in Gloucestershire. Most of the common land in the Metropolitan Police District was regulated as open spaces under an Act of 1866. Banstead Common in Surrey and St Paul Crays Common in Kent fell within this category.

The Addison Committee recommended that all commons should be surveyed and their type of administration recorded. This would prepare the way for a national parks authority or some other body to acquire common land or regulate its use in the national interest. This proposal received a great deal of support in a debate in the House of Commons in 1936, but the Ministry of Agriculture claimed the cost of a survey would be out of all proportion to the consequent benefits. The task would have to be undertaken by the county councils and financed by the rates. The Ministry warned that lords of the manor, landowners and commoners would object to the heavy legal fees entailed in defending their respective rights.[34]

Many of the areas recommended for protection were requisitioned by the military authorities during the Second World War. The West Wales Field Society, for example, protested over the use of Grassholm as a practice bombing range, which threatened a gannetry of over 12,000 birds. During a visit in 1945, J. S. Huxley, John Buxton, R. M. Lockley and E. M. Nicholson discovered numerous bomb craters and the corpses of over a hundred freshly-killed gannets.[35] The tracts of thinly populated countryside, marginal to cultivation, were not only outstanding for their amenity and wildlife but also for military use. Over half of the Isle of Purbeck, a proposed scientific area, was used for battle training. There were especially fears that the tanks, guns and infantry movements would ruin the wildlife interest of the proposed national nature reserve between Studland Bay and the Arne peninsula.[36]

Most of the requisitioned land remained in military hands long after the war ended. The War Office promised not to do anything 'which can reasonably be regarded as objectionable'.[37] But these assurances did little to allay anxiety on the part of naturalists. An anti-tank gun range, for example, was located between the important bird sanctuaries of Ross Links, the Snook and Holy Island in Northumberland. There were fears that the sound of gunfire would disturb the migratory and nesting birds, and that the heavy-wheeled traffic would damage the sands and flats, leading to the extinction of already rare and extremely localised plants. In common with all requisitioned land, the future military use of the area was reviewed in the late 1940s and, at an enquiry, the Bishop of Newcastle and the county natural history society fiercely opposed the retention of the site by the military. But they lost their case, largely because it was the most suitable anti-tank gun range in Britain. The revival of the Territorial Services in late 1946 made it essential that large training areas were retained in England, within easy reach of men living in the major urban centres.[38]

In any case, the military authorities claimed that gunfire and military training caused very little disturbance to wildlife. Many ranges were only used in summer, after the breeding season, and most species soon became accustomed to the noise and disturbance. Admittedly, tanks seriously damaged the vegetation, but otherwise military use was quite compatible with nature preservation. It caused far less destruction than building or industrial development, cultivation or afforestation.

Rather begrudgingly, the voluntary bodies came to accept this view. Herbert Smith, on behalf of the SPNR, commented that military training might after all be a 'blessing in disguise': the Army seemed to cause far less damage than unrestricted public access.

The Management of People on Reserves

Once the reserve had been acquired, the next task was to appoint a committee or individual person to warden the site. There would have been no difficulty in securing wardens if the voluntary bodies had been able to offer a wage. The following letter was the first application for the post of warden to be received by the SPNR. The applicant wrote in 1914:

> . . . my business is that of a Grocer's Assistant. I am deeply interested in, and have a love of wild life and natural science. I haven't the means or the time to help in the preservation of our beautiful country from the hands of the despoiler. If however I can be employed as a caretaker to a Wild Life Sanctuary, I should be pleased if you would consider me as an applicant for such a post.
>
> The necessity to work for my existence has prevented me from doing anything for the benefit of posterity which has been my dream from youth to middle life.
>
> Birds, animals, trees and flowers have been my friends in all my spare moments for half a life time, and although caged animals at the Zoo and stuffed specimens in our museums are helpful for the student they do not supply the longing of a natural naturalist. If you are able to help me to help in your movement I shall be very grateful.[39]

Unfortunately, the voluntary bodies found it impossible to pay their wardens a living wage, and those employed by the SPNR received only annual honoraria. At Meathop Moss, the Society engaged the local gamekeeper as warden of the reserve, but it was soon discovered that he spent most of the critical months of June and July rearing pheasants. He was subsequently replaced by the owner of a local café. On the Calf of Man, the National Trust allowed the warden of the reserve to run a small farm. About £300 was spent in 1928 in stocking the holding and repairing the farm buildings.[40]

There seemed no alternative but to exclude the public 'with its myriad feet' from any reserve where scarce flowers and shy birds were being preserved. Anthony Collett remarked in 1932 that there was always a temptation to pick flowers or throw stones at the squirrels and birds, in addition to the 'involuntary disturbance and defacement' caused by large numbers of visitors. In his words, 'even on the large expanse of Hampstead Heath the thickets are trampled bare and hollow, and few, if any, of the warblers which come in early summer succeed in nesting. Epping Forest, though so wild to the eye, is all but gutted of small wild life.'[41]

Some reserves were established with the prime objective of keeping the public out. This led to fears that the public would come to regard nature reserves as just another form of game preserve, and watchers or wardens as another kind of gamekeeper. C. S. Elton warned against 'a new feudal aristocracy of the scientific age'. The grounds must not become the secret haunt of a small band of intellectuals: they should remain open to scientists and students, local residents and anyone interested in nature study.[42]

The dilemma over public access was most clearly seen where a reserve had been acquired through public subscription, and the subscribers naturally wanted to see the results of their beneficence. Accordingly, a compromise had to be found. The SPNR recommended the sub-division of most reserves into two parts, one of which would be 'an inviolable inner sanctuary' where the public would be excluded, especially in nesting time and when the wild flowers were in bloom. R. B. Burrowes recommended the layout of a series of pathways across each site so that visitors could see each part of the reserve without actually disturbing the wildlife. The Huxley Committee sup-ported this kind of approach, and suggested the publication of short, simple handbooks, giving a general account of the scientific value of each reserve. They should be easy to read, attractive and cheap to buy.[43]

Usually a permit was required before entering a reserve, and the secretary of the SPNR, Herbert Smith, recommended that the rules governing their issue should at first be very strict, for it was easier to relax rather than tighten up the rules at a later date. Nevertheless, C. S. Elton was critical of the arbitrary way in which permits were issued. No one had any idea how many people could visit a reserve before causing damage to the various forms of wildlife. Was it, for example, possible to grant one permit for every ten acres of land, and thereby allow 200 visitors to visit a reserve of 2,000 acres in a year? Could this figure be supplemented by visits of small parties of school children and naturalists, conducted round the reserve by a warden?[44]

The watchers or wardens spent most of their time excluding visitors without a permit. The RSPB found that permits were no deterrent to the determined collector or casual visitor. Soon after the Society took over Brean Down, a young peregrine falcon was taken from its nest. Accounts of the theft vary, but according to one version the warden discovered where the bird was hidden, and motored with the police to a village six miles away. The bird was recovered and the warden, 'with some difficulty and exertion placed it once more under the care of the mother falcon: she, after a moment or two of doubt, recognised and joyfully fed her nestling'.[45]

The SPNR encountered great difficulties in preventing flowers being picked on its more accessible reserves. During the 1930s and Second World War, many of the grasslands containing fritillaries and cowslips were ploughed up and people who had previously picked these flowers every year converged in greater numbers on the few remaining old grasslands. The problem was especially serious on the fritillary meadow at Mickfield in Suffolk where the warden erected a poster in 1943 which announced 'Private Reserve. Fritillary and all wild flowers strictly preserved.' He inserted a notice in the *East Anglian Daily News* in April 1952 warning that proceedings would be taken against anyone 'damaging or taking roots, bulbs, flowers, trees, shrubs, wildbirds, or their eggs'. This had little effect, however, on 'local hooligans'.[46]

In 1938, the SPNR asked its honorary solicitors what should be done when a warden reported a trespasser. The solicitor observed 'there is no really effective method of excluding trespassers' except where they are in pursuit of game. They are not compelled to give a name and address to the warden, but if they did so the Society was advised to write and 'point out that the property is part of the Society's reserve, explain why it is so desirable to exclude trespassers and request that the addressee will in future have regard to the Society's wishes'. The solicitor warned against threatening legal proceedings unless a second 'offence' was committed.[47] He concluded:

> . . . a notice in the current form 'Trespassers will be prosecuted' which has properly been described as a 'wooden lie' usually has no deterrent effect. Possibly the public might be more impressed by a notice which was in the form of a request and explained why trespassing was undesirable.

The voluntary bodies found it especially difficult to regulate the activities of those people who had traditionally visited the grounds of the reserves. The National Trust found it very hard to control the activities of wildfowlers who had visited Blakeney Point for many years. It tried to regulate numbers by issuing permits, but this was difficult to enforce since the reserve was so extensive and the warden could not catch every 'unlicenced sportsman'. In addition, the Trust could not stop anyone shooting the birds below high tide mark although this caused almost as much damage to the birds as shooting on the reserve itself. At Meathop Moss, the SPNR came near to despair in trying to eradicate the traditional practice of collecting gulls' eggs. Local people regarded gulls as vermin and farmers traditionally fed the eggs to cattle and chicken. The Society seriously considered terminating the lease on the reserve in 1927 and 1934 because its scientific value was jeopardised by trespassers.[48]

The problem of controlling public access became so serious at Brean Down that the RSPB decided to abandon the reserve in 1950. The Down was overrun with trippers from May until September, and the warden found it impossible to control them. The nests of the peregrine falcon were on an overhanging cliff and consequently safe from collectors: the raven had reared its young before the trippers arrived in large numbers. The Society consequently decided to hand the land over to Weston-super-Mare, which had promised to maintain existing conditions and protect the birds wherever practical.[49]

The Management of Wildlife on Reserves

The voluntary bodies had to pay honoraria to some of their wardens and meet the burden of drainage rates and road charges. They had to discharge the normal responsibilities of landowners in keeping the boundary hedges and ditches in good order. But they were less prepared for the heavy cost of conserving the wildlife on the reserves, whether by manipulating plant succession, water regimes, or by the predator–prey relationships. The need for managing reserves was highlighted by the Woodwalton Fen nature reserve owned by the SPNR. Together with the other reserves of the SPNR and RSPB, it provided a valuable body of experience, which was drawn upon by the various committees of enquiry which sat during the 1940s and drew up plans for a series of national nature reserves and an official body to administer them.

At first, the National Trust and SPNR believed the sale of such produce as reeds and coppicewood from the reserves would help to cover costs. Consequently, the donor of Wicken Sedge Fen in 1912 was not required to endow his gift, since the National Trust expected the sale of sedge and litter for animal bedding to amply offset the cost of looking after the water-courses and vegetation. However, the demand for sedge and litter declined in the 1920s, and prices slumped. Meanwhile, the cost of labour rose and the voluntary bodies discovered that the reserves needed far more attention and investment than they had expected. By 1928, the National Trust was forced to launch an appeal for funds to endow Wicken Fen.[50]

In the light of this experience, the National Trust refused to accept any liability for the outgoings and costs of management of further gifts of land and, for this reason, it initially refused the gift of Lapwing Fen until the donors had established an endowment. Very often this stipulation proved a formidable obstacle in safeguarding areas from destruction. During the 1930s, about £11,000 was raised by public subscription for the purchase and preservation of Selsdon Woods in Surrey (page 177). The Trust, however, refused to accept the woodland until further money had been raised for an endowment fund. There ensued a long period of crisis which was only resolved when the Corporation of Croydon, and the urban district councils of Coulsdon and Purley, agreed to provide the necessary funds on the condition that they held the woods on a long lease. This was agreed, and a management committee was formed: two-thirds of its members represented the local authorities, and the remainder were nominated by the National Trust.[51]

The SPNR was even more cautious in accepting gifts of land since the Society was designed to promote rather than own reserves. It accepted Sharpham Moor Plot in Somerset only on the condition that the donors met the full cost of liabilities, otherwise the Society reserved the right to sell the land. The Executive Committee even refused the gift of Woodwalton Fen from N. C. Rothschild until he had included with the gift the sum of £3,000 of five per cent War Loan Stock as an endowment. For a time, the revenue from this investment covered costs, but soon the Society faced a crisis. The cost of drainage rates and management increased and exceeded income. The Society had to draw on its general fund in order to supplement the endowment.[52]

In many cases, the traditional use and management of the sites ceased once they had become nature reserves. In some cases, this was intentional. James Ritchie told the Addison Committee in 1929, for example, that sheep and goats should be removed from any protected sites in the Highlands in order to restore the vegetation to its former, natural condition.[53]

But this *laissez-faire* policy soon led to the invasion of scrub and the elimination of those species which had been the object of preserving the sites. This was demonstrated by changes in the plant communities on Woodwalton Fen. During the 1880s, most of the site was grazed or mown for hay, a small part was arable, and the remainder was 'in a relatively primitive condition, having only been used for peat cutting, which did not seriously interfere with the vegetation'. Indeed, A. J. Wilmott noted how the rare and distinctive *Viola stagnina* flourished on the most recently worked peat excavations, where there was less competition from other species. The arable areas fell out of cultivation in the late nineteenth century and were colonised by fen plants, so that by 1905 the site was comprised of four communities, namely:

   i) a flourishing reed bed or swamp;
  ii) marsh grasslands;

iii) patches of scrub or carr, largely composed of sallow;
iv) mixed sedge fen of *Cladium mariscus* and a scatter of reeds and other plants.

The vegetation of types (i) to (iii) was largely secondary in character, made up of species which had spread from type (iv) and from the dense network of water courses.

Striking changes took place in the distribution of these communities between 1906 and 1915, following the cessation of grazing, hay-making and peat-cutting. Almost all the marsh grasslands and mixed sedge were transformed into reed swamp. From 1915 onwards, the reed swamp was in turn invaded by sallow carr so that by 1931 the greater part of the reserve was occupied by 'dense impenetrable thickets of sallow bushes', with an undergrowth of *Calystegia sepium*. In a report, J. C. F. Fryer and H. M. Edelsten remarked that a nature reserve covered by bushes hardly justified the name 'reserve'; clearly the SPNR had to arrest and reverse these harmful changes.

Although marsh vegetation was naturally unstable, Fryer and Edelsten were alarmed at the rapidity of the changes which they attributed to the break down of drainage on the reserve. The area was drained by dykes which had been regularly cleared of silt and vegetation when the land was cultivated, grazed, mown and exploited for peat. This had the effect of maintaining a high and relatively stable water table which benefited the species of the mixed sedge and marsh grassland. But the dykes soon fell into neglect once these activities ceased and by the 1930s most were blocked. This caused a greater fluctuation in water levels, promoting periods of severe flooding and drought which encouraged the rapid conquest of the reserve by sallow carr.[54]

There was also little active management on the reserve at Meathop Moss in Westmorland, and in 1945 a correspondent to the SPNR complained:

> ... after July it is seldom possible to get on to the Moss. The paths are quite overgrown—in some cases with bracken 7 or 8 feet high. Many drains and ditches are grown over and need clearing. Cotton grass in some places is swamping everything: one part of nearly 40 acres which is a gullery is quite covered with it. The birches and conifers which formed a ring round the place have seeded for years and are spreading all over, largely altering the nature of the flora.

The SPNR learnt of a similarly grim situation at Sharpham Moor Plot in Somerset. Although a local management committee had been established in the early 1920s for the reserve, it had never functioned and following the death of the only active member in 1940 no further management work was undertaken. By 1948, the site was so overgrown with tall carr, and the prospect of securing anyone to help with management work was so bleak, that the Executive Committee of the SPNR considered selling the reserve. A. G. Tansley supported this course of action, but the Executive Committee finally decided to keep the site for a few more years since no expenditure was incurred.[55]

Several of the National Trust properties were faced with the same kind of crisis. C. P. Castell described in 1947 the plight of Bookham Common, Surrey, which had been left to Nature for more than twenty years. He wrote:

> . . . two large ponds were formerly a great attraction, but neglect of the embankments has lowered the water level and, to make matters worse, the ditches which drained into them are now thoroughly blocked by vegetation and mud. Horsetail and bur-reed have spread from the margins across the ponds still further reducing the volume of water. Soon, patches of marshy ground will be all that is left to mark the sites of the ponds. The many acres of marshy open grassland are now only occasionally grazed by cattle and an army of hawthorns is advancing across the area from the adjacent woodland. In another more heathy area, bracken and birches are fast taking possession. In the woods, groves of young oaks have sprung up, choking one another and casting such dense shade that little can live under them.[56]

In its memorandum of 1944, the British Ecological Society issued an urgent warning: most plant and animal communities have evolved because man had prevented natural succession taking place. They owed their existence to such practices as grazing, burning, mowing, coppicing or selective felling, and if these forms of management ceased, natural succession would again take place, and the species and their communities would disappear.[57]

Management was especially important for the conservation of invertebrate fauna. J. C. F. Fryer and H. M. Edelsten described in 1941 how a change from short to long grass could bring striking changes in the insect life of a pasture. The owners of a fen or marshland reserve should maintain full control over the water regime. A moorland reserve had to be kept free from bracken. A shifting form of cultivation had to be continued or re-introduced on the grass-heaths of the Breckland in order to sustain their entomological interest. They summarised how:

> . . . the characteristic fauna reaches its highest development on land which has been in temporary agricultural use and has then

been allowed to revert. This system of husbandry was rather general in the past: three or four crops being taken on a piece of breckland, then the latter was allowed to fall out of cultivation for a period. Provision for something of this sort in a reserve is desirable.[58]

There was, of course, no single management programme that could be imposed on all reserves—each site had to be managed according to the declared objectives of the reserve and the character of the soil, drainage and wildlife communities. For many local committees, this was a completely new field of work. The botanical sub-committee of the Cotteswold Naturalists' Field Club was made responsible for the management of Badgeworth Marsh: previously it had been solely concerned with the preparation of a new county flora.[59]

It was often difficult to find a management plan which would satisfy all the parties that had contributed to the purchase of the site. Several local authorities had played a major role in acquiring Belfairs Great Wood in Essex, and they wanted to open the area to the public, create a playground, meandering paths, and plant some areas with exotic trees. Naturalists, on the other hand, wanted to continue the traditional coppicing cycle and limit public access. The management committee eventually found a compromise whereby the site of forty acres was subdivided into eight compartments, which were to be cut on a six-year rotational basis, and a further area was to be set aside as a playground for the children.[60]

There was sometimes a conflict in objectives among the naturalists. Mickfield Meadow in Suffolk was acquired in 1938 in order to protect the fritillary (page 57), and the warden reported that there were between 800 and 1,000 pink and full purple flowers, seventeen pure white, and two white and purple flowers in bloom in April 1944. The warden also tried to establish a bird sanctuary on the meadow and planted various shrubs and saplings for this purpose. He was successful, and soon the number of birds rose and the bushes spread. But there were soon complaints of the pigeons and other birds damaging the plants, and of the bushes invading and displacing the grasslands containing the fritillaries. Clearly, the owner of the site, the SPNR, had to decide between wild plants and birds. J. S. L. Gilmour and S. M. Walters made an inspection of the meadow in 1953 and recommended that the scrub should be removed and the hedgerows cut down so as to improve the quality of the pasture and discourage the birds. In this way, the fritillaries could be conserved.[61]

There was a great deal of controversy as to the amount of protection that should be given to the birds within reserves. L. R. W. Loyd criticised the RSPB for protecting all the birds on Lundy Island, which had resulted in a phenomenal increase in the number of herring gulls. These birds not only damaged the crops on the mainland but also destroyed the eggs of the kittiwakes, guillemots and razorbills, which were already endangered by oil pollution. Loyd warned that this form of indiscriminate bird protection would accelerate the decline and possible extinction of such species.[62]

On the other hand, E. M. Nicholson was critical of those who advocated the eradication of hawks, owls and gulls on account of the damage they inflicted on less common and often smaller birds. Nicholson regarded these ornithologists as being little better than game-keepers: from a hawk's point of view, there would be no difference being shot by a gamekeeper than by a watcher on a sanctuary. Although hawks and gulls might kill other birds or take their eggs, they were hardly 'feathered robbers'. After all, 'a jay which lives on sucked eggs is no more a robber than a swallow or a spider-hunting wren is a murderer'. Each played a crucial role: the hawks, and to a lesser extent the owls, weeded out the unfit and weakling adolescents. Crows and gulls destroyed the degenerate and the unguarded or badly concealed nests, to the benefit of the entire bird population.[63]

Whilst the RSPB supported this view, it was forced to take exceptional steps on Havergate Island in Suffolk during the late 1940s, when the avocet *Avosetta recurvirostra* once again began to establish a breeding colony. The birds were seriously disturbed by large numbers of rats and carrion crows, and, after a long debate, the Council of the Society decided to intervene: the rats were eradicated, and the crow population was severely reduced.[64]

Many landowners and farmers complained that the reserves were becoming nurseries of weeds, pests and diseases, and the various reserve management committees had to go to great lengths to refute these allegations. During the 1920s, the local fishermen accused the National Trust of protecting excessive numbers of terns at Blakeney Point which damaged the fishing of that part of the Norfolk coast. The Trust asked the SPNR for help in investigating the complaints, and a watcher was employed for several years, who concluded that the birds caused no damage whatever to the local fishing.[65]

Most voluntary bodies found it easier to win the confidence of their neighbours if the reserves were managed in a positive manner, with the periodic clearance of scrub and roding of ditches and drains. The control of rabbits and wood pigeons was essential. This did not conflict with the scientific purpose of the reserves: the Huxley Committee emphasised that reserves should contain a balanced population. They should be managed as rigorously as the best farmland. The reserves would fail if one species became so abundant and dominant that it even caused damage to crops on neighbouring farmland.[66]

Gradually, the SPNR and other voluntary bodies adopted a more active management programme. In their report of 1931, J. C. F. Fryer and H. M. Edelsten recommended the preservation of four types of community at Woodwalton Fen, namely a mixed sedge, marsh grasslands, reed swamp and a small area of sallow carr. Such diversity would benefit the rare and distinctive fenland flora and fauna. To achieve this end, most of the carr had to be cut down and the dykes of the reserve cleared of silt and vegetation. There were also plans to excavate a mere or small pond on the reserve in order further to increase the diversity of the habitat, but this ambition was not realised for many years.[67]

Wherever possible, the management work was intended both to preserve and to enhance wildlife. The RSPB reserve on Dungeness included quarries where blue flints had been dug from the shingle for sale to the Staffordshire Potteries. At one time, 5,000 tons of shingle were excavated in one year, and the extensive pits soon became flooded. A local correspondent reported in 1925 how snow buntings visited the site in winter, and how water rail, icterine warblers and firecrests, together with other small migrants, had frequented the tracts covered by willow bushes. Many of the bushes had been cut down for firewood. The RSPB proposed digging further pits to encourage bird life, and planned to plant more gorse, blackthorn and bramble, variegated with willow and reeds, as covert. This would not only extend the feeding, breeding and nesting grounds, but the sale of blue flints would provide a valuable source of revenue.[68]

There were many discussions as to whether species should be introduced to reserves, especially where the plants and animals had become extinct. In 1919, G. C. Druce discussed the feasibility of such an exercise with a party of foreign botanists visiting Woodwalton Fen. During the 1920s, *Peucedanum palustre* was introduced from Wicken Fen, *Cicuta virosa* from the Norfolk Broads, *Sonchus palustris* from near Oxford, *Senecio paludosus* from near Also Dabas, Hungary, and *Senecio saracenicus* from Wilstone, near Tring, in Hertfordshire.[69]

The SPNR allowed the Committee for the Protection of British Lepidoptera (page 52) to re-introduce the large copper butterfly in 1927 to part of Woodwalton Fen. The new stock *Lycaena dispar* Haw *Batavus* was almost indistinguishable from the *Lycaena dispar* Haw which became extinct in the Huntingdonshire fens during the mid-nineteenth century. Experiments were undertaken to discover the most suitable habitat for the new breeding stock: during the winter of 1926–7, the marsh grasslands were cleared of sallow and, between 1927 and 1930, the grassland was half, or summer cut, whereby the upper half of the herbage was 'hooked off' so as to check reed growth. In 1931, alternate strips were mown down, and from 1932 the field was subdivided into twenty-one sections, separated by shelter belts of reed and sallow, which were called hedges. The food plant *Rumex hydrolapathum* was planted and the trials were considered successful, although the number of butterflies was reduced by larval parasites.[70]

These experiments allowed the SPNR to present nature preservation in a more positive and constructive light, rather than as simply an attempt to preserve the *status quo*. But they were extremely expensive and doubts were soon expressed as to the wisdom of spending large sums of money in trying to arrest natural succession. In 1928, Mrs Rothschild asked whether the expense of establishing food plants for the large copper butterfly could be justified when it was clear that rank vegetation would soon overwhelm the food plants.[71]

Natural succession was not the only problem encountered on reserves. The gannet colony on Grassholm was threatened in June 1930 by a fire started by picnickers. The grass fire approached the nesting birds, and devastation might have ensued if a small party of fire-fighters had not been joined by sailors who fortuitously happened to be in the area. Meathop Moss was often threatened by peat-fires, started on the adjacent peat-workings and places frequented by the general public. Fire swept through the only locality of *Plejobus argus* in 1947, and about fifteen acres of the reserve were burnt in May 1940. A correspondent in 1945 recorded how cotton grass invaded the burnt areas, which were characteristically inhabited by fewer native species.[72]

The SPNR and other bodies discovered that it was not enough to own a site and pursue an adequate management policy: it also had to guard against harmful external influences. During the 1930s, the drainage board and neighbouring farmers improved the outfall of watercourses draining Woodwalton Fen, causing the water levels on the reserve to fall dramatically, thereby affecting the plants and animals characteristic of damp conditions. The cost of maintaining and restoring the water levels was prohibitively high, but a 'modest though useful programme was possible for £200'. In 1934, a dam was built across Colemans Drain and in 1935 a Blackstone portable pump was installed in order to help maintain levels.[73]

These events highlighted the need to make continuous and adequate records of changes on each reserve. The RSPB encouraged its watchers to keep day-to-day diaries of their observations, and surveys were mounted of those plant and animal communities which might be displaced. In 1949, Norman Birkett warned in the *Entomologist's Magazine*:

> ... at the present time the extensive and unique mosslands of North Lancashire and South Westmorland are suffering severely from the inroads of peat-cutters. These activities completely destroy the peculiar fauna and flora of the areas concerned. It may not be

long before the special characteristics of those areas follow the fenlands of East Anglia into extinction. Before this happens, if it unhappily should, a full record of the fauna and flora of the areas is desirable.

F. Balfour-Browne shared Birkett's pessimism, and drew attention to the decline in the wildlife interest of Wicken Fen since the days when the area was first studied. He appealed to the SPNR to make a detailed survey of Woodwalton Fen before a similar decline occurred as a result of scrub invasion and improvements to drainage. The Society accordingly engaged a botanist in the summer of 1939 to make a detailed survey of the reserve, but unfortunately little had been accomplished before the surveyor was recalled to the navy for war service. No further progress was possible until the early 1950s when M. E. D. Poore undertook a detailed ecological survey of Woodwalton Fen.[74]

Such surveys provided both a record of contemporary wildlife and also data on the establishment and behaviour of animals and plants, which were highly relevant when drawing up management programmes. The RSPB, for example, admitted that it knew very little about the habits of the Cornish chough. Although the birds had been carefully watched, 'it must be admitted that the increase is very slight and out of all proportion to the number of young hatched out annually. . . . Perhaps the well-known quarrelsomeness of the chough, especially during the breeding season, coupled with its excessive fastidiousness in the selection of a breeding site, may account for a good deal.' Botanists at Badgeworth Marsh in Gloucestershire were similarly puzzled by the behaviour of the snakes-tongue buttercup which flowered in comparatively few years. It was particularly abundant in 1930 and 1933, but only two plants bloomed in 1931 and one plant in 1932. There was need to record the incidence of flowering each year, so that the pattern could be related to any changes in physiographic or biotic conditions.[75]

The Huxley Committee, in its report of 1947, underlined the need to understand the behaviour of individual species and communities, otherwise reserves would fail in their objectives. The Committee observed, 'most changes in nature are slow, insidious and not readily detectable; and they are often irreversible. A slowly dropping water-table; a change in the balance of power between small organisms the very existence of which is unknown except to a few; these are potent factors in the destruction of the country'. According to C. S. Elton, a member of the Committee, ecological surveys were at the core of all management programmes. They had to be undertaken at three levels, by the various university departments, the scientists in charge of the individual reserves, and by the wardens of those reserves. Whilst the warden 'should be firmly protected against too much paper work', he had a duty to keep weather records, phenological records of selected species, and a daily log book of other observations.[76]

The practical value, and yet heavy investment in labour and resources required, in making continuous surveys of wildlife communities was demonstrated by a project mounted on the estate of the University of Oxford, at Wytham Woods in Berkshire. The estate of about 1,000 acres was bounded on two sides by the River Thames and comprised 'quite an ordinary representative bit of English Midlands', which had been 'only moderately spoiled' by modern farming and forestry. About 220 acres of woodland, limestone grassland, marsh and stream course were set aside from ordinary estate management and managed as a series of scientific reserves. The area had been long studied by Oxford naturalists, but detailed surveys of the Woods did not begin until 1942, when members of various university departments and students from Britain and overseas began to make intensive field studies, resulting in the publication of about 400 scientific papers by 1975.

In 1945, C. S. Elton organised an ecological survey in the Bureau of Animal Population of the Department of Zoological Field Studies. The survey sought to channel the results of all the studies made of Wytham Woods into one clearing house, and to carry out field work. The large body of information which accrued over the first twenty years formed the basis of a book, *The Pattern of Animal Communities*, which was published by Elton in 1966. In this book, Elton described how the first ten years of the survey concentrated on devising practical methods of handling the enormous amount of data derived from the individual, and often disparate, field investigations in order to meet worthwhile objectives and secure a synoptic view of the communities and ecosystems. During the second ten years, these methods were used as a means to understanding the components of the ecosystem, including the open ground and meadow, scrubland and hedgerows, and the forest canopy.[77]

Beside providing a blueprint or plan for the organisation of wildlife communities on Wytham Hill, the survey was relevant to the establishment of reserves elsewhere, demonstrating how continuous observations and systematic record-keeping could provide a more accurate, detailed and comprehensive insight into 'the sharing of matter and energy between species, and their movements through consumer layers and habitat components, from the living and dead resources, by day and night and by season'. Such knowledge would form the basis for effective management plans wherever nature conservation was the first priority of land ownership.

Chapter Eight

The Conservation of Nature

At first, everything was concentrated on preserving rare or distinctive plants and animals by means of legislation, supported by publicity campaigns. With the development of ecology as a science, the overriding need to protect the habitat of the individual species became more apparent. At the same time, there was growing concern over the increasing rate of destruction of the habitat through changes in land use and management. This fear encouraged the establishment of more nature reserves, and during the 1940s proposals were made for series of national nature (or habitat) reserves.

Although the owners of the reserves knew they would have to grapple with the normal problems of estate management, they did not at first appreciate the difficulties of managing the wildlife communities. They did not realise that a tract of open grassland or a sedge fen could demand as much investment as a field of wheat. Whereas the farmer could draw on a vast body of research for help, the managers of nature reserves had almost no expertise or experience in sustaining and enhancing the wildlife communities of the reserves.

It was clearly not enough to designate a reserve in order to preserve species from current and potentially harmful practices: the communities had to be conserved by means of scientifically formulated management programmes, and the appreciation of this greater task was illustrated by a change in terminology: in 1941, the SPNR convened a Conference on nature *preservation* in post-war reconstruction, and in 1945 a Wild Life *Conservation* Special Committee was formed. In 1949, the Nature Conservancy was established.

Nature conservation required far greater resources than had previously been deployed in preserving species through legislation and the earlier sanctuaries. Men had to be permanently employed on the reserves, working under expert scientific guidance and requiring expensive machinery and facilities. The gradual perception of these practical problems stimulated discussions as to whether the government should completely take over the administration of national nature reserves and play a far greater role in publicising the need for conservation throughout the countryside. This chapter will indicate how an official body, the Nature Conservancy, was created, and how the voluntary bodies subsequently adapted themselves to meeting the far greater challenge of nature conservation, complementing and supplementing the functions of the Nature Conservancy.

A Wildlife Conservation Council

Soon after the SPNR was set up in 1913, N. C. Rothschild wrote to the Board of Agriculture, asking for its support in protecting wild plants and animals. Ray Lankester, in an article for *Nature*, drew attention to the fact that the German government had set up a special department of state to assist in the protection of nature and that it had already created over a hundred nature reserves. The SPNR believed the British government should give similar assistance, perhaps through the appointment of an officer to be attached to the staff of the Natural History Museum.[1]

For a short period, Rothschild was optimistic of government help, especially after the appointment of R. E. Prothero as President of the Board of Agriculture in December 1916, but it soon became clear that no practical aid was forthcoming. The Board, for example, refused to send out circulars to county councils, urging them to create nature reserves.

No one envisaged the government taking over responsibility for wildlife preservation: commentators simply wanted the government to provide generous assistance. The British Correlating Committee, in its evidence to the Addison Committee in 1929, advocated the creation of a statutory body which would make grants to voluntary organisations and individual persons on a pound for pound basis. The statutory body would consist of representatives of government departments and learned societies.[2] In its report of 1931, the Addison Committee recommended that the proposed national parks authority should fulfil this role by making small grants and by helping to devise by-laws for the protection of wildlife. The actual task of selecting and managing the reserves would be left to expert naturalists and their societies.[3]

Even with government assistance, the limitations of the voluntary bodies were clear to see. The SPNR, for example, could only acquire reserves where there were sufficient people living in the vicinity of the sites to organise the purchase and maintenance of the land, and who would undertake the essentially heavy management work. These were necessary stipulations for a society relatively poor in resources and without any permanent staff, but they meant a heavy loss of sites which were, in all other respects, ideal for nature conservation. In contrast, a government body would not be so dependent on local interest and support. It would be easier for an official body, financed by the Treasury, to adopt a national programme of acquisition and management, based on a more objective and scientific choice of sites.

Once the government accepted a responsibility for national parks, it automatically assumed some responsibility for nature conservation because wild plants and animals were regarded as an essential ingredient of the parks. Nature reserves would have to be established to act as refuges and breeding places, and this raised two fundamental questions: who would buy the reserves and who would manage them? The Standing Committee on National Parks doubted whether the national parks authority would have the competence to undertake this specialist work. The creation and control of nature reserves would require 'expert guidance'.[4]

Geoffrey Dent put forward a solution to these questions in 1942, when he suggested than an official Central Nature Reserves Board should be created, made up of a wide range of scientists who would advise the government and other interested parties on the selection and management of reserves. It would appoint a chief conservator, twelve to fifteen district conservators, and a number of watchers to look after individual reserves. The conservators would be responsible for the overall management of the reserves and the effective implementation of wildlife legislation in their respective districts. They would advise and assist the police and, in some cases, they might even be appointed special constables.[5]

The NRIC discussed the value of a government body responsible for nature conservation during the latter part of 1942. Diver declared there was no point in selecting potential reserves until the question of their administration had been settled. Members feared that a national parks authority and local authorities would be unable to provide the reserves with adequate scientific support, and so the NRIC decided to recommend a separate statutory National Nature Reserves Authority, equal in status to the proposed national parks commission.[6]

This new Authority would be staffed by persons 'with expert knowledge of plants and animals and their natural communities', together with 'such administrative officers as may prove necessary'. The National Nature Reserves Authority would act as 'a centre of scientific knowledge and opinion', and have powers to create reserves in the national parks and elsewhere. This would not preclude the national parks commission, the Forestry Commission, or any other landowner from setting up their own reserves: indeed, the Authority would actively encourage this, making available its expertise and experience wherever requested.

This idea was considered at a meeting with H. G. Vincent of the Ministry of Works and Planning in January 1943. According to the minutes of the meeting, Vincent expressed surprise at this novel suggestion and warned that 'the number of suggested National Authorities to be concerned with amenity questions was already large'. The NRIC responded by drawing a distinction between those authorities and 'a single scientific body, primarily for scientific purposes', which alone could provide 'expert uniform control over the scattered sites' of nature reserves. It would be uniquely equipped to select the reserves on a scientific basis and engage 'in conservation work to preserve species'. An independent statutory body was the safest way of ensuring a continuous long-term policy 'which was essential to the success of any conservation programme'.

Vincent proposed three alternatives: First, he suggested that the national parks commission should be responsible for the reserves, but the NRIC regarded this as completely impracticable. The management of land for recreation was quite different from that 'required for nature reserves set up primarily for scientific purposes'. Secondly, Vincent proposed that an expert committee might be set up to advise the Minister in the same way as the Ancient Monuments Board advised the Office of Works on archaeological and historical questions. The NRIC rejected this: whereas the Office of Works was competent to preserve ancient buildings, the Ministry would have 'no expert knowledge of nature preservation'. Thirdly, Vincent suggested that the control of the reserves might be vested in the learned societies represented, for example, on the NRIC. The latter rejected this on the grounds that the societies had no powers to make or enforce by-laws, and that it was essential that a National Nature Reserves Authority was part of the post-war national planning scheme.[7]

The NRIC's views on the need for a separate authority were set out in its memorandum published in March 1943. One of the most vehement critics was John Dower who accused the NRIC of demanding 'a large and expensive structure of expert salaried staff'. He believed a National Nature Reserves Authority would never 'get through Whitehall and Westminster except as a pendant to national parks'. Far from dismissing the use of the national parks commission, he thought this would be 'entirely practicable and probably desirable'. The commission should administer both the national parks and the nature reserves in order to avoid the expense and waste of two separate organisations. The question of wildlife impinged on the work of so many government departments and local authorities that there would be a serious risk of an overlap of responsibilities if a serparate authority were created. An advisory committee, composed of experts in the relevant scientific fields, would exert far more influence than a new, relatively small and inexperienced executive authority.[8]

To this end, Dower recommended the establishment of a Wild Life Conservation Council with advisory, educational and co-ordinative roles, within the national parks commission. National Nature Reserve Advisory Committees would be set up for each national park which 'would undertake the expert management of nature reserves, singly or in groups, under the executive responsibility of the National Parks Commission, through its regional or local officer'. He thought local naturalists would provide all the expert advice and management required, provided that the park wardens enforced the by-laws and made sure that 'habitat conditions were maintained'.

Dower agreed that some reserves should be established outside the parks, but insisted that the national parks commission should also have control over them. The commission would establish the reserves on the advice of the Wild Life Conservation Council, and then delegate their management to the appropriate local authority or voluntary body.

These proposals were included in Dower's report to the Minister of Town and Country Planning, and in making his request to the Reconstruction Committee of the War Cabinet for a preparatory national parks commission, W. S. Morrison noted 'it is my intention to ask the Preparatory Commission to form a Committee, consisting of one or two of their members with a sufficient number of experts in the main branches of natural history to advise on all questions of wild life conservation and in particular on the possibilities of National Nature Reserves'. Clearly, the Minister had accepted Dower's point of view that the national parks commission should take charge of nature conservation.[9]

The Reconstruction Committee refused, however, to approve a preparatory national parks commission (page 109), and simply called upon the Minister to appoint a national parks committee to provide further help in establishing and administering the parks and nature reserves. Morrison had no alternative but to accept this recommendation, and he accordingly appointed a National Parks Committee under Sir Arthur Hobhouse.

The Delay of Two Years

The delay imposed by the Reconstruction Committee in setting up a national parks commission had important long-term consequences for both national parks and nature conservation. During the two years required by the Hobhouse Committee to make its report, the Town and Country Planning Act was passed, which transformed the planning functions of a future national parks commission. In the same period, ecologists persuaded the government that the Lord President of the Council, rather than the Minister of Town and Country Planning, should be responsible for the government's involvement in nature conservation.

It is first necessary to trace the development of post-war town and country planning, for it provides the background to the decisions taken with respect to national parks and nature conservation between 1945 and 1950. In order to facilitate the rapid and comprehensive re-development of areas affected by the blitz and urban blight, the Town and Country (Interim Development) Act was passed in 1943 (page 99) and, in 1944, a further Town and Country Planning Act provided greater powers for urban authorities to compulsorily acquire land and buildings for redevelopment. Statutory undertakings were made subject to planning control, and provisions were made for the designation and preservation of buildings of special architectural and historical interest. The latter was perhaps a valuable precedent for the national parks and nature conservation movements.[10]

At last the extensive redevelopment of urban centres was possible, but the effectiveness of the 1944 Act and other legislation was limited by the chronic problems of compensating those adversely affected by planning decisions and the need to offset costs by levying a betterment charge on those benefiting from the decisions. In this context, considerable use was made of the Final Report of the Uthwatt Committee, published in September 1942. This recommended that the State should take over development rights on all land outside built-up areas, on payment of fair compensation; there should be a periodic levy on those who benefited from the increase in the value of the land. This proposal led to considerable controversy, and most of the members of the War Cabinet wanted to put off tackling such an intricate and far-reaching measure until the war was over, but W. S. Morrison, the Minister of Town and Country Planning, insisted that planning could not become a reality until this had been resolved.[11]

In June 1944, a compromise was struck whereby the Minister and the Scottish Secretary published a Command Paper which took the form of a discussion paper on the control of land use. In a foreword, they noted how the subject had aroused 'keen political controversy' for many years, but emphasised 'that the collaboration of all Parties in a National Government offers a fresh opportunity for finding some common measure of agreement'. They described how post-war reconstruction would have an uneven impact on land values in each area, and how the award of compensation and the imposition of betterment charges were necessary to ensure that each region or locality bore a similar burden and reaped no unfair advantages. To achieve this, all development should be subject to planning consent. If approval was given, a betterment charge of eighty per cent of the value of the land would be levied: if refused, the applicant would receive appropriate compensation. The payment of compensation and collection of betterment would be undertaken by a Land Commission, rather than by the local authorities.

Beside discussing this proposal, the Command Paper was vitally important for emphasising the government's support for planning and the optimum use of land. It stated:

> . . . provision for the right use of land, in accordance with a considered policy, is an essential requirement of the Government's programme of post-war reconstruction. New houses, whether of permanent or emergency construction; the new layout of areas devastated by enemy action or blighted by reason of age or bad living conditions; the new schools . . . the balanced distribution of industry . . . the requirements of sound nutrition and of a healthy and well-balanced agriculture; the preservation of land for national parks and forests, and the assurance to the people of enjoyment of the sea and countryside in times of leisure; a new and safer highway system . . . the proper provision of air fields— all these related parts of a single reconstruction programme involve the use of land, and it is essential that their various claims on land should be so harmonised as to ensure, for the people of this country, the greatest possible measure of individual well-being and national prosperity.[12]

Soon after the general election of July 1945, the new Minister of Town and Country Planning, Lewis Silkin, submitted a large programme of proposed legislation for the consideration of the Committee of the Lord President. He envisaged a Bill to resolve the compensation and betterment issues in the 1945–6 session, another to secure the establishment of satellite towns and the central purchase of land in 1946–7, another to set up national parks and extend public access to open land in 1947–8, and a final Bill in 1948–9 to consolidate all planning legislation.[13]

Discussion in the Lord President's Committee centred on the first and most fundamental measure, the payment of compensation and collection of betterment charges. The State, rather than local authorities, would purchase land required for public use, and a Land Commission would be established for this purpose. Once again, several Ministers expressed concern over the complexity of the issues and doubted whether the Bill could be made workable. Accordingly, the Lord President, Herbert Morrison, decided to refer the entire question to a sub-committee, composed of the Chancellor of the Exchequer, President of the Board of Trade, Ministers of Agriculture, Health, and Town and Country Planning, and the Scottish Secretary. This had the effect of delaying progress over the entire planning field, with the significant exception of the planning of satellite towns. Silkin persuaded the Committee to allow a relatively short and uncontroversial measure to be introduced, which became the New Towns Act of 1946, setting up the machinery for acquiring the necessary land and building the new towns around London and elsewhere.[14]

Meanwhile, a Town and Country Planning Bill was drafted and received the royal assent in August 1947. It awarded unprecedented powers for the control and guidance of development throughout the country. The Acts of 1932 and 1943 were repealed, and the powers conferred by that of 1944 were absorbed into this wider measure. The 145 county councils and county borough councils replaced the 1,441 smaller district councils as the more important planning bodies. It was hoped this would secure a broader regional approach to planning and facilitate the provision of adequate resources and professional expertise in drawing up schemes.

No changes in land use could take place without the consent of a council. A developer could appeal to the Minister in the event of a refusal. In order to strengthen central planning, the minister could 'call in' any planning application for decision by himself. The beneficiaries of a planning decision were liable for development charges, which would equal the increase in the value of the land. Where land was required for the completion of a redevelopment plan, the planning authorities were empowered to make a compulsory purchase at a price equal to the existing-use value, plus the cost of disturbance.[15]

Meanwhile, the Hobhouse and Douglas Ramsay Committees were preparing their reports on the selection of a series of national parks and the establishment of a national parks commission. At first, the reports were expected in 1946, but a long delay ensued and they were not published until the Town and Country Planning Act was virtually secured. In some ways, this measure facilitated the creation of national parks since it set up machinery for protecting all land. On the other hand, the Act made it much harder to single out individual areas for special treatment. This was because it awarded the county councils, acting separately or as joint planning boards, unprecedented planning powers, and the Standing Committee on National Parks was afraid the councils would be very reluctant to cede any of their newly-won powers to a national parks commission, set up at a later date.[16]

Throughout 1946–7, the Standing Committee urged the government to introduce a National Parks Bill so as to ensure the separate status of the national park areas within the framework of town and country planning. The Committee was particularly worried over Section 4 (2) of the Town and Country Planning Bill which gave the Minister powers to establish joint planning boards wherever he believed areas falling within the jurisdiction of two or more county councils should be administered as one unit for planning purposes. Clearly, such areas as the Peak District were likely to fall within this category, and the Standing Committee was afraid the creation of such boards would prejudice the freedom of action of a national parks commission within the potential parks. The Standing Committee tried to secure the amendment of this clause so as to exclude potential national parks, but it failed.

Soon the worst fears of the Standing Committee seemed to be realised. During December 1947, a deputation met the Minister and was told that the national parks commission would have no planning powers. The county councils now had sufficient powers, staff and resources to safeguard the park areas, and they should be given a chance to prove their worth. Now that the Town and Country Planning Act had been passed, it was politically impossible for the Minister to transfer some of the planning powers of twenty of the sixty-three councils to a new, non-elected body called the national parks commission. Instead, the Minister believed the commission could play an important role as adviser to the county councils, and its main task would be in managing the parks through the provision, for example, of holiday accommodation and sports facilities.[17]

After further delay, the National Parks and Access to the Countryside Act was passed in 1949. This set up a National Parks Commission with powers to designate parks in England and Wales for the protection of their natural beauty and for the provision of opportunities for outdoor recreation. The Commission would be responsible:

a) for the preservation and enhancement of natural beauty in England and Wales, and particularly in the areas designated under this Act as National Parks or as areas of outstanding natural beauty;

b) for encouraging the provision or improvement, for persons resorting to National Parks, of facilities for the enjoyment thereof and for the enjoyment of the opportunities for open air recreation and the study of nature.

Far from the Commission having complete and direct control over the preservation and enhancement of the park areas, it was simply required to advise and assist the county councils. Where a park occurred entirely within one county, the park would be administered by a committee or sub-committee of the county council under Part II of the

First Schedule of the 1947 Act. Where the park extended into two or more counties, the Act expected the appropriate county councils to establish a joint planning board under Section 4 of the 1947 Act in order to administer the park as a single planning unit. But this provision could be waived by the Minister under special circumstances. Where this happened, the park could be administered simply by a joint advisory committee under Part III of the First Schedule of the 1947 Act, or by the county councils administering their appropriate areas separate from the remainder of the park area. The councils and National Parks Commission had to reach a decision as to how each park was to be administered within three months of the parks being designated.[18]

In addition to national parks, the National Parks Commission was made responsible for identifying Areas of Outstanding Natural Beauty, located outside the parks. The Minister had to confirm the designation of each area after there had been the closest consultation with the appropriate planning authorities. The latter were expected to make a special effort to prevent any harmful changes of land use taking place in the AONB's and, wherever possible, to take every step to enhance their natural beauty.

The National Parks Act of 1949 did not extend to Scotland, except with respect to nature conservation. The Scottish Home Department had censured the Dower report in 1943 for adopting a conservative approach to the countryside. There was an insistence in the report on the preservation of traditional features and a bias against industrial development and anything 'savouring of urban ways of life'. The scope for future conflict between a national parks commission and the North of Scotland Hydro-electric Board had also been clearly demonstrated in the report of the Douglas Ramsay committee in 1945, which urged the government to allow only 'really small-scale undertakings'. The Home Department warned that a Scottish national parks commission was likely to take the same view and try to restrict the operations of the Hydro-electric Board.[19]

In an attempt to allay any fears that the national parks would turn the Highlands into depopulated recreation areas for townspeople, the second Douglas Ramsay committee proposed that a Scottish national parks commission should provide generous aid to agriculture, stimulate tourism, and encourage the establishment of light industries in each proposed park. In 1948, a meeting convened by the Scottish Economic Conference set up a Working Party to produce detailed recommendations on meeting the requirements of visitors and satisfying the economic and social needs of the local population in the five parks proposed by the Douglas Ramsay committees. Whilst these gestures helped to reduce fears that the parks would become 'lifeless museums', the promise of aid aroused opposition in another quarter. The inhabitants of neighbouring areas, which were equally in need of rehabilitation and development, resented being excluded from this help simply because their scenery and recreational facilities were not equally outstanding.[20]

In the event, a Scottish national parks commission was not established, and no parks were created. It was noted that the Secretary of State already had very wide-ranging powers for controlling land use, which provided him with the opportunity to reconcile the various demands made on the countryside by the urban dweller and rural resident.

A Biological Service

The two-year delay imposed by the Reconstruction Committee resulted in the eventual National Parks Commission for England and Wales having far fewer powers than its proponents had originally anticipated. Equally significant changes occurred in the perception of national nature reserves. Instead of nature conservation being an adjunct of town and country planning, it came to be regarded as the province of the Lord President of the Council, who 'represented' science in the Cabinet. Instead of being a planning issue, nature conservation was to be administered by scientists who alone had the expertise to implement an effective land use and management policy for the conservation of wildlife and geological and physiographical features.

The question of the administration of nature conservation became fused with a wider desire to adopt a more scientific approach to government. As early as 1934, J. S. Huxley had drawn attention to this need: he became 'more than ever impressed with the fact that both our existing structure of civilisation and our hope of progress are based on science and that the lack of appreciation and understanding among business men, financiers, educational authorities, politicians and administrators, was a serious feature of our present situation'.[21]

The ecologist felt particularly neglected, and in 1940 the annual meeting of the British Ecological Society passed a resolution calling on the government to make greater use of biologists in the war effort. In a report on the organisation of biological sciences after the war, the Biological Committee of the Royal Society emphasised the need for a new organisation to guide fundamental research and to establish an institute of terrestrial ecology.[22]

In this context, the proposal for a series of national nature reserves, selected and controlled by a national parks commission, was just one more example of planning without appreciating the wider scientific implications. In the view of the British Ecological Society, Dower's proposals for a Wild Life Conservation Council of experts to advise on the choice and administration of the reserves were quite useless. There were no experts since no one had very much experience of conserving plants and animals. A large research programme was required to answer even the most elementary questions related to wildlife management. The reserves would be a failure unless a permanent scientific research staff and trained technical assistance were appointed. In the same way as the Ministry of Agriculture would be responsible for ensuring efficient farming in the park areas, so an independent scientific body should be responsible for nature reserves.

During this period, the Bureau of Animal Population at Oxford was carrying out research on rodent control, with the aid of the Agricultural Research Council, and, in the course of this work, C. S. Elton became impressed by the potential of a research council for co-ordinating and leading the research effort in this and other fields of biological investigation. Not only could a council take up initiatives in the theoretical and practical aspects of science with the minimum of 'red tape', but it had, unlike most government departments, responsibilities on both sides of the Scottish border.

These observations may have contributed to the substance of a memorandum circulated by the Universities Federation for Animal Welfare (UFAW) in September 1943, which stressed the need for an official body to reconcile the potential conflict between the protection of wildlife and other forms of land use. Some species were treated as pests or hunted for sport, and any statutory wildlife authority would have to be above these sectional interests in order to act as arbiter. Clearly, the National Parks Commission would be inappropriate, and the Federation recommended placing the statutory authority under the Lord President of the Council, who was already responsible for the various research councils.[23]

Following consultations with the Federation in 1943, the Council of the British Ecological Society formed a special committee under the chairmanship of A. G. Tansley to review the whole question of nature conservation and ecological research (page 102). This special committee recommended the establishment of an Ecological Research Council to take charge of nature reserves, undertake surveys of the fauna and flora of Britain, and establish an institute of terrestrial ecology. The Research Council would help ecology in the same way as the Agricultural Research Council and Medical Research Council aided their own respective fields of interest and, like them, it would also be responsible to the Lord President.

The British Ecological Society set out these ideas in two memoranda, and Tansley discussed them in a more general fashion in his book *Our heritage of wild nature* published in 1945. The concept of an Ecological Research Council was opposed by the Royal Society, Agricultural Research Council and the Treasury: there were, for example, fears that the work of the new Council would overlap that of the Agricultural Research Council which was also concerned with living organisms and such problems as pest control. The British Ecological Society therefore reviewed such alternatives as the creation of an ecological committee within the Development Commission, or a wildlife conservation board directly under the Lord President.[24]

The most important task of the Huxley Committee was to reconcile these two approaches to nature conservation, namely the need to protect wildlife as part of the amenity of the countryside, and the need to safeguard wildlife for its contribution to scientific research, educational needs, and the economic well-being of the nation. Should the reserves be left to a national parks commission, or be controlled by an entirely new government body with much broader environmental responsibilities?[25]

Whilst recognising these two different objectives, the Huxley Committee was at pains to point out that the two approaches were not entirely in conflict. Both wanted to conserve 'the rich variety of our countryside and sea-coasts' and to increase 'the general enjoyment and understanding of nature'. This could only be achieved through protecting and managing wildlife on a scientific basis. Good estate management was not enough.

In order to secure both objectives, the government had to accept responsibility for (i) the protection and management of nature reserves, (ii) the conservation and control of wildlife over the entire country, and (iii) the conduct, support and encouragement of the research and survey work made necessary in order to discharge these responsibilities. The Huxley Committee insisted that these three responsibilities should be given to a single organisation with an administrative role and a scientific capacity. This would ensure that administrators asked the right scientific questions, and scientists appreciated the problems of administration. Experience in other fields of government 'had shown that it was essential to have some scientific and technical personnel in an executive body if a satisfactory degree of integration was to be achieved and expert advice was to be translated into action'.[26]

These tasks were too large to be simply delegated to the National Parks Commission. Bearing in mind the other responsibilities of the Commission, only a few biologists would be appointed, and 'the work was far too extensive, varied and complex to be successfully dealt with in this way'. A much larger staff and budget was required for the acquisition and management of reserves, completely out of proportion to the other branches of work of the National Parks Commission.

At the same time, there was no suitable candidate for this role in the existing scientific field. The Natural History Museum, the Royal Botanic Gardens at Kew, and the National Museum of Wales were primarily concerned with nomenclature, classification and other aspects of taxonomic research. Whilst these subjects were relevant to nature conservation, the institutions were hardly equipped to take on the role of selecting and managing reserves.

The Committee decided that an entirely new body was required, and it began to search for a formula whereby the organisation obtained a competence in both the planning and scientific fields. Figure 13 indicates the Committee's first solution, whereby the Ministry of Town and Country Planning would establish both a National Parks Commission and a Wild Life Conservation Commission of equal status,

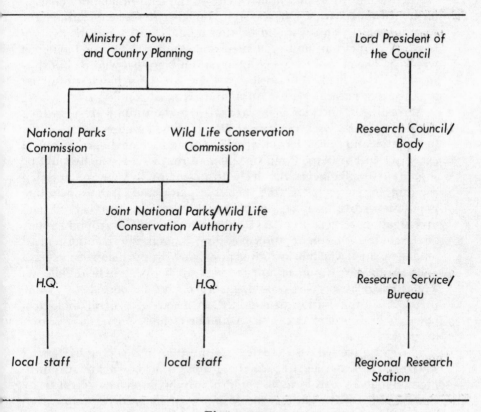

Figure 13

A formula considered by the Huxley Committee for the administration of national parks, national nature reserves and ecological research

which would create a joint Wild Life Conservation Authority to be responsible for nature reserves and nature conservation in general. There would be the closest liaison with any research council or institute of terrestrial ecology created by the Lord President.[27]

But the Committee soon recognised the limitations of this formula when it began to study how the Wild Life Conservation Commission would undertake its research programme. The Huxley Committee had already stressed the need to select and manage reserves within the context of protecting and controlling wild species throughout the country. To achieve this, the Commission would require a wide range of scientists, with appropriate qualifications, 'effectively equipped for survey and research, both in the field and in the laboratory, directed to determining the distribution, ecology, genetics, general structure and behaviour of natural populations, and the physical conditions in which they live'.

These scientists would, in fact, require the kind of facilities characteristic of universities and research councils. At the same time, the Commission's scientists would be offering universities and the existing research councils an unprecedented opportunity to further biological research. The nature reserves would not only protect wildlife but they would become field laboratories for studying 'the behaviour of living organisms in natural, semi-natural and artificial conditions'.

Accordingly, a new formula was devised in the autumn of 1945 which ensured an even closer link between the proposed organisation and the universities and research councils. The Committee envisaged a central executive authority to administer the nature reserves, which would be supported by a Biological Service with a responsibility for 'maintaining a continuing survey of all wild species of plants and animals including population, distributional and other studies; the conduct of such investigations as were necessary for the formation of Government policy on the control and conservation of national populations and the general management of wild life, including pests; and the provision of a general information bureau and advisory service on all aspects of field biology'. The Biological Service would, in turn, be supported by 'some permanent organisation to consider the needs of general biological research' and would work closely with one or more terrestrial research institutes.

This formula led the Huxley Committee into an embarrassing situation. It was reporting to the Minister of Town and Country Planning, and yet its formula could hardly be implemented solely by that Minister. For example, the Minister could hardly set up a Biological Service which not only helped his Ministry but other government departments as well. This was much more the responsibility of the Lord President, and yet the committee could hardly submit a detailed programme of recommendations to the Lord President on ways of amending and extending his powers in the field of science. That was the responsibility of his own advisers, the Scientific Advisory Committee which had been established in 1940.[28]

This committee had also been studying the question of nature conservation, primarily in the context of post-war biological research. It had received copies of the memorandum of the Biological Committee of the Royal Society and those from the British Ecological Society. In September 1945, J. C. F. Fryer, who was by then secretary of the Agricultural Research Council and therefore a member of the Scientific Advisory Committee, was invited to compile a paper on *Nature conservation and research on the British terrestrial flora and fauna*. In submitting his paper to the Scientific Advisory Committee, Fryer summarised the various proposals that had been made for the organisation of nature conservation. Far from being revolutionary, the proposals would merely allow Britain to catch up with such countries as the United States, which already had 167 national parks and nature reserves, occupying 21,600,000 acres. The United States National Park Wildlife, Fish and Wildfowl Service undertook surveys and research on game and other birds, fur and other animals, marine and freshwater life.

From October 1945 onwards, the Scientific Advisory Committee and the Huxley Committee were in close contact, and it was decided at a meeting in March 1946 that both Committees should continue to pursue their separate investigations and keep the other informed of their conclusions. By October 1946, the enquiries of the Scientific Advisory Committee were complete, and the chairman, Sir Henry Dale, submitted a report on the need for a national biological policy to the Lord President, who in turn forwarded copies to the Ministry of Town and Country Planning and Scottish Secretary for submission to their respective committees.[29]

In its report, the Scientific Advisory Committee recommended: (i) the establishment of a series of national nature reserves; (ii) the creation of one or more institutes of terrestrial ecology to undertake fundamental research in ecology—they should ideally work in conjunction with universities and make full use of the facilities offered by the nature reserves; (iii) the setting up of a Service of 'fully qualified scientific officers charged with the duties of managing the reserves, advising any body whether governmental, local authority or private upon problems of nature conservation'.

Having made reference to the pending report of the Huxley Committee, the Scientific Advisory Committee made the following interim suggestions, namely that the new Service should cover England, Wales and Scotland, and start from 'small beginnings', initially attached to an existing government organisation. The secretariat of the Agricultural Research Council was the most suitable body since its responsibility also extended to Scotland and there was some risk of the work of the new Service overlapping with that of the Council. The Committee suggested that the legal and land agency functions of the Service in connection with the administration of the nature reserves might be performed on an agency basis by another official or semi-official body.

By the autumn of 1946, the enquiries of the Huxley Committee were almost complete, and a third formula was proposed which was in many ways very similar to that recommended by the Scientific Advisory Committee. Under this formula, the government was advised to set up a Biological Service which would be responsible for selecting, acquiring and managing the reserves, and for undertaking the necessary survey and research work. It would act as a central bureau of information, operate an advisory service, and encourage educational work. The Service would initiate legislation for the preservation of wildlife and ensure the enforcement of existing laws. Unlike the Scientific Advisory Committee, the Huxley Committee recommended that the Biological Service should carry out its own legal and land agency work.[30]

At first, the majority of the Ritchie Committee wanted a completely separate organisation for Scotland in the form of a Scottish Wild Life Service, equal in status to a Scottish National Parks Commission. This reflected the general desire to administer Scotland separately in the planning field. It would also be easier to closely supervise the reserves, and more attention could be given to the distinctive ecological problems encountered in Scotland.

In a review of these proposals, the Douglas Ramsay Committee challenged the need for both a Scottish National Parks Commission and a Scottish Wild Life Service, and suggested fusing them into one body. The Ritchie Committee vigorously opposed this, but agreed that the Scottish National Parks Commission could be made responsible for all publicity and educational work, and for the wardening of both national parks and nature reserves. This proposal profoundly disturbed the Huxley Committee since it feared the close links between the Scottish National Parks Commission and Wild Life Service would discourage the government from setting up a Biological Service in England and Wales, completely separate from the National Parks Commission.

There were, however, dissensions in the Ritchie Committee itself. F. Fraser Darling claimed that a Scottish Wild Life Service, no matter how attractive in administrative terms, was indefensible on ecological grounds. If Scotland was to keep abreast with the research being undertaken in Great Britain, the Service had to be part of the Biological Service. At a meeting in April 1947, this view was endorsed by the Huxley Committee, which also pointed out that a Biological

Service, under a research council, could be set up straightaway without an Act of Parliament, whereas the proposals of the Ritchie Committee could only be implemented by a separate National Parks Act for Scotland. In the meantime, many important sites might be destroyed.

After further reflection, the Ritchie Committee finally agreed to the formation of a single Biological Service for England, Wales and Scotland, on the condition that the Scottish part, based in Edinburgh, would have a greater degree of autonomy. This would help to win the whole-hearted support of the Scottish people for the new body.[31]

Both the Huxley and Ritchie Committees suggested that the Biological Service should subdivide the country into conservancies, and a competent field naturalist with proven ability in land management should be appointed to each as a conservator. Wardens would undertake the day-to-day management of the reserves. One or more senior conservators would be appointed to co-ordinate the conservancies and serve as a link with headquarters, which would act as a clearing house for information.

The scientific staff of the Biological Service would be responsible for research on the special problems presented by each reserve and for formulating suitable management programmes for the plant and animal communities. The staff would be recruited from ecology, plant and animal physiology, genetics, soil science, climatology and statistics. In view of the Service's responsibilities for geological monuments, some geologists and physiographers would also be needed. There were fears lest the Service should divert scientists skilled in their various disciplines from other important work, especially in the agricultural field, but the Huxley Committee dismissed such fears as groundless, provided that the government implemented the proposals set out in a Command Paper on the Scientific Civil Service, published in September 1945.[32]

Although the Biological Service would provide some research facilities, the Huxley and Ritchie Committees hoped the institutes of terrestrial ecology, as proposed by the Scientific Advisory Committee, would also be established for the 'study of biological, geographical, physiographical and climatic factors'. The relationship between the institutes and the Biological Service was not precisely defined: although they would work very closely with the staff of the Service, the committees thought it would be wrong for the Biological Service to 'dictate the research to be undertaken'.

In addition to one institute in Scotland, the Huxley Committee proposed four in England and Wales: one would be in the Isle of Purbeck and concerned with 'intensive pure research' on the various habitats of that part of Dorset and Hampshire. Another would be based in or near Cambridge, and have at least four out-stations in the Broads, Fens, Breckland and East Anglian heaths and coasts, and undertake extensive and comparative work. A third institute would be based on Oxford and undertake fundamental research and act as a centre for post-graduate and other training courses. Lastly, an institute would be established in Snowdonia or the Lake District, where it would work closely with the Freshwater Biological Association. It would play an essential role in advising the Biological Service on the management of wildlife in the proposed series of upland national parks.[33]

Both Committees recommended that the Biological Service should be 'attached' to the government through a Nature Conservation Board, made up of scientists and a few members with experience in the educational and recreational fields. This Board would initially be responsible to the Agricultural Research Council, although the Huxley Committee hoped it would soon become 'self-contained and independent'.

The members of the Hobhouse Committee were generally sympathetic to the Huxley Committee's report, but John Dower was highly critical of the proposals for the Nature Conservation Board, which he thought 'threw a bucket of cold water over the whole thing, quite needlessly'. He thought the Board should be completely independent within the framework of the Privy Council. The Agricultural Research Council was an entirely unsuitable nursemaid for 'once in the Agricultural Research Council's grasp, the Biological Service would never be allowed to achieve independence, and would inevitably have its work twisted so as to be of prime service to agriculture . . . they would finish the ride with the lady inside, and a smile on the face of the tiger!'[34]

In the light of its discussions with the Scientific Advisory Committee, the Huxley Committee replied to these criticisms by stressing the need to be realistic: it was simply 'not practicable politics' to recommend a completely new and large organisation for a new field of government work. The committee was much more likely to achieve its objectives by recommending a slow and determined build-up of staff, resources and expertise and, for this purpose, attachment to the Agricultural Research Council was ideal. The Council would have no influence over policy: it would 'merely be assuming temporarily an additional function'. It may have been also significant that Sir John Fryer, a leading member of the NRIC, was secretary of the Agricultural Research Council until his death in November 1948.[35]

While the government modified and even rejected some of the proposals of the Hobhouse and Douglas Ramsay Committees, it largely accepted those of the Huxley and Ritchie Committees. Whereas the provision of parks and greater public access to the countryside aroused keen debate, comparatively little attention was given to nature reserves. The reserves affected fewer people, a much smaller area of land, and were generally cheaper to establish. The concept of national nature reserves fitted much more easily into the planning framework envisaged by the Town and Country Planning Act of 1947. There would be no conflict with the powers awarded to the county councils in the planning field.

In 1947, the Minister of Town and Country Planning invited members of the Huxley Committee to act as Wild Life Scientific Advisers until their recommendations had been considered and, where appropriate, adopted. The Advisers thereafter met at regular intervals under the chairmanship of A. G. Tansley and spent most of the time assessing threats to proposed reserves, organising fresh surveys, and considering the biological interest of 'newly-discovered' sites. C. S. Elton, for example, made a two-day visit to the proposed reserve at Ainsdale in Lancashire, where he made a vegetation map on the basis of RAF air photographs and a ground survey. This made it possible to determine the precise boundaries of the potential reserve for the first time. Meanwhile, the Ministry's Regional Planning Officers were asked to make every effort to prevent any harmful developments taking place on the proposed reserves, and the co-operation of the Ministry of Agriculture and Interdepartmental Committee on Service Land Requirements was obtained.

In January 1948, the Lord President of the Council, Herbert Morrison, accepted responsibility for following-up the recommendations of the Huxley Committee, and on 29 April he informed parliament that the government had accepted the recommendations for a Nature Conservancy Board and a Biological Service, which would be responsible to the Agricultural Research Council. Both would cover England, Wales and Scotland, although special arrangements would be made for Scotland. Soon afterwards, he announced that the Board would have a 'more convenient title', namely the Nature Conservancy, and that A. G. Tansley would be the first chairman. On 1 November 1948, C. Diver became the first Director-General.[36]

By the beginning of 1949, it was clear that the Nature Conservancy had to be given separate legal status from the Agricultural Research Council, and in March an Order in Council was issued which made the Nature Conservancy responsible to a new Committee of the Privy Council for Agricultural Research and Nature Conservation.

A royal charter was secured, which set out the responsibilities of the Nature Conservancy: these were 'to provide scientific advice on the conservation and control of the natural flora and fauna of Great Britain; to establish, maintain and manage nature reserves in Great Britain, including the maintenance of physical features of scientific interest; and to organise and develop the research and scientific services related thereto'.

The Nature Conservancy derived its statutory powers from the

National Parks and Access to the Countryside Act of 1949. Although this Act was primarily concerned with amenity and public access to the countryside, the Conservancy was required to select and manage its reserves on purely scientific criteria. The Act defined the purpose of the National Nature Reserves as (i) providing, under suitable conditions and control, special opportunities for the study of, and research into, matters relating to the fauna and flora of Great Britain and the physical conditions in which they live, and for the study of geological and physiographical features of special interest in the area, or (ii) preserving flora, fauna or geological or physiographical features of special interest in the area.

The Nature Conservancy would own or lease the reserves, or enter into a Nature Reserve Agreement, whereby the landowner, lessee or occupier would allow the Conservancy to implement a management programme for nature conservation on their property. The Act granted the Conservancy powers to acquire land by compulsion and to formulate by-laws for the protection of each reserve.

The Nature Conservancy

It is not the intention of this book to examine in detail the events before and during European Conservation Year, or the developments of the 1970s. This section will simply summarise the main events in the life of the Nature Conservancy, and relate them to the proposals made in the earlier period.

The first chairman of the Nature Conservancy, A. G. Tansley, forecast in 1953 that the number of National Nature Reserves in England and Wales was unlikely to exceed one hundred.[37] By 1963, forty-seven National Nature Reserves had been declared and a further eighty-one areas were designated as proposed National Nature Reserves. By January 1975, a total of ninety-nine reserves had been established in England and Wales, with a further forty-one in Scotland (Figure 14). The lists of proposed reserves, drawn up in the 1940s, served as the basis of the acquisition programme, and eighty of those identified in the earlier lists eventually became National Nature Reserves (Table 8). Many of the remainder were found to be no longer worth protecting owing to a diminution of their scientific interest. In the course of fieldwork, further important sites, worthy of protection, were discovered and, in some cases, were declared National Nature Reserves. For example, Lullington Heath in Sussex was not recommended by the Huxley Committee for protection, probably because chalk heathland communities were comparatively extensive in lowland England at that time. But the decline in the area of heathland in the post-war period was so dramatic that the Nature Conservancy decided to acquire 155 acres of Lullington Heath as a National Nature Reserve in 1956.

Whereas the Huxley and Ritchie Committees recommended 101 reserves of about 181,000 acres, there were 140 reserves by January 1975, occupying an aggregate area of 282,980 acres. The Committees assumed that most of the reserves would be purchased or held on very long leases. In a few cases, where the 'proprietor was anxious to collaborate in the conservation of wild life', it might be possible to draw up a nature reserve agreement instead. In the event, these agreements became an extremely important method of acquiring reserves. Of the 140 National Nature Reserves in Britain by January 1975, forty-one were held on the basis of a Nature Reserve Agreement, thirty-eight were leased, twenty-seven owned, ten were partly owned/agreement, ten were owned/leased, nine were owned/lease/agreement, and five were leased/agreement. In Scotland, as many as twenty-three of the forty-one reserves were held on the basis of a Nature Reserve Agreement. Although the Nature Conservancy was granted powers to acquire land by compulsory purchase under the 1949 Act, these powers were never used to override the wishes of a landowner or occupier.

There was room for only a small proportion of the sites proposed by the NRIC regional sub-committees in the acquisition programme of the Nature Conservancy. It was hoped that the county councils would designate many of the remaining sites as Local Nature Reserves. The 1949 Act enabled them to establish such reserves on any land under their jurisdiction. The first were established in 1952 at Aberlady Bay in East Lothian and at Gibraltar Point in Lincolnshire (page 168). In the event, only forty Local Nature Reserves were declared by 1975, of which only two were in Scotland and two in Wales. Almost half of those in England were situated in the Greater London area, Kent, Surrey, Sussex, Essex and Hertfordshire (Figure 14). Their aggregate area of 13,800 acres represented only five per cent of the area occupied by National Nature Reserves.

The Huxley and Ritchie Committees emphasised the importance of the Forestry Commission's property for wildlife conservation. In 1954, the Commission and Nature Conservancy entered into an agreement whereby 200 acres of woodland at Waterperry in Oxfordshire were to be managed in the interests of nature conservation, ecological research *and* timber production. Since the two parties to the agreement were Crown bodies, it was decided not to declare the wood a National Nature Reserve, but to devise a new category of land holding, namely a Forest Nature Reserve. Another twelve Forest Nature Reserves were designated in the period up to 1975, with an aggregate area of 2,400 acres. They were owned by the Forestry Commission, Depart-

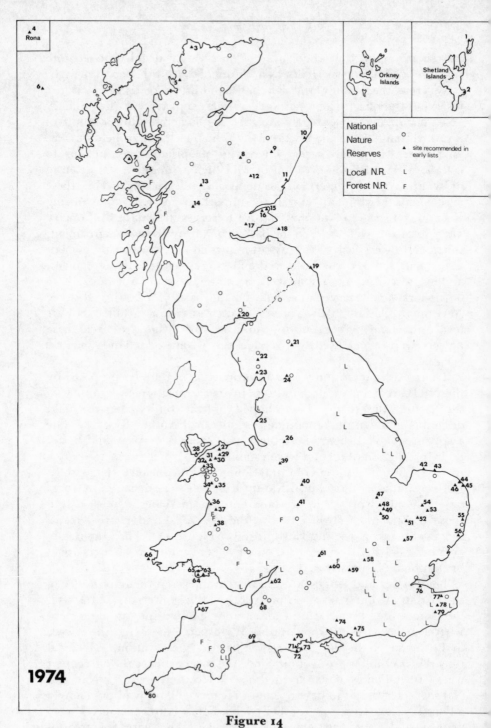

Figure 14

Distribution of National Nature Reserves, Local Nature Reserves and Forest
Nature Reserves in 1974, indicating those sites recommended in earlier lists
of proposed reserves (Table 8)

Number on map	National Nature Reserve designated between 1949 & 1975	Nominated in: 1 1915 by SPNR 2 1929 by British Correlating Committee 3 1943 by British Ecological Society 4 1945 by NRIC 5 1947 by Huxley Committee 6 1949 by Ritchie Committee
1	Hermaness	6
2	Noss	6
3	Inchnadamph	1, 6 (Special Conservation Area)
4	Rona & Sula Sgeir	6
5	Inverpolly	6
6	St Kilda	1, 6
7	Rhum	6
8	Cairngorms	3, 6 (National Park Reserve)
9	Dinnet Oakwood	6 (Nature Conservation Area)
10	Sands of Forvie	6
11	St Cyrus	6
12	Caenlochan	1, 2, 6 (NCA)
13	Ben Lui	1, 2, 3
14	Rannoch Moor	1
15	Tentsmuir	2, 6
16	Morton Lochs	6
17	Loch Leven	1, 6
18	Isle of May	6
19	Lindisfarne	5 (Scientific Area)
20	Caerlaverock	6
21	Upper Teesdale	1, 2, 3, 4 (Conservation Area), 5 (SA)
22	North Fen	3, 4, 5
23	Roudsea Wood	1, 3, 4, 5
24	Colt Park Wood	2, 3, 4, 5
25	Ainsdale Sand Dunes	1, 3, 4, 5
26	Rostherne Mere	1, 3, 5
27	Newborough Warren— Ynys Llandwyn	1, 3, 4, 5
28	Coed Gorswen	
29	Coed Dolgarrog	
30	Cwm Glas, Crafnant	Snowdonia identified in 2, 3, 4, 5
31	Coed Tremadoc	
32	Cwm Idwal	1, 2, 3
33	Y Wyddfa—Snowdon	

34	Rhinog	3, 4 (in CA), 5 (in SA)
35	Cader Idris	3
36	Dyfi	3
37	Coed Rheidol	3
38	Cors Tregaron	1, 3, 4, 5
39	Wybunbury Moss	1, 5
40	Chartley Moss	2
41	Wrens Nest	5
42	Scolt Head	3, 4, 5
43	Holkham	5
44	Hickling Broad	4, 5 ⎱ Broads identified in
45	Bure Marshes	3 ⎰ 1, 2, 3, 4, 5
46	Winterton Dunes	1, 4, 5
47	Castor Hanglands	4, 5
48	Holme Fen	1, 4, 5
49	Woodwalton Fen	1, 3, 4, 5
50	Monks Wood	4, 5
51	Chippenham Fen	1, 4, 5
52	Cavenham Heath	2, 4, 5
53	Thetford Heath	4 (in CA), 5 (in SA)
54	Weeting Heath	4 (in CA), 5 (in SA)
55	Walberswick	4 (in CA), 5 (in SA)
56	Orfordness—Havergate	1, 4, 5
57	Hales Wood	4, 5
58	Tring Reservoirs	4, 5
59	Cothill	1
60	Aston Rowant	3, 5
61	Wychwood	1, 4, 5
62	Avon Gorge	1, 3, 5
63	Oxwich Point	1, 5 ⎱ Gower identified
64	Gower Coast	⎰ in 2, 4, 5
65	Whiteford	3
66	Skomer Island	5
67	Braunton Burrows	1, 2, 3, 4, 5
68	Shapwick Heath	1, 2, 4, 5
69	Axmouth—Lyme Regis Undercliffs	1, 2, 4 (in CA), 5 (in SA)
70	Morden Bog	1, 3, 4, 5
71	Hartland Moor	4 (in CA), 5 (in SA)
72	Studland Heath	1, 3, 4, 5
73	Arne	4, 5
74	Old Winchester Hill	5
75	Kingley Vale	1, 2, 3, 4, 5
76	High Halstow	5

77	*Blean Woods*	*1, 2, 4, 5*
78	*Wye and Crundale Downs*	*1, 3, 4, 5*
79	*Ham Street Woods*	*4, 5*
80	*Lizard*	*1, 2, 3, 4 (in CA), 5 (in SA)*

Table 8

The National Nature Reserves designated between 1949 and 1975, which were proposed as nature reserves in surveys undertaken between 1915 and 1949

ment of Agriculture and Fisheries for Scotland, and the Duchy of Cornwall.

The National Parks Act of 1949 did not implement the concept of scientific areas. There were fears that this would conflict with the broader planning powers recently awarded the county councils. But another proposal of the Huxley Committee, namely the creation of Sites of Special Scientific Interest (SSSI's), was adopted to provide some protection for areas outside the statutory reserves. The Act of 1949 laid down that:

> . . . where the Nature Conservancy are of opinion that any area of land, not being land for the time being managed as a nature reserve, is of special interest by reason of its flora, fauna, or geological or physiographical features, it shall be the duty of the Conservancy to notify that fact to the local planning authority in whose area the land is situated.

Once established, the Nature Conservancy began the task of scheduling the bulk of the sites proposed for protection by the regional sub-committees of the NRIC and, by 1963, over 1,420 sites had been scheduled in England and Wales. By 1975, the number of SSSI's had risen to 2,422 sites in England and Wales, with a further 787 in Scotland. Of the total of 3,209 sites, 819 were notified for their geological or physiographical interest. Many of the scheduled sites contained a variety of interest: the schedule, compiled in 1963, for Cheshire noted that each of the twenty-six sites in the county had more than one type of interest, and one had as many as seven. Twenty-one sites were important botanically, nineteen for ornithology, fourteen for hydrobiology, thirteen for educational use, seven for entomology, and six for palaeobotany.

About 2,361,491 acres of land had been scheduled in England and Wales by 1975, and a further 1,375,690 acres in Scotland.[38] There was a considerable range in the size of sites: of the thirty-nine sites in Essex, the smallest three were less than two acres in extent. They were notified for their geological importance. The largest site in the county was over 13,000 acres; four sites were between 5,000 and 10,000 acres, and five were between 1,000 and 5,000 acres. In the Lake District, fifteen of the sixty-two sites contained over 42,000 of the 45,593 acres of scheduled land in the National Park. Twenty-four of the SSSI's in England and Wales were over 10,000 acres in January 1975 and, in many respects, they met the objectives of the scientific areas, as originally proposed by the Huxley Committee. The most extensive sites in lowland England included woods, marshes and reservoirs, and those in upland Britain covered moorland and mountainside.

The county schedules were revised up to four times between 1950 and 1975, and many fresh sites were added as a result of further field-work. On the other hand, over 113 sites in England and Wales were removed from the schedules, and over eighty-seven were reduced in area.

The threat to wildlife posed by changes in the use of farmland was first discerned between the wars, and in 1944 the NRIC described farming as the most serious threat to wild plants and animals. But most observers believed the extensive reclamation of land during the war would end once peace returned. The ploughing up of old grasslands and the exploitation of marginal timber reserves would cease. A. G. Tansley wrote in 1945 that 'it is scarcely probable that the extension of agriculture will go much further, for the limits of profitable agricultural land must have been reached in most places'. The Hobhouse Committee of 1947 confidently believed that the Ministry of Agriculture, through its county agricultural committees and other means, would prevent any attempt to reclaim sites that were of wildlife interest.[39]

This attitude toward the future of agricultural development influenced the content of much post-war legislation: the Town and Country Planning Act of 1947 placed no restrictions on land reclamation or afforestation, and consequently farmers and foresters did not have to seek the consent of local planning authorities before ploughing up old pasture, installing underdrains or felling woodland. This meant that the notification of Sites of Special Scientific Interest was completely ineffective in preventing these fundamental changes in land management taking place on key biological sites.

The limited value of scheduling was highlighted by the destruction of Waddingham Common in 1963. The site was first proposed as a nature reserve in the early 1940s as the only surviving example of a peat bog overlying limestone in Lincolnshire. It contained Grass of Parnassus *Parnassia palustris* and other wetland species. The Nature Conservancy scheduled the site in 1951, and the Lincolnshire

Naturalists' Trust began to negotiate a nature reserve agreement with the parish council when a local farmer, to everyone's surprise, proved that he owned the common. He decided to plough up the site, and the Nature Conservancy first learned of the threat to the wildlife when the Ministry of Agriculture informed it of an application from the farmer for a grant of £12 per acre toward the cost of reclamation. Both the Conservancy and Trust appealed to the farmer to spare the common, and the Trust offered to purchase the land or provide compensation for any losses the farmer might incur by leaving the site intact. The farmer refused, and the Trust and a local member of parliament then appealed to the Ministry of Agriculture to withhold the grant, thereby hoping to dissuade the farmer from proceeding. They drew attention to the anomalous situation where one government body scheduled the site for protection and another used public funds to destroy it. The Ministry was sympathetic and admitted the anomaly, but found that under existing legislation it could not withhold the grant where reclamation was technically feasible. Soon afterward Waddingham Common was ploughed up and its wildlife was irretrievably destroyed. Subsequent attempts in parliament and elsewhere to grant greater security to scheduled sites failed.[40]

The experience of the 1930s had emphasised the need to carefully manage the nature reserves in order to sustain the diversity and richness of their wildlife communities. In accordance with this view, the Nature Conservancy would have preferred to delay acquiring reserves until it was fully equipped to manage them, but the general increase in the cost of land made such a policy imprudent. A compromise was struck whereby the reserves were acquired as quickly as possible, and as much management work was undertaken as practicable.

From the late 1950s, formal management plans were drawn up for many reserves, setting out the objectives of acquiring and managing the sites, providing basic data on topography, geology, climate, soils, vegetation, fauna, land-use history and archaeology, describing the potential for research work on the site, and concluding with sections on land agency problems, public access, and wardening. It was intended to revise every management plan periodically, as fresh information and experience were gained. A detailed survey of the ecology of each reserve was a very high priority: this would be the task of the warden and the regional staff of the Conservancy, supported by specialists from the experimental stations of the Conservancy and university departments.

The Huxley and Ritchie Committees had envisaged the necessary survey and experimental work being undertaken directly by the Biological Service and a series of institutes of terrestrial ecology. In the event, the Nature Conservancy established a number of stations, the first of which were at Merlewood in the Lake District and Furzebrook in the Isle of Purbeck. The largest was at Monks Wood in Huntingdonshire.

As early as 1953, research was in progress on ways of halting the degradation of high peat-moor, on the dynamic plant/soil relationship in woodlands, and on recent coastal changes and the spread of *Spartina townsendii*. The Annual Report of the Nature Conservancy in 1960 noted the growing concern over the impact of various toxic chemicals used in the countryside on wildlife, and a Toxic Chemicals and Wild Life Group was accordingly established to undertake the essentially ecological and long-term research required to answer such questions as: (i) what are the long-term effects of sub-lethal poisoning? (ii) are observed declines in animal populations due to toxic chemicals or in part to other coincidental factors? and (iii) to what extent can populations of different organisms adapt themselves to different chemicals?

In 1965, the Nature Conservancy became a component part of a new research council, the Natural Environment Research Council. The government's responsibility for nature conservation was thereby transferred from the Lord President of the Council to the Secretary of State for Education and Science, but the Conservancy's responsibility for establishing and managing reserves, and for undertaking relevant research, remained virtually unchanged.

A more fundamental change occurred in 1973 when the Nature Conservancy was abolished, and a new Nature Conservancy Council (NCC) was created as a grant-aided body, financed by and responsible to the Department of the Environment. The new Council was responsible for establishing, maintaining and managing National Nature Reserves, providing advice and disseminating knowledge about nature conservation, and for commissioning or supporting research relevant to nature conservation. The research staff, numbering about a hundred scientists, of the former Conservancy remained in the Natural Environment Research Council and became the Institute of Terrestrial Ecology.[41]

The relationship between the NCC and the new Institute was defined as that of a customer and contractor. The Council would be the executive and general advisory body in the nature conservation field, and would commission or support research from experts within the Institute or elsewhere. Whereas all the research under the Nature Conservancy had been previously financed from the government's science vote, a proportion of the funds required by the Institute would be obtained from contracts placed by the Council and other bodies.[42]

This separation of responsibilities represented a completely new approach to the government's involvement in nature conservation: the Nature Conservancy Council Act of 1973 marked the beginning of a new phase in the British conservation movement.

The County Naturalists' Trusts

The creation of the Nature Conservancy and the powers awarded by the National Parks Act created an entirely new situation for the voluntary movement. The RSPB and SPNR were no longer alone in pleading the case for nature conservation. The Conservancy would protect key sites and deploy officers and wardens in each region to manage the reserves and generally keep wildlife under surveillance. In addition, powers had been granted to local authorities to create their own reserves and generally adopt a more positive approach toward the protection of wildlife.

From thenceforth, the prime task of the voluntary bodies was to supplement and complement the functions of the Nature Conservancy. Accordingly, the RSPB urged all its members in 1949 to maintain their vigilance and report any threats to the survival of individual species or key ornithological sites. The Society asked for details of any threat, the name of the organisation or individual responsible, and information on the species endangered. It concluded its appeal by noting that 'in general, the Society is better able than individual members to organize opposition to serious threats. Members are therefore urged to leave the main defence to the Society, and not to compromise the position by hasty or ill-organized action. Members can perform invaluable service by the provision of expert information and by the establishment of liaison with other voluntary bodies interested in the preservation of a threatened area.'[43]

Local societies and field clubs had a special role in persuading local authorities to establish local nature reserves. As early as 1944, L. A. Harvey had warned that the authorities would be very reluctant to allocate funds and undertake the administration of reserves, and it was up to local naturalists and their organisations to convince council members and ratepayers of the great benefits of a series of local reserves.[44]

It was hoped the regional sub-committees of the NRIC would play an active role, and the Berkshire and Oxfordshire sub-committee, for example, recruited new members, including the county planning officers of the respective counties, but in general little was achieved. The government failed to award them any official status and most sub-committees failed to meet. The SPNR reviewed the situation in 1954 and discovered only three of the original twenty-four sub-committees were still active. It decided to 'suppress' all of them and encourage the more active committees to be 'resurrected under a different name'.[45]

Fortunately, three counties had already taken the initiative in safeguarding wildlife. A Norfolk Naturalists' Trust was formed in 1926 with four main objectives, namely to protect areas of natural beauty or for 'ornithological, botanical, geological, zoological, or scientific interest', secondly to establish and maintain reserves for plants and animals, thirdly to encourage the breeding of wild birds which were harmless, beautiful or rare, and fourthly to prevent the slaughter of species for their fur, feathers or skins.

The Norfolk Trust had been formed for the following reasons. In 1910, Lord Calthorpe had granted a lease for Blakeney Point to be used for 'marine horticulture' and, on his death in 1912, the peninsula was purchased privately and donated to the National Trust. In 1923, Scolt Head Island was offered for sale on generous terms: an appeal was launched and the island was acquired and then handed over to the National Trust. Soon afterwards, naturalists were given an opportunity of securing the Cley marshes as a third reserve in Norfolk, but on this occasion the National Trust refused to accept the land. Accordingly, S. H. Long and others created the Norfolk Naturalists' Trust, specifically to acquire and manage the marshes as a reserve. The Trust was made a limited company for this purpose.

The Cley marshes were expected to be only the first of many reserves acquired by the Norfolk Trust, and F. W. Oliver commented, 'if the enterprise succeeded one would look forward to the time when every county would have its County Trust which would hold and administer the areas it acquired'. He noted how much easier it would be for a County Trust to manage the sites, rather than a body based in London. The National Trust had already devolved much of its management work to local committees, 'and one might even look forward to a time when many of the properties now held by the National Trust could be handed over (or at any rate leased) to the County Trusts, as soon as they qualify by work done and financial stability'. By 1941, the Norfolk Trust had acquired seven reserves, namely the Cley Marshes, Alderfen Broad, Lakenheath Warren, Blo' Norton Wood, East Wretham Heath, Weeting Heath and the Martham Marshes, Brancaster Staithe, and Burnham Overy.[46]

But no further county trusts were formed until 1946 when the Yorkshire Philosophical Society, based on its museum at York, founded the Yorkshire Naturalists' Trust. During the war, Sidney Smith had persuaded the Society of the urgent need to preserve nearby Askham Bog, with its outstanding invertebrate fauna. This was very urgent as the drains were becoming blocked and scrub was invading all parts of the site. Sir Francis Terry, the chairman of the Society, entered into negotiations with the owner and succeeded in acquiring the Bog for the Society in 1946. The Society immediately asked the Norfolk Trust for advice as to how the reserve should be administered and managed. The Norfolk Trust suggested that a county naturalists' trust should be formed as a limited liability company, with powers to own Askham Bog and other sites. On this advice, the Yorkshire Naturalists' Trust was founded, to a large extent on the Norfolk model, and soon afterwards a warden was appointed and boy scouts undertook some rudimentary management work on the new Askham Bog reserve.[47]

In Lincolnshire, the county Naturalists' Union decided in 1946 to form a permanent committee to take charge of nature conservation in the county. Whilst this helped to keep the issue alive, there was soon need for a larger, independent organisation, with powers to actually own and manage property. Accordingly, the Lincolnshire Naturalists' Trust was founded in December 1948 with an annual subscription of ten shillings per annum. Membership rose from 131 in December 1949 to 360 by 1954. The secretary, A. E. Smith, noted that members joined 'for what the Trust is doing rather than for what it provides them'. Six of the sixteen places on the Trust's council were filled by representatives of the Naturalists' Union, but a considerable amount of work was undertaken by people who were not primarily naturalists. They were simply deeply interested in conservation and furthering the Trust's aims.

One of the first tasks of the Trust was to amend the list of proposed reserves compiled by the Lincolnshire sub-committee of the NRIC. A new list of twenty-four sites was issued in 1950, which were soon designated as Sites of Special Scientific Interest by the Nature Conservancy. By 1954, the Trust managed Gibraltar Point, Scotton Common and an old duck decoy at Friskney as reserves, and was negotiating for a further ten reserves in the county.

The designation of Gibraltar Point as a reserve illustrated the potential role of the Trusts in stimulating local authorities. The Lincolnshire Naturalists' Union drew attention to the value of the site for educational purposes in 1949 (page 168), and one of the first priorities of the Trust was to persuade the Lindsey County Council, which owned Gibraltar Point, to declare it a nature reserve. In 1952, the site became the first Local Nature Reserve to be declared under the 1949 Act in England and Wales. Subsequently, the Skegness Urban District Council made an adjacent area of sand dunes a reserve. The Trust was responsible for managing the entire area, and a field station and bird observatory were soon established.[48]

A. E. Smith noted that the Nature Conservancy, far from discouraging the development of the county trusts, provided a fresh incentive, and in 1956 the Leicestershire and Cambridgeshire Trusts were founded. There followed a trust for the West Midlands in 1957, Kent in 1958, Surrey and Berkshire, Buckinghamshire and Oxfordshire (BBONT) in 1959, and Essex, Bedfordshire and Huntingdonshire, and Hampshire and the Isle of Wight in 1960. The West Wales Field Society became the West Wales Naturalists' Trust in 1956, and a Scottish Wildlife Trust, covering the whole of Scotland, was established in 1964.

The formation of the Manx Nature Conservation Trust in 1974 brought the number of trusts to forty. The Essex Trust was the first to obtain 5,000 members, and by the end of the same year, 1973, 85,000 people belonged to a trust. By 1975, the membership had risen to 100,000. The number of reserves rose from under fifty, covering 4,000 acres, in 1960, to 850, occupying 58,222 acres by January 1975 (Figure 15). Of this area, 12,132 acres were owned, 20,071 acres were leased, and 26,019 acres were managed under an agreement between the appropriate trust and landowner.[49]

With regard to the conservation of specific forms of wildlife, the RSPB underwent a remarkable growth in membership from 6,000 in 1946 to 29,000 in 1965, and it surpassed 117,000 in 1972 and 180,000 in 1974. By January 1975, the Society owned forty-eight reserves (Figure 16), occupying over 32,000 acres, and the annual report described the appointment of further staff to undertake the management of existing reserves, surveys of newer ones with a view to the production of management plans, and the construction of new display centres. In 1961, the headquarters of the Society moved to the Old Lodge, Sandy in Befordshire, the subject of correspondence with the SPNR in 1915 (page 62).

Many of the reserves managed by the Trusts and RSPB fell into the category of local reserves, as envisaged by the NRIC and Huxley Committee: they complemented and supplemented the National Nature Reserves administered by the Nature Conservancy. In Bedfordshire and Huntingdonshire, for example, the Trust established twenty reserves by 1975, in addition to the National Nature Reserves declared by the Conservancy at Knocking Hoe, Monks Wood, Holme Fen and Woodwalton Fen. The Trust's reserves included the largest tract of unreclaimed marshland in mid-Bedfordshire, and a woodland mentioned in the medieval cartulary of Ramsey Abbey. In addition to these long-established wildlife communities, the reserve series also included a reserve situated on the material excavated from a railway tunnel in 1857, and fifty-two acres of flooded gravel pits which were excavated in the late 1930s in order to provide gravel for the concrete runways of local airfields.

One of the most famous reserves of the RSPB is the Minsmere Level

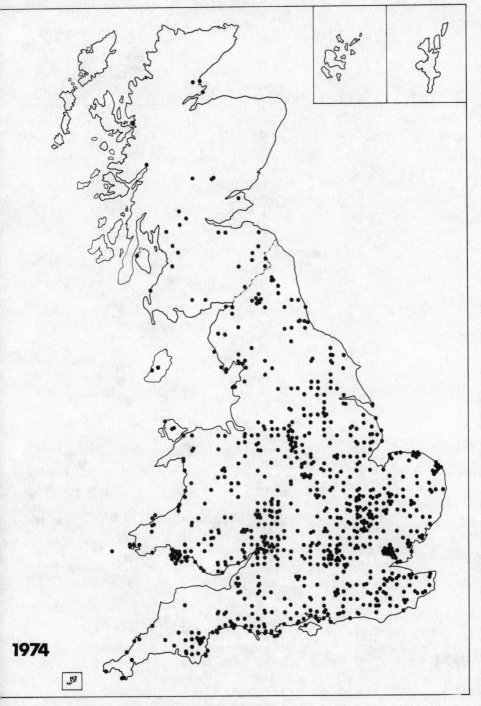

1974

Figure 15
Distribution of nature reserves of County Naturalists' Trusts in 1974

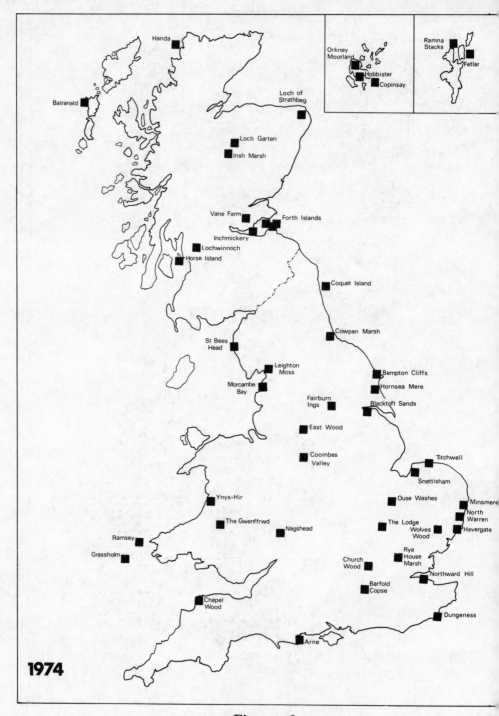

Figure 16

Distribution of nature reserves of the RSPB in 1974

of Suffolk, which was flooded by seawater in 1940 as part of the military defence system of the North Sea coast. It was proposed as a national nature reserve by the NRIC in 1945 on account of the exceptional variety of bird life in the marshes, adjacent to the heaths and woods of the Norwich Crags. Soon after the war ended, part of the Levels was reclaimed for agriculture, but the RSPB secured a lease on the remainder in order to preserve the shallow lagoons, which were becoming increasingly brackish. At first, most attention was centred on the value of the reserve as a refuge for the avocet *Avosetta recurvirostra*, which nested at Minsmere and Havergate Island for the first time in many decades in 1947. But interest in the reserve soon widened, and by 1973 over thirty species of marshland bird were nesting on the site, including the Marsh Harrier and Savi's Warbler.

The Minsmere reserve provides a recent example of how the voluntary bodies had to implement management programmes quickly and participate in discovering new techniques. Within ten years, about a quarter of the open water at Minsmere became covered by reed, and the accretion of humus from the dead plants raised and dried out the slightly undulating land sufficiently for shrubs and alder carr to invade the previously open and varied habitat. A system of sluices and ditches had to be installed to improve water control. Water levels had to be kept high in late winter and spring, and then allowed to fall, by evaporation and draining into the sea, from mid-summer onwards. Artificial 'scrapes' were excavated to increase the area of open water and mud flats.[50]

Although the acquisition and management of reserves absorbed most of their resources, the trusts were keenly concerned with the conservation of wildlife on all categories of land. By 1969, fifteen agreements were negotiated between the trusts and various highway authorities as to the use of herbicide sprays on roadside verges. When the authorities began to use mechanical methods for maintaining the verges, the trusts entered into further agreements, controlling the timing and frequency of cutting the grass in the interests of wildlife. Surveys were made of the most important verges for wildlife, and maps were submitted to the appropriate authorities, marking the most important sites for plants, insects, birds and mammals. By 1969, about twenty Highway Authorities had entered into such agreements and, in Sussex, fifty-seven verges were protected, with an aggregate length of 10.1 miles. In Lincolnshire, the twenty-four protected verges included the most northerly breeding colony of the chalkhill blue butterfly *Lysandra coridon*.[51]

Liaison with local authorities, and private landowners and occupiers, highlighted the continuing need to stimulate interest in wildlife, and nature conservation in particular. It was noticed how many adults and children began to take an interest in wild plants and animals, following a visit to a reserve. During the 1960s, several trusts opened up nature trails on their reserves: this was a concept first mooted in the 1930s and successfully developed in America. One of the first trails in Britain was set out in 1963 by the Berkshire, Buckinghamshire and Oxfordshire County Naturalists' Trust (BBONT), in conjunction with the Council for Nature, at Coombe Hill in Buckinghamshire. The site was owned by the National Trust and was already used for public recreation. A series of illustrated notice boards guided visitors round the trail, explaining differences in the wildlife characteristic of the top and sides of the hill. The need to manage the vegetation was explained, and attention was drawn to the consequences of a recent fire. In spite of bad weather, 200 visitors used the trail on the first weekend, and 700 visitors were recorded on a day later in the year.[52]

In the place of the Bird and Tree Competition, the RSPB established first a Junior Bird Recorders' Club, and then the Young Ornithologists' Club, which had over 64,000 members by 1975, made up of children of primary and middle school age. Members received a bi-monthly colour magazine and could participate in both residential courses on ornithology and local group activities, often linked with other outdoor pursuits. Parties of school children were encouraged to visit reserves and the increasing number of Nature Centres, equipped with Nature Discovery Classrooms. Wardens and a growing number of qualified teacher/naturalists took the parties round the reserves and centres. The educational department of the RSPB provided courses for teachers and supplied films, posters and pamphlets for use in the classrooms.

By 1975, the RSPB employed a full-time staff of 200, and about 100 people on a part-time basis. Thirty-four of the forty County Naturalists' Trusts had appointed administrative officers. But the strength of the voluntary bodies was the extent to which they involved their membership in a wide range of activities, contributing toward nature conservation. About seventy RSPB members' groups, with an aggregate membership of 10,000, had grown up largely spontaneously in various parts of the country, publicising the work of the Society, undertaking practical conservation work, beside organising bird-watching parties.[53]

The participation of members of the County Naturalists' Trusts may be illustrated by the Cambridgeshire and Isle of Ely Naturalists' Trust (CAMBIENT), which had twenty-four local management committes in 1975, each responsible for a nature reserve. The members wardened the reserves, drew up management plans in liaison with the Trust's Scientific Advisory Committee, and implemented those plans. The large reserve of Hayley Wood (125 acres) had a committee of twelve in 1975, which dealt with coppicing, fencing, draining, planting, pest control and maintaining the nature trail. At the other extreme, Heydon Chalk Pit of one acre had a management committee of three, which dealt with trespassing, litter clearance and the control of scrub. A trust could utilise almost every talent offered by its members. In CAMBIENT, members undertook the clerical tasks, delivered newsletters, and manned the weekly market stall in Cambridge market, which not only sold £1,000 worth of goods in 1974 but also formed a valuable way of publicising the Trust and recruiting new members. Not only were all those contributions vital to the running of the voluntary bodies, but they demonstrated how the trusts provided an outlet for those people who were convinced of the need for nature conservation, and who asked, 'What can I do to help?'[54]

The SPNR and Council for Nature

From 1946 onwards, the future intentions and organisation of the SPNR came under surveillance. The work of the NRIC was completed and the creation of the Nature Conservancy was assured. In the international field, steps were being taken to strengthen liaison through the creation of the International Union for the Protection of Nature (IUPN). The SPNR could take a great deal of credit for these achievements, but its own future was far from clear.

The first step was to review the Society's commitments, and a subcommittee was set up in 1946 primarily to advise on the future of the Woodwalton Fen nature reserve. Although the Society's income had risen sharply since the Druce bequest of 1939, the outgoings and cost of management of the reserve made serious inroads. The funds were insufficient to arrest the rapid deterioriation of the reserve, caused by falling water levels and the spread of scrub. The Society decided to seek the help of the Nature Conservancy, and in 1954 the reserve became a National Nature Reserve: although the SPNR retained the freehold, the Conservancy took over the cost of upkeep and the management of wildlife.[55]

This resulted in about half the funds of the SPNR being released for other purposes, and immediately the Society became more generous in making grants. The Lincolnshire Naturalists' Trust received a grant of £200 for the acquisition of Scotton Common, and in 1956 the Society offered up to £500 on a pound for pound basis for the purchase of Linwood Warren in the same county. Instead of simply waiting for requests, the Society began to publicise its willingness to make grants for the acquisition and management of reserves. But the opportunities to give assistance were comparatively few, and by the mid-1950s there was a growing surplus of unspent revenue. E. M.

Nicholson, who was Director-General of the Nature Conservancy by this time, deplored this trend, especially as the Conservancy was so short of funds and had recently taken over the burden of Woodwalton Fen. Every effort had to be made to spend all the current income of the SPNR on worthwhile projects.

Some members of the SPNR suggested that the Society should take over and manage new reserves where no local body could be found to undertake the work. Accordingly, Blackmoor Copse in Wiltshire was acquired in 1956, primarily in order to preserve the purple emperor butterfly *Apatura iris*, but the Society tried to avoid this kind of commitment because of its lack of resources for managing the reserves. J. S. L. Gilmour had recently made a survey of Mickfield Meadow, Badgeworth Marsh and Sharpham Moor, and had emphasised the need for heavier investment and much closer supervision of the management work.

In order to prevent the reserves of the voluntary movement becoming the poor relations of the National Nature Reserves, they had to be managed on a scientific basis by a permanent salaried staff. Herbert Smith and C. Diver agreed, but warned that the Society could not afford the expense. It was completely dependent on the revenue from its investments, and the prospect of further generous bequests seemed to be very remote. Under its royal charter, the SPNR could not raise an annual subscription. There was no alternative but to leave the acquisition and management of reserves to others.

Clearly, it was the responsibility of the SPNR to help those who could take on these tasks. By 1957, there were five trusts and a promise of further trusts being founded in the near future. They were financed by members' subscriptions and, as membership grew, so the trusts would become more prosperous and able to acquire more land and invest in management programmes.

The SPNR could support the trusts in two ways. First, it could offer expert advice on land agency problems and scientific management. This could be achieved by reforming the structure and composition of the Society's Council so as to ensure the maximum representation of experts who were prepared to take an active role in promoting reserves. A special reserves committee should be formed to deal with specialised aspects of this work. Regular visits to reserves would be organised and meetings would be convened between the wardens of each site so as to ensure a free interchange of ideas and experience. Secondly, the SPNR should mount a publicity campaign to focus public attention on the role of the trusts in protecting wildlife. The Society had considered for several years the publication of a popular handbook setting out the need for nature conservation. E. M. Nicholson proposed an even larger educational programme which would include the publication of a monthly journal providing the public with information on reserves and wildlife in general.

The County Naturalists' Trusts themselves proposed a third task for the SPNR, namely as a co-ordinating body for the trusts. A meeting of representatives from the Lincolnshire, Cambridgeshire and Leicestershire Trusts was held in Cambridge in June 1957 which concluded that greater co-operation would lead to greater efficiency, the formation of further trusts, and the promotion of nature conservation generally. The view was endorsed and amplified at a larger meeting at Hickling Broad in September, attended by representatives of all the trusts. Four counties began to issue a joint bulletin, and there was general agreement that the next logical step should be federation under the SPNR.

The SPNR set up a sub-committee in 1957 to review these proposals, consisting of H. W. Miles, W. H. Pearsall and N. D. Riley, who had succeeded Herbert Smith as secretary of the Society in 1953. Although not a member, C. Diver exerted an influential role. The sub-committee endorsed the need for the SPNR to provide expert advice to the trusts and other bodies on the acquisition and management of reserves, but it believed the task of publicising and winning support for the nature conservation movement would overwhelm both its legal powers and financial resources. Instead of undertaking this task itself, the SPNR should promote a new body which would canalise opinion, give voice to and publicise the wide range of voluntary bodies concerned with the protection of wildlife.

The proposed new body was soon called the Council for Nature. It was noted how the analogous National Council of Social Service helped in defending the interests of its constituent charitable bodies, and how the National Audubon Society had helped to win popular support and more funds for its component parts. E. M. Nicholson stressed the value of the Council in supporting and complementing the work of the Nature Conservancy. The case for preserving sites would be greatly strengthened by the support of both the official and voluntary bodies. A Council for Nature could undertake work which was normally outside the scope of an official body: it could mobilise public opinion, lobby members of parliament, and participate in press controversy. It could employ voluntary labour, people who had a great deal of enthusiasm and energy, local and empirical knowledge. Although the Conservancy had established regional offices, it had to work to a national programme, whereas the work of a Council for Nature could reflect much more closely the individual wishes and character of each region.

The SPNR decided to promote the Council for Nature and provide it with initial financial support. Although the financial demands were daunting, a working party argued that since racing pigeon clubs raised over £2.5 millions per annum for transport charges surely a Council for Nature could amass even greater funds for nature conservation. At a meeting in early 1958, it was decided to widen the objectives of the Council so as to promote public interest over the entire field of natural history. Membership was to be open to those organisations not specifically concerned with nature conservation.

The Council for Nature was finally established in late 1958, and by 1963 it had obtained the support of 390 national and local organisations, which probably represented 100,000 naturalist members. A grant of £5,000 per annum for five years from the BBC made it possible to set up an Intelligence Unit under the direction of R. S. R. Fitter, which acted as an information bureau on all questions related to natural history in the British Isles.

It was immediately apparent that the Council for Nature could not be adapted to serve as the 'federal centre' for the County Naturalists' Trusts, and accordingly A. E. Smith proposed the creation of a new committee within the SPNR to fulfil this role. The Society agreed, and the first meeting of the County Naturalists' Trust Committee was held in November 1958, with all trusts represented. It soon began providing expert guidance on the formation of new trusts, recruitment of new members, and on a wide range of financial and land agency problems. It became a clearing house for the trusts, initiating such new ventures as a joint newsletter.

A permanent secretariat was appointed to the SPNR in 1965 and an increasing proportion of the resources of the Society was devoted to helping the County Naturalists' Trust Committee. As vacancies occurred on the SPNR Council, each trust was invited to nominate a member, and by 1973 every trust was represented. The process of integration of the SPNR and trust movement was almost complete: the County Naturalists' Trust Committee was dissolved and the Society became in effect the Association of County Trusts (ACT). By 1975, steps were being taken for a revision of the SPNR charter of 1916 to formalise these changes.

Beside arranging meetings and conferences on topics of common concern, the SPNR made every effort to secure financial help for the trusts. Over £400,000 were spent by the Society and trusts in acquiring reserves in the 1960s. Through the SPNR, for example, the World Wildlife Fund helped most purchases: the Nuffield Trust provided the Society in 1961 with a revolving loan-fund of £20,000, which had been used at least six times by 1975 in providing interest-free loans to the trusts for reserve acquisition. Between 1969 and 1975, the Carnegie United Kingdom Trust provided £40,000 to enable trusts to appoint paid administrative or conservation officers, and to set up such educational projects as nature trails, visitor centres and mobile displays.

Toward 1970

This book has concentrated on the documentation of the British nature conservation movement and has made comparatively little reference to developments overseas. Concern has always been shown in Britain for the preservation of wildlife overseas, whether exotically coloured birds or tigers, elephants and other beasts of the tropics. The Society for the Protection of Birds (1889) and the Society for the Preservation of the Fauna of the Empire (1903) were founded expressly to promote their protection. The incidence of oil pollution at sea and slaughter of birds on migration reminded naturalists, and especially ornithologists, of the need for a supra-national organisation. The International Council for Bird Preservation was founded in 1922, and some support was given to the concept of a Central Correlating Committee for other forms of wildlife in the inter-war period.

But Britain continued to pursue a comparatively insular approach to wildlife preservation until the late 1940s, when the closer liaison between nations engendered by the war and the inception of the United Nations and its agencies stimulated further attempts to create an international wildlife body. In 1946, the Chairman of the Scientific Commission of the Swiss National Park invited J. S. Huxley and other members of the Hobhouse and Huxley Committees to inspect the Swiss National Park. The invitation was accepted, and during the course of the visit the Swiss League for the Protection of Nature organised an informal meeting of representatives from seven countries to discuss ways of extending international collaboration. There was general agreement on the need for 'an active international organisation, widely international and representative in character'.[56]

A year later, the Swiss League arranged a formal conference at Brunnen, attended by representatives of twenty-four countries, which accepted proposals for an International Union for the Protection of Nature. Meanwhile, Huxley had become the first Director-General of UNESCO, which formally accepted a definitive draft constitution for the Union, prepared by the British Foreign Office. Membership was open to official and voluntary bodies, both national and international in character. The name of the Union was changed to the International Union for the Conservation of Nature and Natural Resources (IUCN) in 1956.[57]

The SPNR and Nature Conservancy gave considerable material aid to the Union in its initial scientific and technical work, which sought to identify which species were threatened with extinction and ways of averting such a danger. By 1961, the scale of the crisis was clear: sixteen distinguished scientists, naturalists and businessmen in that year produced a manifesto describing how 'vast numbers of fine and harmless wild creatures' were losing their lives or homes as a result of thoughtless and needless destruction. The devastation of the 1960s was expected to surpass all previous records. The manifesto emphasised that sufficient skill and devotion were available to avert such a disaster: the over-riding need was for money to carry out the necessary mercy missions and to meet conservation emergencies. The Union was ill-equipped to take on the necessarily skilled task of campaigning and fund-raising in individual countries, and accordingly a separate organisation, called the World Wildlife Fund, was established. Working in close harmony with the IUCN, it assisted 682 projects between 1961 and 1974 for the conservation of wildlife in over sixty countries.[58]

The IUCN played an important role in focusing attention on conservation problems through the organisation of technical meetings. These often provided the first opportunities for an international exchange of ideas on topics of common concern: the meeting at The Hague in 1951 took as its theme the 'Rural landscape as a habitat for flora and fauna in densely populated countries'; the themes of the Salzburg conference of 1953 were 'Protection of nature and tourism', and the 'Protection of fauna and flora at high altitudes'; and the Copenhagen meeting of 1954 examined 'Arctic fauna' and 'The effects of modern insecticides on mammals, birds and insects'.[59]

Not only did representatives from many countries participate, but a wide range of disciplines and land-users became involved in the discussions. At the Edinburgh meeting of 1956, the themes included the 'Relationship of ecology to landscape planning', and 'The problems arising from deep and open cast mining'. Papers covered such topics as 'Shelterbelts in cleared landscapes', 'Plant nutrition on ash', and 'Hydro-electric schemes in the North of Scotland'.[60]

Within Britain itself, the value of the Council for Nature in co-ordinating the work of its member bodies was demonstrated in May 1963 when it sponsored a National Nature Week. Displays and activities were arranged throughout Britain drawing attention to wildlife and the countryside. The largest exhibit was organised by *The Observer* at Alexandra Palace in London. The event aroused great public interest and equally significantly it provided an opportunity for those concerned with amenity and wildlife to meet and debate with other land- and resource-users.

In order to extend these contacts, the Council for Nature immediately made plans for convening a study conference where a fuller exchange of data and ideas could take place. Meanwhile, the

Royal Society of Arts had just published a survey of the inter-relationship of industry and the countryside, undertaken by H. E. Bracey, and it planned to hold a conference to examine Bracey's findings in the light of the recommendations of the Scott committee of twenty-one years previously. In view of the common interest between both intended conferences, it was decided to hold a single meeting in November 1963, organised by the Nature Conservancy. This was attended by representatives of ninety organisations, who examined the question, 'What sort of countryside do we all want to see in 1970?' The year 1970 seemed near enough to make realistic forecasting possible, but was 'tinged with just a little of the apprehension aroused by George Orwell's 1984'.[61]

The meeting, under the presidency of the Duke of Edinburgh, sub-divided itself into three working parties to cover the inter-related aspects of conservation, organisation and research. Its success in securing representatives from the entire environmental spectrum may be illustrated by the working party on conservation, which included representatives from agriculture and forestry, mining and the power industries, statutory water undertakings and the military authorities, and those organisations concerned with outdoor recreation, amenity and wildlife. There was general agreement on the need for a more positive approach to planning, greater liaison between planning authorities, amenity societies and the developers, and the potential value of universities and colleges offering courses on conservation. For most participants, the meeting was an unprecedented opportunity 'to examine the role and principles of conservation in the modern world, and how these and the demands which society makes on the resources of the countryside' could be reconciled.[62]

The apparent benefits of a wide range of disciplines and organisations discussing such practical issues stimulated the appointment of twelve study groups in late 1964 to examine in depth the legislation, administration, the use of the countryside, the impact of technology, various aspects of education and training, and ways of disseminating information. Their reports formed the substance of a second 'Country-side in 1970' conference in November 1965.

One of the study groups reviewed the efficacy and comprehensiveness of legislation in the environmental field, and recommended, for example, the replacement of the National Parks Commission by a Countryside Commission with nation-wide responsibilities for the conservation of fine landscapes and provision of facilities for outdoor recreation. It proposed further powers for local authorities to acquire and manage land for amenity, access and recreation. These proposals were in large part implemented by the Countryside Act of 1968 which set up a Countryside Commission for England and Wales, and gave local authorities powers to establish Country Parks. In the previous year, the Countryside (Scotland) Act had provided for a Countryside Commission for Scotland.[63]

This important study group of the second 'Countryside in 1970' conference also made recommendations which did not require fresh legislation. These included a proposal that county councils should appoint Countryside Committees. The study group remarked that 'Parliament may legislate; government departments may declare national policies; countrywide bodies may advise and exhort; yet national laws and policies may remain but imperfectly implemented unless backed by strong local determination.' The group believed that such Committees, containing members of the county council and local voluntary bodies, would help to utilise and channel local initiatives for such projects as tree planting, the creation of nature reserves, and identification and preservation of countryside treasures. Within two years, such committees had been appointed by fifteen county councils.

The third and final 'Countryside in 1970' conference was held in 1970, and concluded by examining how each organisation and person could help conserve the environment. It outlined the choices and opportunities presented to mankind in the 1970s. F. F. Darling gave the BBC Reith Lectures for 1969 and took as his theme 'Wilderness and Plenty', also emphasising how man's increased control over the world's resources had brought with it increasing responsibilities for conserving the intrinsic dynamism, richness and diversity of the planet. Steps had to be urgently taken to reduce pollution and the destruction of habitat, and above all to curb the largely uncontrolled rise in human population. Man had to become once again 'an integrated functional member of the plant and animal world'.[64]

On British initiative, the Council of Europe designated 1970 as European Conservation Year. A European Conservation Declaration was made, President Nixon described the need for conservation in a Message to Congress, and in Britain the first ever reference to environmental conservation was made in the Queen's Speech in that year. Although the terms environment and conservation came to be used ever more loosely, wildlife and nature conservation were recognised as important components of the total problem.

Precedents and Initiatives

During the 1960s and 1970s, wildlife was increasingly affected by changes in land use and management, and perhaps most significantly by the ploughing up of old grasslands, drainage schemes, the application of fertilisers and herbicides, and woodland planting programmes. Many of these changes were piecemeal and aroused little immediate concern. Large-scale industrial ventures encountered greater opposition, as when the Tees Valley and Cleveland Water Board succeeded in gaining approval for a reservoir at Cow Green in order to provide water for industrial and domestic use of Teesside. Part of Cow Green was in the Upper Teesdale National Nature Reserve, and the remainder had been notified as a SSSI. Parliament decided in 1967 that the urgent need for water overrode the irreparable loss of the plant communities of the site and the disruption of the National Nature Reserves series.

In addition to the loss of habitat, wildlife was also affected by the incidence of pollution, which was equally varied and complex in its impact on individual species. The wreck of the oil tanker *Torrey Canyon*, off Lands End in 1967, was an obvious disaster for maritime life. About 100,000 tons of crude oil escaped into the sea, producing oil slicks which eventually affected the coasts of the South-West Peninsula and France. In addition, about 1,756,000 gallons of emulsifier-solvent mixture were used to reduce the extent and intensity of oil pollution at sea and on the beaches. The impact of the oil and chemicals on wild birds, fish and shell fish may be illustrated by the loss of guillemots and razorbills. It was estimated that about 20,000 guillemots *Uria aalge* perished, which was equivalent to the aggregate breeding population between the Isle of Wight and Cardigan Bay in that period. About 5,000 razorbills *Alca torda* died, equal to a third of the breeding population of the same area.[65]

Other pollutants, derived from industrial or agricultural sources, had an indirect or sub-lethal effect on wildlife, but they were nevertheless an equally serious threat in the long-term. Organochlorine compounds are so persistent that even relatively small quantities could have widespread and significant impact. Damage may be caused in a variety of ways: ovulation might be delayed, eggs might be infertile, or their shells too thin for successful incubation. Some pollutants might have no effects on a species in normal conditions, but cause deaths during a stress period, such as adverse weather conditions or shortages of food. Whereas many species experience periodic natural disasters and a marked fluctuation in population, pollutants derived from pesticides or some other source might turn a disaster into an irreversible loss.

Against this background, the period of the 1960s and 1970s was marked by an improvement in understanding of the complex man-environment relationship. Instead of regarding wild plants and animals as being simply provided for the amusement of naturalists and senti-mental country-lovers, wildlife was recognised as an essential part of this relationship. Their decline and displacement were symptomatic of the harmful side-effects of human activity, and sharp reminders of the need for man to pay greater heed to conserving his own habitat. The conservation of wildlife was only one part of the overall task of husbanding the resources of the world. The penalties of neglect or abuse were not only the loss of various wild plants and animals, but also a world-wide shortage of basic foodstuffs, fuel and the other prerequisites of human life.

In spite of these changes in the real world and our perception of this world, the present-day nature conservation movement draws much of its strength from the events, initiatives and experiences of the past. When itemised, these events would include the first wild birds protection act of 1869, the Conference on nature preservation in post-war reconstruction in 1941, and the issue of a royal charter establishing the Nature Conservancy in 1949. Important initiatives would include those taken by N. C. Rothschild in the early part of the century, the attempts of Geoffrey Dent and Herbert Smith to secure agreed policies on nature preservation in the early 1940s, and the role of A. G. Tansley and the British Ecological Society in emphasising the need for a series of national *habitat* reserves administered by an official body with a scientific capacity. The early experience in suppressing egg-collecting and managing such reserves as Woodwalton Fen is still recalled by those battling with similar problems today.

There have been few dramatic changes in the methods of protecting and managing wildlife. The legislation to protect deer (1959 and 1963), seals (1970) and badgers (1973) was based very largely on the experience of earlier wild birds protection acts. There were attempts to protect other forms of wildlife, but parliament, whilst sympathetic, became increasingly uneasy over the way in which each species was considered individually and in a piecemeal fashion. Accordingly, there was widespread support for a private member's Bill in 1975 which established 'a framework for conservation'. It made it illegal to kill, harm, possess or offer for sale any plant or creature included in the schedules to the Act, or any species subsequently added to these schedules. No unauthorised person could uproot any wild plant without reasonable excuse. The sponsors realised that it would be very difficult to enforce such an Act, but felt 'that existing legislation in this field had had a real effect, perhaps largely because of the educative influence that it had on society'.[66]

The scale of operation, rather than the objectives, has changed. Whereas sixty-one sites were identified by their owners in 1941–2 as nature reserves, there were over 1,000 reserves in 1975. Instead of the modest *Bird Notes and News*, members of the RSPB received in 1975 an extremely lavish magazine, called *Birds,* which included many coloured photographs. Television has revolutionised the task of giving everyone the experience of looking at wildlife: outstanding films and informed discussion have played a major part in winning public support for conservation.

There is far greater public participation in nature conservation: the expertise derived from the science of ecology is applied more effectively. Nevertheless, the proponents of nature conservation must continue to operate within the broader field of environmental concern. In the 1930s, they participated with the advocates of amenity and outdoor recreation in the debates and campaigns for a series of national parks: in the 1970s, they assist official and voluntary bodies in drawing up regional planning studies.

Nature conservation remains intimately involved in the wider political, social and economic affairs of the nation. In the 1940s, it drew strength from the opportunities presented in the field of town and country planning. In this way, Lord Reith and John Dower, the Town and Country Planning Act, and the National Parks Act, had a tremendous influence on the objectives and resources of nature conservation in the post-war years. Likewise, in the 1970s, the influence of external factors is strong, whether measured by the size of the grant made by the Department of the Environment to the Nature Conservancy Council each year, or by the funds given to the voluntary bodies by industry and charitable organisations.

We continue to pursue policies broadly similar to those devised earlier in the century: we are simply more effective in implementing them. Consequently, it remains relevant to ask how, why and when nature conservation evolved in Britain. Nature conservation may be a comparatively young interest, but it already has a history.

Notes and References

1   J. Gilmour, 'How our flora was discovered', in J. Gilmour & M. Walters, *Wild Flowers* (Collins, London), 1972, 22–44

2   R. Gray, *The birds of the west of Scotland* (Murray, Glasgow), 1871, 436

3   An acte agenst destruccyon of wyldfowle, 1533–34, 25 Henry VIII, c. 11

4   R. S. R. Fitter, *Wildlife in Britain* (Penguin, London), 1963, 94–105; A. C. Smith, 'On the ornithology of Wilts', *Wiltshire Archaeological and Natural History Magazine*, 1, 1874, 41–5

5   O. H. Mackenzie, *A hundred years in the Highlands* (Bles, London), 1956, 221 pp.

6   J. R. Jeffries, *The Open Air* (Chatto & Windus, London), 1885, 112–38

7   C. Waterton, *Essays on Natural History* (Longman, London), 1838, 153–60

8   J. Cordeaux, 'Notes from Flamborough Head', *Zoologist*, 2, 1867, 1008–11; *Bird Notes and News*, 4, 1910–11, 26–7

9   *Report on the British Association for the Advancement of Science*, 38th meeting, 1868, 108–9

10 W. H. Hudson, *The Land's End* (Hutchinson, London), 1908, 204–21

11 SPNR archives, Box 23, 119 & 126

12 Ibid., Boxes 23 & 25; F. H. Davey, *Flora of Cornwall* (Chegwidden, Penryn), 1909, 543; D. E. Allen, *The Victorian fern craze* (Hutchinson, London), 1969, 83 pp.

13 *Bird Notes and News*, 3, 1908, 13–15; RSPB archives, council minutes, 5/12/13

14 E. M. Nicholson, *Birds in England* (Chapman & Hall, London),

1926, 152; Gilmour, *loc. cit.*; T. H. Mason, *The Islands of Ireland* (Mercier, Cork), 1967, 131

15 RSPB archives, council minutes 13/4/23

16 E. Parker, *Ethics of egg-collecting* (The Field, London), 1935, 120 pp; Nicholson, *op. cit.*, xii & 247

17 L. R. W. Loyd, *The Protection of birds: an indictment* (Longman, London), 1924, 88 pp.; T. A. Coward, 'Ethics of egg-collecting', *19th Century and after*, 100, 1926, 101–109

18 E. T. Booth, *Rough notes on the birds observed* (Porter & Dulau, London), 1881–7, vol. 1, Chough, 3 pp.

19 J. Fisher, *Natural History of the Kite* (RSPB occasional publication), 1949, 16 pp.

20 W. G. Sheldon, 'The destruction of British butterflies', *Entomologist*, 58, 1925, 105–112

21 Jefferies, *op. cit.*, 112–38

22 B. Harrison, 'Religion and recreation in nineteenth-century England', *Past and Present*, 38, 1967, 98–125; 'Animals and the State in nineteenth-century England', *English Historical Review*, 88, 1973, 786–820

23 Act to consolidate and amend the several laws relating to the cruelty and improper treatment of animals, 1835, 5–6 William IV, c. 59

24 Hares Preservation Act, 1892, 55 Victoria, c. 8; Wild Animals in Captivity Protection Act, 1900, 63–4 Victoria, c. 33

25 Selborne Society, *Report for 1887*, 1888, 12 pp.

26 *Bird Notes and News*, 4, 1910–11, 37–9

27 Ibid., 19, 1941, 129–32; 25, 1953, 293–5

28 *Annual Reports of the Society for the Protection of Birds*; *Bird Notes and News*, 11, 1924, 19–25

29 RSPB archives, council minutes, 1911

30 An Act to prohibit the importation of plumage, 1921, 11 & 12 George V, c. 16; RSPB archives, council minutes, 18/10/12 & 24/3/25; P. Barclay-Smith, 'The trade in bird plumage', *The UFAW Courier*, 1951, 4 pp.

31 *Bird Notes and News*, 19, 1941, 129–32

32 *Annual Reports of the Society for the Protection of Birds*

33 RSPB archives, council minutes, 24/1/13

34 Ibid., 18/4/13 & 24/4/25; P. J. Conder, 'Protecting birds at lighthouses', *Bird Notes*, 29, 1960, 95–8

35 J. Mothersole, *The Isles of Scilly* (Religious Tracts Society, London), 1910, 244 pp.

36 *Bird Notes and News*, 10, 1922, 49–51

37 RSPB archives, council minutes; SPNR archives, Box 32, 4K

38 Oil in Navigable Waters Act, 1922, 12 & 13 George V, c. 39;
    Public Record Office, HO 45 17389
39 RSPB archives, council minutes, 24/4/25 & 16/10/25
40 Ibid., 6/12/29
41 P. Barclay-Smith, 'The International Council for Bird preser-
    vation', *Biological Conservation*, 5, 1973, 290–1
42 SPNR archives, Box 31, 2/3–30; Box 32, 1
43 Ibid., Box 31, 1 & 2/79; Box 32
44 Ibid., Boxes 24–6

Chapter Two

1   An Act to Prevent the Cruel and Improper Treatment of Cattle,
    1822, 3 George IV, c. 71; An Act to Consolidate and Amend the
    Several Laws related to the Cruel and Improper Treatment of
    Animals, 1835, 5 & 6 William IV, c. 59
2   *Report of the British Association for the Advancement of Science*, 37th
    meeting, 1867, 97
3   Ibid., 38th meeting, 1868, 108–9
4   *Bird Notes and News*, 14, 1930, 137–8
5   Parliamentary Debates, Commons, vol. 194, 1/3/69, 404–6
6   An Act for the Preservation of Sea Birds, 1869, 32 & 33
    Victoria, c. 17
7   T. H. Nelson, *The Birds of Yorkshire* (Brown, London), 1907,
    vol. 2, 711–24
8   An Act for Protection of certain Wild Fowl during the breeding
    season, 1872, 35 Victoria, Bill 46
9   An Act for the Protection of certain Wild Birds during the
    breeding season, 1872, 35 & 36 Victoria, c. 78
10 An Act for the Preservation of Wild Fowl, 1876, 39 & 40
    Victoria, c. 29
11 Wild Birds Protection Act, 1880, 43 & 44 Victoria, c. 35
12 Ibid., 1881, 44 & 45 Victoria, c. 51
13 Wild Birds Protection Bill, 1891, 54 Victoria, Bill 213
14 Ibid., 1893, 56 Victoria, Bill 298; C.M.D., *Lord Lilford* (Smith,
    Elder, London), 1900, 188
15 Wild Birds Protection Act, 1894, 57 & 58 Victoria, c. 24
16 Wild Birds Protection Bill, 1896, 59 Victoria, Bill 282; Wild Birds
    Protection Act, 1896, 59 & 60 Victoria, c. 56
17 Wild Birds Protection Act, 1902, 2 Edward VII, c. 6
18 Ibid., (St Kilda), 1904, 4 Edward VII, c. 10
19 Wild Birds Protection Act, 1904, 4 Edward VII, c. 4; W. H.

Hudson (ed.), *The barn owl* (Society for the Protection of Birds), 19, 1902, 11 pp.

20 Wild Birds Protection Act, 1908, 8 Edward VII, c. 11

21 Ibid., 1925, 15 & 16 George 5, c. 31

22 Game Preservation Act, 1930, Saorstat Eireann, no. 11; Wild Birds Protection Act, 1920, Saorstat Eireann, no. 16

23 Parliamentary Debates, Dail Eireann, vol. 33, 12/2/30, 77–104

24 P. G. Kennedy, *An Irish Sanctuary* (Colm O Lochlainn, Dublin), 1953, 168 pp.

25 RSPB archives, council minutes, 6/10/11 & 19/4/12

26 A Bill to consolidate and amend the law relating to the Protection of Wild Birds, 1899, 62 Victoria, Bill 83

27 E. S. Montagu, *Report of the Departmental Committee on the Protection of Wild Birds*, Cmd 295, 1919, 44 pp.; Minutes of evidence taken before the Departmental Committee, Cmd 189, 1919, 193 pp.

28 Public Record Office (PRO), HO 45 17925

29 Wild Birds Protection Bill, 1927, 17 & 18 George V, Bill 8

30 Parliamentary Debates, Senate (Northern Ireland), 13, 25/3/31, 103–14; Commons (N.I.), 13, 29/9/31, 2113–28; Wild Birds Protection Act (Northern Ireland), 1931, 21 & 22 George V, c. 14; Wild Birds Protection Act (N.I.), 1950, 14 George VI, c. 26, & 1968, 16 & 17 Elizabeth II, c. 5

31 S. McClelland, 'Wild bird protection in Northern Ireland', *Bird Notes*, 25, 1953, 205–8

32 Protection of Lapwings Act, 1928, 18 & 19 George V, c. 2; PRO, HO 45 12981; Protection of Birds Act, 1933, 23 & 24 George V, c. 52; PRO, HO 45 15326; Quail Protection Act, 1937, 1 & 2 George VI, c. 5; Wild Birds (Duck & Geese) Protection Act, 1939, 2 & 3 George VI, c. 19

33 Nicholson, *op. cit.*, 1926, 20–1

34 PRO, HO 45 17925

35 Parliamentary Debates, Lords, vol. 179, 3/12/52, 703–46; Protection of Birds Act, 1954, 2 & 3 Elizabeth II, c. 30; Lord Tweedsmuir, *One Man's Happiness* (Hale, London), 1968, 181–7

36 Parliamentary Debates, Lords, vol. 246, 14/2/63, 1062–3; Protection of Birds Act, 1967, c. 46

37 Grey Seals (Protection) Act, 1914, 4 & 5 George V, c. 3; Parliamentary Debates, Lords, vol. 16, 12/5/14, 176–8; PRO, HO 45 15043; Scottish RO, AF 1443–6

38 Grey Seals (Protection) Act, 1932, 22 & 23 George V, c. 23

39 Parliamentary Debates, Commons, vol. 793, 12/12/69, 792–800; Conservation of Seals Act, 1970, c. 30

40 Deer (Scotland) Act, 1959, 7 & 8 Elizabeth II, c. 40; Deer Act, 1963, c. 36; Badgers Act, 1973, c. 57
41 Local Government Act, 1888, 51 & 52 Victoria, c. 41
42 SPNR archives, Boxes 23 & 25-6
43 Malicious Damage Act, 1861, 24 & 25 Victoria, c. 97; Larceny Act, 1861, 24 & 25 Victoria, c. 96; 6 & 7 George V, c. 50
44 SPNR archives, Box 25, 1/217-23 & 3
45 Ibid., Boxes 24-6; Wild Plants Protection Bill, 1967, Bill 39
46 RSPB archives, council minutes, 11/4/30 & 11/10/29
47 *Bird Notes and News*, 16, 1933, 14
48 RSPB archives, council minutes, 6/12/12; *Bird Notes and News*, 3, 1909, 81-2
49 *Bird Notes and News*, 3, 1908, 13-15; PRO, HO 45 16785; M. Taylor, *The history of the Association of Bird Watchers and Wardens* (unpublished manuscript), 1971, 21 pp.
50 *Daily News*, 17/2/08; RSPB archives, council minutes, 22/4/10 & 13/7/28
51 *Bird Notes and News*, 11, 1924, 19-25; RSPB archives, council minutes, 12/12/30
52 SPNR archives, Box 33, NRIC report, no. 2
53 J. S. Huxley, *Conservation of nature in England and Wales*, Cmd 7122, 1947, 106-21
54 *Report of the British Association for the Advancement of Science*, 39th meeting, 1869, 91-6
55 W. H. Hudson, *Birds and man* (Duckworth, London), 1915, 5-6
56 M. C. F. Morris, *Francis Orpen Morris: a Memoir* (Nimmo, London), 1897, 67-111
57 Nicholson, *op. cit.*, 187
58 SPNR archives, Box 22, posters, Box 23, 86-7, Box 25, 1/45-7
59 Ibid., Box 21, protection of mammals; RSPB archives, council minutes, 19/4/12, 28/1/10; *Bird Notes and News*, 12, 1926, 19
60 SPNR archives, Boxes 23-6
61 *Bird Notes and News*, 18, 1939, 143-4
62 SPNR archives, Box 14, 1/29
63 Ibid., Box 25, 2/25
64 Ibid., Box 24, 2/337
65 R. Baden-Powell, *Scouting for boys* (Pearson, London), 1918, 334 pp.
66 RSPB archives, council minutes
67 SPNR archives, Box 21, protection of mammals
68 *Bird Notes and News*, 17, 1937, 187-91
69 RSPB archives, council minutes, 20/7/23; PRO, HO 45 17925 & 19234
70 PRO, HO 45 19001
71 J. S. Huxley, 'The courtship-habits of the Great Crested Grebe',

Proceedings of the Zoological Society of London, 35, 1914, 491–562

72 A. Hibbert-Ware, *Report of the Little Owl Food Enquiry, 1936–7* (Witherby, London, for British Trust for Ornithology), 1938, 74 pp.

73 F. Fraser Darling, *A Naturalist on Rona* (Oxford University Press), 1939, 103

74 SPNR archives, Box 25, 2/38

75 E. J. Salisbury, 'A proposed biological flora of Britain', *Journal of Ecology*, 16, 1928, 161–2

76 W. Gardiner, 'Orme's Head cotoneaster', *Transactions of the Llandudno Field Club*, 1908, 7–14

77 W. G. Sheldon, 'A committee for the protection of British Lepidoptera', *Entomologist*, 58, 1925, 1–2; SPNR archives, Box 32, 4/D & H

78 SPNR archives, Box 25

79 Ibid., Box 24, 2/149–71

Chapter Three

1 SPNR archives, Box 17, Farne Islands

2 *Handbook of the Society for the Promotion of Nature Reserves*, 1928; SPNR archives, Box 8

3 W. M. Webb, 'The nature reserves in Britain', *Journal of Ecology*, 1, 1913, 46

4 SPNR archives, Box 27, 1/51

5 *Bird Notes and News*, 17, 1937, 112–3

6 SPNR archives, Box 14, Meathop Moss, 2/39–40; Box 17, Braunton Burrows, Box 34, 1/46–7

7 SPNR archives, Box 14

8 Public Record Office (PRO), HLG 52, 713, minutes of 6th meeting

9 SPNR archives, Box 15

10 Ibid., Box 24, 1/75–87, 2/132–40; Box 34, 6/90

11 Ibid., Box 14, 2/81

12 J. Ritchie, *The influence of man on animal life in Scotland* (Cambridge University Press), 1920, 550 pp.

13 G. Shaw Lefevre (Lord Eversley), *English Commons and Forests* (Cassell, London), 1894, 391 pp.

14 R. Fedden, *The continuing purpose* (Longman, London), 1968, 226 pp.

15 National Trust Act, 1907, Local Acts 7 Edward VII, c. 136; National Trust for Scotland Confirmation Act, 1938, Local Acts 2 & 3 George VI, c. 4

16 SPNR archives, Box 54, 1
17 *The Times*, 18/12/12
18 SPNR archives, filing cabinet, envelope I, a, B, m and 35
19 Ibid., filing cabinet, envelope S, y
20 Ibid., filing cabinet, envelope 233 & A, h
21 Ibid., Box 21, Annual Report, 1918
22 *Handbooks of the Society for the Promotion of Nature Reserves*
23 SPNR archives, Box 16, St Kilda
24 Ibid., filing cabinet, envelope M, b
25 *Handbook of the Society for the Promotion of Nature Reserves*, 1931
26 SPNR archives, Box 21, Annual Report, 1920
27 Ibid., filing cabinet, envelope C, x
28 Ibid., filing cabinet, envelope G, i; H, a & C, a
29 Ibid., Box 32, 1/11
30 Ibid., Box 17, Hawksmoor, 6; *Handbook of the Society for the Promotion of Nature Reserves*, 1933
31 SPNR archives, Box 34, 1/42

Chapter Four

1   Access to Mountains (Scotland) Bill, 1884, 47 Victoria, Bill 122; SPNR archives, Box 54, 1/50 & 3/226–33
2   East Sussex Record Office, MSS GA 1341/7; SPNR archives, Box 16, West Wittering
3   *The Times*, 6/6/19
4   P. Abercrombie, *The Preservation of Rural England* (Liverpool University Press & Hodder & Stoughton, London), 1926, 56 pp.
5   SPNR archives, Box 54, 8/664
6   Thames Valley Branch of the Council for the Preservation of Rural England, *The Thames Valley from Cricklade to Staines*, prepared by Earl of Mayo, S. D. Adshead & P. Abercrombie (London University Press), 1929, 106 pp.
7   Public Record Office (PRO), F 19, 9
8   PRO, F 18, 162
9   C. Addison, *Report of the National Park Committee*, Cmd 3851, 1931, 131 pp.
10 Council for the Preservation of Rural England, *The case for national parks in Great Britain*, 1938, 15 pp.
11 *The Times*, 8/10/29
12 C. Stewart, *In the Evening* (Murray, London), 1909, 51–64
13 Addison, *op. cit.*, appendix 2; PRO, HLG 52, 717, minutes
14 *The Times*, 8/10/29
15 PRO, HLG 52, 717, minutes of 2nd and 5th meetings

16 SPNR archives, Box 36, national parks, 12; Addison, *op. cit.*, appendix 2/15
17 SPNR archives, Box 36, national parks, 17
18 Addison, *op. cit.*, 1931, sections 3 & 7
19 PRO, PREM 1, 100; HLG 52, 723
20 PRO, HLG 52, 552
21 Town and Country Planning Bill, 1931, 21/7/22 George V, no. 210; Town and Country Planning Act, 1932, 22 & 23 George V, c. 48
22 PRO, HLG 52, 714
23 P. M. Stewart, *Second report of the Commissioner for the Special Areas (England and Wales)*, Cmd 5090, 1936, 67; *Third report*, Cmd 5303, 1936, 67–8; Parliamentary Debates, Commons, vol. 318, 9/12/36, 2077
24 Parliamentary Debates, Commons, vol. 304, 9/7/35, 236
25 PRO, HLG 52, 715
26 Ibid., 716
27 PRO, PREM 1, 82
28 PRO, HLG 68, 56
29 G. Ryle, *Forest Service* (David & Charles, Newton Abbot), 1969, 340 pp.
30 PRO, F 19, 21–2
31 Ibid., 10; H. H. Symonds, *Afforestation in the Lake District* (Dent, London), 1936, 97 pp.
32 PRO, F 19, 37–8
33 PRO, F 18, 289 & 19, 21–2 & 37
34 Addison, *op. cit.*, appendix 2
35 PRO, F 19, 9–10; J. Walton (ed.), *Guide to the Argyll National Forest Park* (HMSO, London), 1938, 29 pp.
36 PRO, F 19, 10; Forestry Commission, *Post-war forestry*, Cmd 6447 1943, 77–80
37 Scottish Record Office, HH 1, 1102; Access to Mountains Bill, 1938, 2 George VI, Bill 7
38 Access to Mountains Act, 1939, 2 & 3 George VI, c. 30

Chapter Five

1 E. M. Nicholson, *The system* (Hodder & Stoughton, London), 1967, 256–77; H. Macmillan, *Winds of change* (Macmillan, London), 1966, 373 & appendix
2 M. Barlow, *Report of the Royal Commission on the distribution of the industrial population*, Cmd 6153, 1940, 320 pp.

3 J. S. W. Reith, *Into the Wind* (Hodder & Stoughton, London), 1949, 403–47; Public Record Office (PRO), CAB 118, 79
4 PRO, CAB 67, 8
5 PRO, PREM 4, 92, 9
6 PRO, CAB 67, 8
7 PRO, CAB 21, 1583
8 PRO, CAB 67, 9 & 65, 17; HLG 86, 2, 3, 5 & 8
9 Parliamentary Debates, Commons, vol. 370, 19/3/41, 250–1
10 PRO, CAB 117, 123
11 RSPB archives, NRIC file; council minutes, 30/1/41 & 17/4/41; *Bird Notes and News*, 24, 1950, 80–2
12 SPNR archives, Box 34, 3, 6
13 Ibid., Box 27, Report on the Conference on nature preservation in post-war reconstruction, number 1
14 Ibid., Box 27, 1–3
15 *Conference on nature preservation in post-war reconstruction*, memorandum 1, 1941, 8 pp.; SPNR archives, Box 27, 3–4
16 SPNR archives, Box 27, 4, 87–8, 99, conference report, no. 4
17 Minister of Works and Planning Act, 1942, 5 & 6 George VI, c. 23
18 SPNR archives, Box 27, 5; PRO, HLG 92, 18, 3
19 Parliamentary Debates, Lords, vol. 122, 21/4/42, 669–70; Commons, vol. 379, 29/4/42, 976 & 1,036
20 PRO, CAB 117, 123
21 PRO, HLG 86, 8 & 21; Lord Justice Scott, *Report of the committee on land utilisation in rural areas*, Cmd 6378, 1942, 138 pp.
22 SPNR archives, Box 27, 5/4–6; Scott, *op. cit.*, 179
23 Minister of Town and Country Planning Act, 1943, 6 & 7 George VI, c. 5
24 Mr Justice Uthwatt, *Expert Committee on compensation and betterment: interim report*, Cmd 6291, 1941, 14 pp.; Town and Country Planning (Interim Development) Act, 1943, 6 & 7 George VI, c. 29; Parliamentary Debates, Commons, vol. 395, 30/11/43, 223
25 SPNR archives, Box 27, 5; *Conference on nature preservation in post-war reconstruction*, memorandum 2, 1942, 4 pp.
26 SPNR archives, Box 34
27 Ibid., 2/75, 6/40; Box 28, 10/40–41
28 Ibid., 1/12; PRO, HLG 92, 18, 6; *Conference on nature preservation in post-war reconstruction*, memorandum 3, 1943, 25 pp.
29 PRO, HLG 92, 46
30 PRO, CAB 117, 123
31 PRO, HLG 92, 46
32 *Conference on nature preservation in post-war reconstruction*, memorandum 4, 1943, 11 pp.

33 British Ecological Society archives, minute book; SPNR archives, Box 34, 1/20, 32 & 87

34 British Ecological Society, 'Nature conservation and nature reserves', *Journal of Ecology*, 32, 1944, 45–82; British Ecological Society, *Memorandum on Wild Life Conservation and Ecological Research from the National Standpoint* (BES, London), 1945, 15 pp.

35 SPNR archives, Box 27, 1/62–3 & 69; PRO, HGL 92, 18, 32

36 Ibid., Box 35, 7/9–10, 53, 8/58–9 & 61

37 Ibid., Box 36, geology sub-committee, 18 & 25

38 *Conference on nature preservation in post-war reconstruction*, memorandum 5, 1945, 41 pp.; SPNR archives, Box 36, Bl/36

39 SPNR archives, Box 35, 8 & 10; *Conference on nature preservation in post-war reconstruction*, memorandum 6, 1945, 77 pp.

40 SPNR archives, Box 28, 9/91, 10/40–1

41 Ibid., Box 34, 6/5 & 9; Box 33, NRIC report, no. 6

42 Parliamentary Debates, Commons, vol. 395, 30/11/43, 225–6

43 PRO, HLG 92, 49; J. Dower, *National Parks in England and Wales*, Cmd 6628, 1945, 57 pp.; *Journal of the Royal Institute of British Architects*, 55, 1948, 38–9

44 Scottish Record Office, HH 1, 2587; J. Douglas Ramsay, *National parks*, Cmd 6631, 1945, 27 pp.

45 SPNR archives, Box 43, 2/4

46 Ibid., 1/33

47 Ibid. 1/35

48 PRO, F 18, 162 & 19, 10

49 Ibid., 217 & 19, 10; SPNR archives, Box 43, 2/63; Scottish Record Office, HH 1, 2587

50 PRO, HLG 92, 49

51 PRO, CAB 87, 10

52 A. Hobhouse, *National parks committee*, Cmd 7121, 1947, 134 pp.; J. Douglas Ramsay, *National parks*, Cmd 7235, 1947, 72 pp.

53 PRO, HLG 93, 1 & 51–2; J. S. Huxley, *Conservation of nature in England and Wales*, Cmd 7122, 1947, 139 pp.

54 SPNR archives, Box 35, 10/74, 91, 97 & 100; Box 36, B1/15, 22 & 26

55 Ibid., Box 36, B1/94; B2/48

56 Ibid., Box 35, 9/34; Scottish Record Office, HH 1, 638

57 Ibid., Box 34, 1/26, 39, 74, 2/62, 82, 85, 6/36; Box 35, 9/62; Box 36, B2/94 & Scottish Nature Reserves Committee; Box 36, geological sub-committee, 44

58 J. Ritchie, 'Conservation of nature in Scotland', Ramsay, *op. cit.*, 1947, 57–72; J. Ritchie, *Nature reserves in Scotland: final report*, Cmd 7814, 1949, 34 pp.

59 SPNR archives, Box 34, 1/75

60 R. W. Clark, *The Huxleys* (Heinemann, London), 1968, 283;
    SPNR archives, Box 36, B1/88

61 F. Fraser Darling, *A Naturalist on Rona* (Oxford University Press),
    1939, 104

62 *Spectator*, 4/6/43; A. G. Tansley, *Our heritage of wild nature*
    (Cambridge University Press), 1945, 74 pp.

63 British Ecological Society, 1944, 47

64 H. Conwentz, *The care of natural monuments* (Cambridge University
    Press), 1909, 185 pp.; Huxley, *op. cit.*, 37

65 *Country Life*, 10/5/13

66 A. G. Tansley (ed.), *Types of British vegetation* (Cambridge
    University Press), 1911, 352–66

67 SPNR archives, Boxes 18 & 20

68 Ibid., Box 35, 8/93–4

69 PRO, HLG 93, 48 WLC Inf. 23

70 Ibid., 48 WLC 31

71 Ibid., 49 WLC Ev. 24

72 *Conference on nature preservation in post-war reconstruction*, memo-
    randum 3, 1943, 3–4

73 SPNR archives, Box 34, 4/15

74 Ritchie, 'Conservation', in Ramsay, *op. cit.*, 1947, 58

75 SPNR archives, Box 36, geological sub-committee, 42

76 Huxley, *op. cit.*, 82–5

77 C. Addison, *Report of the National Park Committee*, Cmd 3851,
    1931 appendix 2

78 PRO, HLG 93, 48 WLC, 1; Huxley, *op. cit.*, 86–90

79 SPNR archives, Box 35 & Box 36, geology sub-committee, 17 &
    20

80 Ibid., Box 54, 1/56

81 Ibid., Box 66

82 A. G. Tansley, 'Field study and nature conservation', *Address to
    the Council for the Promotion of Field Studies*, 1946, 4 pp.

83 *Conference on nature preservation in post-war reconstruction*, memo-
    randum 6, 1945, 10–11

Chapter Six

1 E. Lankester (ed.), *Memorials of John Ray* (Ray Society), 1846,
   175

2 F. Willughby, *The ornithology*, ed. J. Ray (John Martyn), 1678,
   18–19

3 J. Fisher, *The Birds of Britain* (Collins, London), 1942, 7–8

4 Huntingdon Record Office, Manchester MSS, 57a; C. Abbot,

Flora Bedfordiensis, 1798, vi; Bedfordshire Record Office, MSS X 48/5, SQ 185 & CC 433–4; L. Linder (ed.), *The Journal of Beatrix Potter* (Warne, London), 1966, 448 pp.

5   E. Newman, *British Butterflies* (Hardwicke & Bogus; London), 1869, 486 pp; E. B. Ford, *Butterflies* (Collins, London), 1957, 7–25

6   R. Smith, 'Botanical survey of Scotland, Edinburgh district', *Scottish Geographical Magazine*, 16, 1900, 385–416; 'Botanical survey of Scotland, North Perthshire district', *Scottish Geographical Magazine*, 16, 1900, 441–67

7   H. Conwentz, *The Care of Natural Monuments* (Cambridge University Press), 1909, 185 pp.

8   SPNR archives, Box 25, 1/119; Fisher, *op. cit.*, 44–5

9   C. B. Crampton, *The vegetation of Caithness* (British Vegetation Committee), 1911, 132 pp.

10   A. G. Tansley, 'The early history of modern plant ecology', *Journal of Ecology*, 35, 1947, 130–7; H. Godwin, 'Obituary for Arthur George Tansley', *Biographical memoirs of Fellows of the Royal Society*, vol. 3, 1957, 227–46

11   *New Phytologist*, 4, 1905–11 & 1912

12   A. G. Tansley, *Types of British vegetation* (Cambridge University Press), 1911, 416 pp.

13   A. G. Tansley, 'British ecology during the past quarter-century: the plant community and the ecosystem', *Journal of Ecology*, 27, 1939, 513–30

14   SPNR archives, Box 54, 1/56

15   Ibid., filing cabinet, envelope R

16   Ibid., filing cabinet, envelope 100

17   Ibid., filing cabinet, envelope S, 5

18   Ibid., Box 30, 7–13; filing cabinet, envelope H, a & R

19   Ibid., Box 30, 2–6

20   Ibid., filing cabinet, envelope 227

21   Ibid., Box 12, forms since 1922

22   C. Addison, *Report of the National Park Committee*, Cmd 3851, 1931, appendix 2; SPNR archives, Box 36, Conference; Earl of Onslow, 'The importance of national parks', *Handbook of the Society for the Promotion of Nature Reserves*, 1938, 25–33

23   Anthony Collett, *The Changing Face of England* (Cape, London), 1932, 229–32

24   SPNR archives, Box 31, 3/16

25   Ibid., Box 27, 5/71; Box 33; Box 34, 1/5–9 & 31; Box 33, report of NRIC, no. 1

26   Ibid., 34, 1/94, 2/5

27   Ibid., Box 34, 1/10

28   Ibid., Box 34, 2/23 & 3/4

29 Public Record Office (PRO), HLG 92, 18/8
30 SPNR archives, Box 34, 2/83; PRO, HLG 92/18/9
31 SPNR archives, Box 34, 2/28; Box 33, NRIC report, no. 2
32 Ibid., Box 34, 2 & 3; Box 33, NRIC report, no. 3
33 *Conference on nature preservation in post-war reconstruction*, memo-randum 4, 1943, 11 pp.
34 PRO, HLG 92, 18/52–55
35 PRO, HLG 92, 18/48
36 SPNR archives, Box 34, 3/69, 4/17; *Handbook of the Society for the Promotion of Nature Reserves*, 1946, 58
37 SPNR archives, Box 34, 6/71; Box 35, 7/73; British Ecological Society archives, minute book
38 SPNR archives, filing cabinet, envelope T, i; Box 33, NRIC report, no. 3
39 Ibid., Box 33, NRIC report, no. 2
40 *Conference on nature preservation in post-war reconstruction*, memo-randum 3, 1943, 25 pp.
41 PRO, HLG 92, 18/38
42 SPNR archives, Box 33, NRIC report, no. 3
43 Ibid., Box 33, Conference report, no. 1
44 Ibid., Box 27, 1/59
45 Ibid., Box 21, *Nature reserves for the Nation*
46 Ibid., Box 34, 3/54
47 Ibid., Box 36
48 Ibid., Box 35, 7/73
49 Ibid., Box 35, 7/80
50 C. P. Castell, 'Nature conservation in the London area', *London Naturalist*, 26, 1946, 17–41
51 SPNR archives, Box 33
52 *Nature*, 157, 9/3/46, 277–8
53 SPNR archives, Box 35, 8/81–3
54 Ibid., Box 34, 3/306
55 Ibid., Box 35
56 *Conference on nature preservation in post-war reconstruction*, memo-randum 6, 1945, 16–17
57 SPNR archives, Box 35, 9
58 Ibid., 9/44–5
59 *Conference on nature preservation in post-war reconstruction*, memo-randum 6, 1945, 77 pp.
60 J. S. Huxley, *Conservation of nature in England and Wales*, Cmd 7122, 1947, appendix 6
61 PRO, HLG 93, 47 WLC, Inf. 4
62 Ibid., 48 WLC, Inf. 22
63 SPNR archives, Box 35, 10/98

64 PRO, HLG 93, 48 WLC, Inf. 33
65 Ibid., 53
66 Huxley, *op. cit.*, appendix 6/3
67 PRO, HLG 93, 48 Minutes 16
68 Ibid., 48 WLC, Inf. 46
69 Ibid., Inf. 15
70 Ibid., 36
71 Ibid., 48 Minutes 1
72 J. Dower, *National Parks in England and Wales*, Cmd 6628, 1945, 57 pp.
73 A. Hobhouse, *National Parks Committee*, Cmd 7121, 1947, 134 pp.
74 *Conference on nature preservation in post-war reconstruction*, memorandum 1, 1942, part II; memorandum no. 3, 1943, 14–16; PRO, HLG 92 18/20
75 British Ecological Society archives, National Habitat Reserves and Scheduled Areas, 1943
76 *Conference on nature preservation in post-war reconstruction*, memorandum 6, 1945, part III
77 SPNR archives, Box 35, 9 & 10
78 Huxley, *op. cit.*, appendix 8
79 PRO, HLG 93, 48 WLC, Inf. 26
80 Ibid., Inf. 38; J. R. Matthews, 'Geographical relationships of the British flora', *Journal of Ecology*, 25, 1937, 1–90
81 Huxley, *op. cit.*, 70
82 SPNR archives, Box 35, 10/44
83 Ibid., Box 31, 3/16
84 Ibid., Box 36, geology sub-committee
85 Ibid., filing cabinet, envelope R, n
86 Huxley, *op. cit.*, appendix 7
87 Ibid., 71 & appendix 8/11
88 J. Douglas Ramsay, *National parks*, Cmd 6631, 1945, 27 pp.
89 J. Ritchie, 'Conservation of nature in Scotland', in J. Douglas Ramsay, *National Parks*, Cmd 7235, 1947, 1; J. Ritchie, *Nature reserves in Scotland: final report*, Cmd 7814, 1949, 34 pp.
90 F. Fraser Darling, *A Naturalist on Rona* (Oxford University Press), 1939, 106
91 SPNR archives, Box 31, 3/160; Ritchie, 'Conservation', in Ramsay, *op. cit.*, 1947, chapter 5
92 PRO, HLG 93, 48 WLC inf. 34
93 SPNR archives, Box 33, report of Lincolnshire sub-committee
94 Ibid., Box 37, Lincolnshire sub-committee, 12

Chapter Seven

1 C. Waterton, *Essays on Natural History* (Longman, London), 1838, 312 pp.; *Bird Notes and News*, 10, 1923, 65–7; P. Gosse, *The Squire of Walton Hall* (Cassell, London), 1940, 324 pp.
2 SPNR archives, Box 33, report of regional sub-committee for Northumberland and Durham
3 E. C. Arnold, *Bird Reserves* (Witherby, London), 1940, 215 pp.
4 SPNR archives, Box 34, 1/94
5 Ibid., Box 27, 1/47 & Box 19, Wicken Fen
6 *Bird Notes and News*, 12, 1926, 17
7 RSPB archives, council minutes, 11/4/24
8 SPNR archives, Box 54, 1/30–37 & 39
9 Ibid., Box 54, 5/457; Box 16, Ray Island
10 Ibid.,
11 *Bird Notes and News*, 5, 1912
12 RSPB archives, council minutes, 24/4/25; SPNR archives, Box 16, Dungeness
13 SPNR archives, Box 16, Dungeness, 5
14 Ibid., Minutes of Council, 1914
15 Ibid., Box 18, Meathop Moss
16 Ibid., Swaddiwell Field
17 RSPB archives, council minutes, 19/2/32 & 16/2/34; *Bird Notes and News*, 17, 1937, 119–20; SPNR archives, Box 16, Dungeness
18 SPNR archives, Box 16, Croxley Green
19 National Trust Act, 1937, 1 George VI, c. 57; National Trust for Scotland, reports from council
20 SPNR archives, Box 19, Lynmouth
21 Ibid., Box 16, Selsdon Wood
22 E. Ray Lankester, 'Nature reserves', *Nature*, 93, 1914, 33–5
23 SPNR archives, Box 24, 2/119
24 G. H. T. Stovin, 'Belfairs Great Wood', *Handbook of the Society for the Promotion of Nature Reserves*, 1938, 16–17; SPNR archives, Box 18, Belfairs Wood
25 SPNR archives, Box 20, Belfairs Wood
26 Ibid., Box 16, Lesness Abbey Woods
27 Ibid., Box 37A
28 *Bird Notes and News*, 16, 1935, 188 & 18, 1939, 113–15
29 RSPB archives, council minutes, 20/7/23
30 *Bird Notes and News*, 11, 1924, 43–6; Sir Lionel Earle, *Turn Over the Page* (Hutchinson, London), 1935, 165–7
31 RSPB archives, council minutes, 22/7/32
32 *Bird Notes and News*, 14, 1931, 200
33 C. Addison, *Report of the National Park Committee*, Cmd 3851,

1931, 53–62: SPNR archives, Box 17, Lakenheath Warren, & Box 19, Breckland

34 Public Record Office (PRO), HLG 52, 715

35 *The Times*, 14/7/45

36 SPNR archives, Box 52, region 19

37 Parliamentary Debates, Commons, vol. 448, 15/3/48, 1779 & vol. 449, 21/4/48, 1808–10

38 SPNR archives, Box 36, B2/51

39 Ibid., filing cabinet, envelope marked 'post as watcher'

40 Ibid., Box 14, & Box 19, Calf of Man

41 A. Collett, *The Changing Face of England* (Cape, London), 1932, 241–2

42 PRO, HLG 92, 48/9

43 SPNR archives, Box 35, 7/73; J. S. Huxley, *Conservation of nature in England and Wales*, Cmd 7122, 1947, 50

44 SPNR archives, Box 5

45 *Bird Notes and News*, 5, 1912

46 SPNR archives, Box 15, 2/1

47 Ibid., Box 18, Meathop 2/19

48 SPNR archives, Box 16, Blakeney Point; Box 14

49 *Bird Notes and News*, 24, 1950, 96

50 SPNR archives, Box 11, 4/70 & 5/28

51 Ibid., Box 16, Selsdon Wood

52 Ibid., Box 8; Box 11, 1 & 4/70

53 PRO, HLG 52, 717, minutes of 10th meeting

54 SPNR archives, Box 1, 4; Box 2, 4/2; Box 3, 3/3; Box 8, 5/3; Box 9, 1/243

55 Ibid., Box 14, 2/4

56 C. P. Castell, 'Nature conservation in the London area', *London Naturalist*, 27, 1947, 27–8

57 British Ecological Society, 'Nature conservation and nature reserves', *Journal of Ecology*, 32, 1944, 45–82

58 SPNR archives, Box 27, 1/59

59 Ibid., Box 14, 1/11–12

60 Ibid., Box 20, Belfairs Great Wood

61 Ibid., Box 15

62 L. R. W. Loyd, *The Protection of birds: an indictment* (Longman, London), 1924, 3–8

63 E. M. Nicholson, *Birds in England* (Chapman & Hall, London), 1926, 200–1 & 206

64 RSPB archives, council minutes, 20/2/52

65 W. E. Collinge, 'An investigation of the food of terns at Blakeney Point', *Transactions of the Norfolk and Norwich Naturalists' Society*, 12, 1924–5, 35–53

66 Huxley, *op. cit.*, 55
67 SPNR archives, Box 3, 3/3; Box 9, 1/243
68 Ibid., Box 16, Dungeness
69 Ibid., Box 1, 2/4 & Box 2, 4/10
70 Ibid., Box 2, 4/10; Box 8, 5/171; E. Duffey, 'Ecological studies of the Large Copper Butterfly at Woodwalton Fen National Nature Reserve', *Journal of Applied Ecology*, 5, 1968, 69–96
71 SPNR archives, Box 8, 5/172; Box 9
72 *Bird Notes and News*, 14, 1930, 46–7; SPNR archives, Box 14, 1/31–5 & 2/16
73 SPNR archives, Box 6, 5; Box 7, 5; Box 9, 11 & 13
74 Ibid., Box 1, 3/1–2; Box 2, 4/9; Box 3, 3/3; Box 6, 1; Box 10, 2/158–89; Box 14, 2/80; M. E. D. Poore, 'The ecology of Woodwalton Fen', *Journal of Ecology*, 44, 1956, 455–92
75 *Bird Notes and News*, 10, 1922, 49–51; SPNR archives, Box 14
76 Huxley, *op. cit.*, 6; PRO, HLG 93, 48 WLC 9
77 C. S. Elton, *The Pattern of Animal Communities* (Methuen, London), 1966, 432 pp.

Chapter Eight

1 *Handbook of the Society for the Promotion of Nature Reserves*, 1947, 9; E. Ray Lankester, 'Nature reserves', *Nature*, 93, 1914, 33–5; SPNR archives, Box 54, 1/147 & 181–4
2 Public Record Office (PRO), HLG 52 717, minutes of 6th meeting
3 C. Addison, *Report of the National Park Committee*, Cmd 3851, 1931, 36
4 Council for the Preservation of Rural England, *The case for national parks in Great Britain*, 1938, 16 pp.
5 PRO, HLG 92, 18/9; SPNR archives, Box 33, NRIC report, no.
6 PRO, HLG 92, 18/24 & 53
7 Ibid., 18/29
8 Ibid., 18/29 & 38
9 Ibid., 49
10 Town and Country Planning (Interim Development) Act, 194 6 & 7 George VI, c. 29; Town and Country Planning Act, 194 7 & 8 George VI, c. 47
11 Mr Justice Uthwatt, *Expert committee on compensation and betterme final report*, Cmd 6386, 1942, 180 pp.; PRO, PREM 4, 92/5 &
12 Minister of Town and Country Planning and Secretary of Si for Scotland, *The control of land use*, Cmd 6537, 1944, 15 pp.
13 Scottish Record Office (RO), HH 1/1105

14   PRO, CAB 71/21 LP (45), 134–6, 27th meeting, 5; New Towns Act, 1946, 9 & 10 George VI, c. 68

15   Town and Country Planning Act, 1947, 10 & 11 George VI, c. 51

16   SPNR archives, Box 43, 4/43

17   Ibid., 5/60

18   National Parks and Access to the Countryside Act, 1949, 12–14 George VI, c. 97

19   Scottish RO, HH 1/2587; J. Douglas Ramsay, *National parks*, Cmd 6631, 1945, 27 pp.; Hydro-electric Development (Scotland) Act, 1943, 6 & 7 George VI, c. 32

20   J. Douglas Ramsay, *National Parks*, Cmd 7235, 1947, 72 pp.

21   R. W. Clark, *The Huxleys* (Heineman, London), 1968, 203

22   British Ecological Society archives, council minutes

23   SPNR archives, Box 35, 7/54, 60–1 & 63

24   British Ecological Society, 'Nature conservation and nature reserves', *Journal of Ecology*, 32, 1944, 45–82; British Ecological Society, *Memorandum on wild life conservation and ecological research from the national standpoint*, 1945, 15 pp.; A. G. Tansley, *Our heritage of wild nature* (Cambridge University Press), 1945, 74 pp.

25   J. S. Huxley, *Conservation of Nature in England and Wales*, Cmd 7122, 1947, 3–10

26   Ibid., 155; PRO, HLG 93, 48 Minutes of 1st meeting

27   PRO, HLG 93, 48 WLC, 14

28   Lord President of the Council, *Scientific research and development*, Cmd 6514, 1944, 12 pp.

29   PRO, HLG 93, 48 WLC, 18 & 48 WLC, Inf. 24

30   Ibid., 12 & minutes of 24th meeting

31   Huxley, *op. cit.*, 157–81; J. Ritchie, 'Conservation of nature in Scotland', in Ramsay *National parks*, 1947, chapter 6

32   Chancellor of the Exchequer, *The Scientific Civil Service*, Cmd 6679, 1945, 16 pp.

33   PRO, HLG 93, 48 minutes of the 11th meeting; Huxley, *op. cit.*, 183–6; Ritchie, *loc. cit.*, chapter 6

34   PRO, HLG 93, 48 WLC BEP 16

35   Ibid., 18 WLC 50

36   SPNR archives, Box 36, B2/79, 84, 86–7; Parliamentary Debates, Commons, vol. 450, 29/4/48, 600–1; Commons, vol. 461, 11/2/49, 104–6

37   A. G. Tansley, 'The conservation of British vegetation and species', in J. E. Lousley (ed.), *The Changing Flora of Britain* (Botanical Society, London), 1953, 188–96

38   Data kindly provided by Nature Conservancy Council

39 SPNR archives, Box 9, 49; A. G. Tansley, *Our heritage of wild nature*

40 *Lincolnshire Times*, December 1963—January 1964; *The Observer*, 23/2/64; Parliamentary Debates, Commons, vol. 687, 17/1/64, 73

41 Natural Environment Research Council, *Report of the Council* (HMSO, London), 1967, 88 pp.; The Nature Conservancy Council Act, 1973, Elizabeth II, c. 54

42 Parliamentary Debates, Commons, vol. 859, 4/7/73, 456–7

43 *Bird Notes*, 22, 1949, 153

44 SPNR archives, Box 35, 8/3

45 Ibid., Box 36, B3/25

46 F. W. Oliver, 'Nature reserves', *Transactions of the Norfolk and Norwich Naturalists' Society*, 12, 1924–9, 317–22

47 Data kindly provided by Mr R. Wagstaffe

48 SPNR archives, Box 49, Lincolnshire, 14

49 Data kindly provided by SPNR

50 H. E. Axell, 'Minsmere: control of reed', in International Waterfowl Research Bureau, *Management of wetland manual*, 1974, file

51 D. T. Streeter, 'Road verges', in J. M. Way (ed.), *Road verges* (Monks Wood Experimental Station, Huntingdon), 1969, 15–19

52 Data kindly provided by Mrs J. Buchanan

53 Data kindly provided by RSPB

54 Data kindly provided by Mr R. Payne

55 SPNR archives, Boxes 12–13

56 PRO, HLG 93, 48

57 E. M. Nicholson, *The Environmental Revolution* (Hodder & Stoughton, London), 1970, 188–238

58 World Wildlife Fund, *Yearbook 1970–71* (World Wildlife Fund, Morges), 1971, 217–21

59 IUPN, *Proceedings and papers of the Technical Meeting held at the Hague*, 1952, 105 pp.; ...*at Salzburg*, 1954, 258 pp.; ...*at Copenhagen*, 1956, 170 pp.

60 IUCN, *Proceedings and papers of the 6th Technical Meeting, Edinburgh*, 1957, 265 pp.

61 H. E. Bracey, *Industry and the countryside* (Faber, London), 1963, 261 pp.

62 Nature Conservancy, *The countryside in 1970: reports and proceedings* (HMSO, London), 1964, 286 pp.

63 'The Countryside in 1970', *Proceedings* (Royal Society of Arts & Nature Conservancy, London), 1966, 178 pp.; Countryside Act, 1968, Elizabeth II, c. 41

64 'The Countryside in 1970', *Proceedings* (Royal Society of Arts,

London), 1970, 193 pp.; F. Fraser Darling, *Wilderness and Plenty* (BBC, London), 1970, 88 pp.

65 S. Zuckerman, *The Torrey Canyon* (HMSO, London), 1967, 48 pp.

66 Conservation of Wild Creatures and Wild Plants Act, 1975, Elizabeth II, c. 48; Parliamentary Debates, Commons, vol. 884, 24/1/75, 2123–50

Index